Beyond Blind Faith

Reasons For The Hope We Have
(1 Peter 3:15)

by Don Davidson, B.A., J.D.

CFT Publishing
Bedford, Texas

Published by CFT Publishing
Bedford, Texas
ISBN 978-0-9992335-0-4

You can contact Don via email at *donatty@flash.net*.

To read Don's blog, and for more information on Don's writings, including some that are available for free, visit *dondavidson.net*.

Other books by Don: *Beyond Shallow Faith: Cultivating Christian Maturity (Ephesians 4:13-15),* which is available on Amazon.com.

All Biblical quotations in this book are from the New American Standard Bible translation. *Italics* are in the original, and indicate that the word is implied, but not literally included, in the original Greek, Aramaic, or Hebrew. ALL CAPS are also in the original, and indicate quotations from the Old Testament.

For my wife, Marsha, the love of my life.

TABLE OF CONTENTS

Preface

I have long believed that there is only one sufficient reason to be a Christian, and that is because it is true. Christianity may be a wonderfully moral religion in which to bring up your kids. And it certainly advocates many useful values, such as peace, kindness, cooperation, and non-violence. But so does Buddhism. If Christianity were not true, I would have no use for it. And in my younger days, I had no use for it.

I converted to Christianity at age 20, in my junior year of college. (My faith journey is discussed in more detail in "About the Author," on page 257.) Before that, I would often challenge Christians with tough questions for which I believed they had no answers—and most of them in fact had no answers.

For example, if it's true that "whoever believes in Him shall not perish, but have eternal life" (John 3:16), why doesn't God show Himself so that everyone would believe—and thus be saved? (See Chapter 4.) Or, why would a loving Father condemn His children to eternal torture in Hell just because they didn't believe the right things? (See Chapter 5.) And, of course, the traditional favorite: if God is both omnipotent and loving, why is there so much evil and suffering in the world? (See Chapter 3.)

The Bible has legitimate answers for these and other questions, and that is the focus of this book. Sound reasons exist for believing that Christianity is true. Yes, it is ultimately a matter of faith, but it need not be blind faith.

Chapter 1
CHRISTIANITY IS DIFFERENT

Whether you are a believer or a skeptic, please don't fall for the lie that Christianity is pretty much like other religions. It isn't. Jesus Christ is unlike any other religious leader in what He says and does. And His followers said some pretty unique things as well. To see what I mean, let's look at some other religions.

Jesus Does Not Resemble Man-Made Gods. When people invent a religion, the gods inevitably think like us and behave like us. Just look at the ancient Greek gods. They were powerful and immortal, but they were also deeply flawed. They fought, killed, kidnapped, and stole. [1] They married, had children, and committed adultery. [2] They exacted revenge, often without regard to fairness or justice. [3]

Similarly, the gods of other religions consistently exhibit human failings. When Krishna, the Hindu god, appears in human form, he steals, he humiliates young girls by taking their clothes while they are bathing naked in a river, and he performs many mischievous acts. The Japanese god, Susa-no-wo, wreaks havoc on the earth, while the god, Oh-kuni-nushi, tries to steal Susa-no-wo's possessions and kidnap his daughter. In Mesopotamian mythology, the goddess Ishtar tries to kill a human, Gilgamesh, as well as his friend, Enkidu, because Gilgamesh would not marry her. The Egyptian god, Osiris, is murdered through the trickery of the god, Set. The Hawaiian goddess, Pele, seduces a young Hawaiian prince, Lohiau, and then leaves him to pine away for her until he dies.

Even in monotheistic Islam, we see these human elements in the Qur'ân's portrayal of Hell, where Allah exacts eternal, excruciating, and pitiless revenge against unbelievers. Similarly, the Qur'ân's view of Heaven is decidedly anthropocentric, with a cornucopia of earthly delights such as abundant food and drink, luxurious clothing, and even sex. [4] Allah caters to human beings in Heaven while acting like a bitter and vengeful human being in Hell.

In each case, it is easy to imagine a human being inventing the religion, because the gods think and behave like humans. In contrast, the Jesus of the New Testament doesn't seem like anything a human being would invent. What normal person would come up with the strange and eccentric idea that people should pray for their enemies? Or act with mercy, kindness, and forgiveness toward those who mistreat them—as Jesus and His disciples advocated? [5] That is not how a normal person thinks or acts.

The New Testament contains many such counter-intuitive notions. While human wisdom tells us to seek happiness and security through wealth and possessions, Jesus taught that poverty is better than riches, because money impedes devotion to God. [6] Contrary to human nature, the New Testament instructs us to avoid judging or condemning others. [7] Few people value qualities such as gentleness and humility, often disparaging them with derogatory terms like "wimp" and "loser." Yet the New Testament champions those who are meek, humble, weak, and self-giving, while reproving the arrogant, boastful, pretentious, and vain. [8]

Jesus and the New Testament authors did not seek acclaim by pandering to public opinion, either. Some of what they said and did was not merely counter-intuitive, but downright unpopular.

Jesus condemned divorce except in cases of adultery. [9] He sanctioned the payment of taxes to the hated Romans, and His disciples encouraged people to obey the oppressive Roman government, [10] the same government that had cruelly and unjustly executed Jesus. He associated freely with the dregs of society: prostitutes, tax collectors, [11] and other notorious people, [12] while aggressively challenging the religious leaders of His day. [13]

And as if trying to scare away followers, He warned about the persecution and suffering His disciples must expect. [14] Indeed, the New Testament frankly states that Christianity is sometimes difficult and that certain sacrifices are necessary. [15] This message of suffering and sacrifice was no more inviting in Jesus's day than it is today.

Jesus's wisdom and cleverness must be considered, because they are extraordinary. Think about the memorable stories He told, such as the story of "The Good Samaritan." Even most unbelievers know this story, or at least know of it, in which Jesus depicts the love we are to show to others through this tale about a man who helps his enemy simply because he is in need. [16] Or consider the story of "the Prodigal Son," in which Jesus illustrates God's love for us through a father's love for a son who made some terrible choices. [17]

Jesus told many wonderful stories like these (known as parables) to teach moral and religious truths in a way people would remember. He even mixes in some humorous images, like a person with a log in his eye trying to take a speck out of his brother's eye, [18] or a person who would carefully avoid consuming a gnat and then blithely swallow a camel. [19]

Jesus was so smart that He consistently outwitted His opponents. For example, the Jewish leaders asked Him if people should pay taxes to Rome. "No" would bring down the wrath of the Romans, who of course insisted that the money be paid, but "Yes" would upset many among the Jewish people, who loathed the Romans and their oppressive taxes. After pointing out that the coins used to pay the tax are Roman coins, Jesus responded: "Then render to Caesar the things that are Caesar's; and to God the things that are God's" (Matthew 22:21). Thus, He silenced his enemies. [20] When Jesus was challenged by the Jewish leaders to state His authority, He cleverly responded with a loaded question of His own which they refused to answer. [21]

Even Jesus's miracles are different. In most religions, the gods' miracles demonstrate their power, but seldom their goodness. In contrast, Jesus's miracles almost always helped people:

healing the sick, feeding the hungry, raising the dead. [22] Never did Jesus use His power to harm a person. [23] He rebuked two of His disciples for merely suggesting that He do so. [24]

And then there is the bizarre and counter-intuitive notion of grace. [25] This principle, which has no parallel in any other major religion, proclaims that we cannot earn God's favor through religious practices, righteous behavior, or charitable deeds—but that God gives us immortality if we will merely love and trust Him. [26]

Of course, the simple fact that much of the New Testament runs counter to the way people normally think and live their lives does not by itself prove that it came from God rather than men. I would not ascribe divinity to a book that advocated wearing wet clothing during bitterly cold weather—although that would certainly be counter-intuitive—for the simple reason that it doesn't work. Yet the principles which the New Testament espouses actually do work, whereas the conventional wisdom does not.

A psychiatrist, J.T. Fisher, has written that Jesus's Sermon on the Mount [27] confirms what science tells us about how to achieve and maintain mental health. In effect, Jesus set forth a concise "blueprint for successful human life with optimism, mental health, and contentment." [28]

You will not find peace or happiness in wealth, but you can find both in Christ. Hatred and revenge solve nothing—the residents of the Middle East have been proving this for many decades, with no end in sight. Yet mercy and forgiveness can change enemies into friends. Arrogance generates resentment and hostility, while meekness and gentleness restore calm and often resolve disputes peacefully.

And as it turns out, the strange doctrine of grace makes far more sense than those religions which try to please God through proper behavior. For we cannot *earn* anyone's love, least of all God's. Nor can we ever be good enough to meet His standard of perfection. Fortunately for us, the New Testament says we don't have to, because He loves us anyway. [29]

Christianity Is Different

Unlike other religions, God in the New Testament is not merely a judge, deciding whether or not our behavior and religious practices measure up. He is instead a loving Father who embraces us even though we do not deserve it. All we have to do is stop resisting (for He will not force Himself on us) and give ourselves to Him.

Jesus is also different in what He says about Himself. Christianity makes two bold assertions, both grounded in historical fact: (1) that its founder, Jesus Christ, claimed to be divine (that is, God, or at least God-like), and (2) that He died, was buried, and then came back to life. The first assertion is made relevant by the second. If Jesus did not rise from the dead, He was merely a charlatan or a deluded madman. But if He came back from the dead, then we must seriously consider everything He said, including what He said about Himself.

Jesus's Claims of Divinity. We will discuss Jesus's resurrection in Chapter 2. But we must first address that other bold assertion—that Jesus claimed to be divine. Did He really say this about Himself, or was this something that, like Buddha, was concluded by His followers long after His death? [30] Well, Jesus made at least nine claims that show that He thought He was much more than a mere man. He seems to have actually believed He was God. Those nine claims are:

1. He thought He was perfect. [31]
2. He claimed to be eternal. [32]
3. He said He was the Christ (Messiah), the Son of God, and He considered Himself equal with God. [33]
4. He taught that following or rejecting Him was the same as following or rejecting God. [34]
5. He insisted that He had come from Heaven, and He spoke about Heaven as if He'd been there. [35]
6. He predicted His own death—and, more importantly, His resurrection. [36]

7. He believed His death was necessary to save the world. [37]
8. He claimed to have authority to forgive sins. [38]
9. He didn't bother to cite any type of authority to validate what He said or did.

The first seven are pretty obvious claims of divinity. If I say I am immortal, or perfect, or equal with God, I'm making claims no ordinary human being has any right to make. And if I say I have come down from Heaven, and that if you reject me you are rejecting God Himself, you would have every right to question my sanity.

But those last two—forgiving sins and not citing authority—don't seem quite so obvious. So let's take a closer look at them.

Forgiving sins would not be anything special if Jesus were merely forgiving wrongs done to Himself. After all, that is what Christians are supposed to do. [39] But as C.S. Lewis pointed out, Jesus did much more—He forgave people for wrongs they had done *to other people.* [40] Only God may do that. Therefore, by claiming this authority, Jesus was placing Himself on an equal footing with God.

The ninth and last claim of divinity is that Jesus never cited authority for what He said. For example, in His famous Sermon on the Mount in Matthew's Gospel, He says:

> "You have heard that it was said, 'YOU SHALL NOT COMMIT ADULTERY'; but I say to you that everyone who looks at a woman with lust for her has already committed adultery with her in his heart."
>
> —Matthew 5:27-28

Here Jesus lays down a new moral rule—or, if you prefer, a new interpretation of an old rule—and provides no authority whatsoever for doing so, other than His own say-so: "You have heard . . . but I say. . . ." Unlike scholars and prophets, Jesus did not claim that His authority came from Scripture or a vision from God, or from any book or person. His word was enough. And He did this repeatedly, in many different contexts. [41] The common people immediately noticed the difference:

> When Jesus had finished these words, the crowds were amazed at His teaching; for He was teaching them as one having authority, and not as their scribes.
>
> —Matthew 7:28-29 [42]

The Jewish religious leaders reacted as we would—they demanded to see His credentials: " 'By what authority are You doing these things, and who gave You this authority?' " (Matthew 21:23) [43] But Jesus didn't tell them. [44] The only authority He ever cited was that of God:

> "For I did not speak on My own initiative, but the Father Himself who sent Me has given Me a commandment as to what to say and what to speak. I know that His commandment is eternal life; therefore the things I speak, I speak just as the Father has told Me."
>
> —John 12:49-50 [45]

If a friend of yours made any of these nine claims about himself, you might assume he was joking. And if he convinced you he was serious, you would think he had lost his mind. But Jesus was entirely serious, and the Jewish leaders took His claims very seriously indeed.

Nor could they dismiss Him as simply a harmless nut case. The Jesus we see in the New Testament is a remarkably wise, clever, insightful, and perceptive individual—most certainly not a lunatic. That left only one alternative in the minds of His enemies: that He was a lying, deceiving, demon of a man. Evil incarnate. And they condemned Him to death because of it. [46] But the Jewish leaders were unwilling to consider the other alternative: what if He was what He said He was? How can we know? Well, if Jesus indeed came back to life after being dead, then we have our answer. And that is what we will discuss in Chapter Two.

Endnotes for Chapter One, "Christianity Is Different"

[1] Zeus and his fellow Olympians came to power by waging war against the Titans and overthrowing them. The Olympians then consolidated their rule by killing the giants who opposed them. Hades, god of the underworld, obtained his bride, the goddess Persephone, by kidnapping her. The messenger god, Hermes, stole cattle from the god Apollo.

[2] Zeus, in particular, had many extramarital liaisons.

[3] For example, Artemis changed the unfortunate Actaeon into a stag when he accidentally saw her naked. And Hera struck poor Tiresias blind for agreeing with Zeus in a dispute between the goddess and her husband.

[4] For more on this, see Chapter 8, "Islam's Credibility Problem."

[5] See Matthew 5:38-41, 5:43-48; Luke 6:27-35; Romans 12:14, 12:17-21; 1 Thessalonians 5:15; 1 Peter 3:8. And on the subject of treating others with mercy, forgiveness, and kindness, see also: Matthew 5:7, 6:14-15, 7:12, 18:21-35; Mark 11:25-26, 12:31; Luke 6:36-38, 9:51-56, 10:25-37, 15:11-32, 17:3-4, 23:33-34; John 8:2-11; 1 Corinthians 4:12-13, 6:7; Galatians 5:22, 6:10; Ephesians 4:31-32; Colossians 3:12-13; 1 Thessalonians 5:15; James 3:17-18; 1 Peter 3:8.

[6] For example, when a man came to Jesus asking what he must do to receive eternal life, Jesus told him to sell all of his possessions, and then remarked on how hard it is for the rich to enter the kingdom of God. See Luke 18:18-27. Similarly, see: Matthew 6:19-21, 6:24, 6:31-34, 19:16-21, 19:23-24; Mark 4:18-19, 10:19-27; Luke 6:20-21, 6:24-25, 8:14, 12:15-21, 12:22-23, 12:33-34, 14:33, 16:13-15; Philippians 4:11-12; 1 Timothy 3:3, 6:6-10, 6:17-19; Hebrews 13:5; James 2:1-6, 4:3-4, 5:1-6; 1 John 2:15-16, 3:17; Revelation 3:17-18.

[7] See, for example: Matthew 7:1-5; Luke 6:36-38; Romans 2:1-3, 14:1-4, 14:10-13; 1 Corinthians 4:5, 5:12-13; James 4:11-12, 5:9.

[8] See the following verses: Matthew 5:5, 5:21-22, 6:1-6, 6:16-18, 7:12, 11:25-26, 18:1-4, 19:30, 20:25-28, 22:39, 23:1-7, 23:11-12; Mark 9:33-37, 10:13-15, 10:31, 10:42-45, 12:31; Luke 6:29, 7:36-50, 9:46-48, 10:21, 11:43, 13:29-30, 14:11, 16:15, 18:9-17, 22:24-26; John 13:12-15; Romans 11:17-21, 12:3, 12:10, 12:16, 1 Corinthians 1:18-21, 2:3-5, 3:18-20, 4:6-7, 4:10, 8:8-13, 10:24, 10:32-33, 13:4-5; 2 Corinthians 6:1-10, 10:17, 12:7-10, 13:4; Galatians 5:22-23,

5:26, 6:10; Ephesians 4:1-3; Philippians 2:3-4, 4:5; Colossians 3:8, 3:12-13; 1 Timothy 3:2-3, 6:11; 2 Timothy 2:24-26; Titus 3:1-2; Hebrews 12:14; James 1:21, 3:5-10, 3:17-18, 4:6, 4:10; 1 Peter 2:13-14, 3:8, 3:14-17, 5:5-6.

[9] Matthew 5:31-32, 19:9; Mark 10:2-12; Luke 16:18; 1 Corinthians 7:10-11.

[10] Luke 20:19-25; Romans 13:1-7; 1 Peter 2:13-14

[11] The Roman government often hired people from the local population to collect Roman taxes, and set an amount that had to be collected and delivered to the Roman government. The tax collectors were allowed to keep any monies which they were able to amass in excess of the required amount. The Jewish people despised the tax collectors because they were usually greedy, corrupt, and wealthy, and because they were viewed as collaborators with Rome.

[12]Matthew 9:10-13; Mark 2:15-17; Luke 5:29-32, 19:1-7

[13] For example, see: Matthew 6:1-6, 6:16-18, 21:23-46, 23:1-7, 23:13-35; Mark 7:5-13, 11:27-12:12, 12:38-40; Luke 6:6-11, 11:37-54, 19:1-7, 20:1-19; John 9:39-41.

[14] See, for example: Matthew 5:10-11, 10:17-23, 10:28, 23:34; Mark 13:13; Luke 6:22-23, 12:4-5, 21:12-19; John 15:19-20, 16:2. That the disciples did in fact suffer persecution is shown by: Romans 8:16-18; 1 Corinthians 4:9-13; 2 Corinthians 6:1-10, 12:7-10; 2 Timothy 1:8-9, 2:3, 3:12; Hebrews 13:12-13; James 1:2-3, 1:12; 1 Peter 1:6-7, 2:19-20, 3:14-17, 4:12-16, 5:8-10; 1 John 3:13; Revelation 2:10.

[15]See: Matthew 10:37-39, 16:24-26, 18:8-9, 25:31-45; Mark 8:34-38, 9:42-48, 10:42-45; Luke 9:23-26, 9:59-62, 14:26-33; John 12:25; Romans 15:1; 1 Corinthians 8:8-13, 10:24; Philippians 3:8-9.

[16] See Luke 10:29-37.

[17] See Luke 15:11-32.

[18] Matthew 7:1-5

[19] Matthew 23:24

[20] Matthew 22:17-22; see also Mark 12:13-17 and Luke 20:21-26.

[21] Jesus asked, "Was the baptism of John from heaven or from men?" (Luke 20:4) The Jewish leaders did not believe John the Baptist was a true

prophet, but they were afraid to say so publicly for fear of the people's reaction. See Matthew 21:23-27, Mark 11:27-33, and Luke 20:1-8.

[22] See Matthew 4:23-24, 8:1-3, 8:5-17, 8:28-32, 9:2-7, 9:18-25, 9:27-30, 9:32-35, 10:1, 12:9-13, 12:15-16, 12:22, 14:14-22, 14:34-36, 15:21-38, 17:14-18, 19:1-2, 20:29-34, 21:14; Mark 1:23-26, 1:30-34, 1:39-42, 2:3-12, 3:1-5, 3:9-10, 5:1-13, 5:22-42, 6:5, 6:7-13, 6:35-44, 6:53-56, 7:25-30, 7:32-35, 8:1-9, 8:22-25, 9:14-29, 10:46-52; Luke 4:33-35, 4:38-41, 5:12-13, 5:17-25, 6:6-11, 6:17-19, 7:1-15, 7:21-22, 8:26-33, 8:41-55, 9:1-6, 9:10-17, 9:37-42, 10:1-9 and 10:17, 11:14, 13:10-16, 13:31-32, 14:1-5, 17:11-19, 18:35-43, 22:49-51; John 4:46-53, 5:2-16, 6:1-2, 6:5-14, 9:1-34, 11:1-44.

[23] He did, however, curse a fig tree (Matthew 21:18-19, Mark 11:2-14 and 19-21), and He indirectly caused the death of some swine when he cast demons into them, ultimately resulting in their death by drowning (Matthew 8:28-32; Mark 5:1-13; Luke 8:26-33).

[24] Luke 9:51-56

[25] "Grace" means "unmerited favor." Grace refers to any benefit that we receive from God which we do not deserve (which arguably is *any* benefit that we receive from God).

[26] See: Acts 15:11; Romans 3:24-26, 3:27-30, 4:1-5, 4:16, 4:22-25, 5:1-2, 5:15-21, 6:23, 10:8-13; 2 Corinthians 5:18-21; Galatians 2:15-16, 3:24-25; Ephesians 2:4-9; Philippians 3:8-9; 2 Timothy 1:8-9; Titus 2:11-12, 3:3-7; Hebrews 11:6; James 4:6; 1 Peter 5:10. Also note the element of grace which is implicit in these Scriptures, in which people win Jesus' approval through love or faith, rather than by any good deeds or religious behavior: Matthew 20:1-16, 21:28-32; Luke 5:29-32, 7:36-50, 17:7-10, 18:9-14, 19:1-7.

[27] Matthew chapters 5 through 7

[28] Fisher, J.T. and L.S. Hawley, *A Few Buttons Missing* (Lippincott, Philadelphia, 1951), p. 273, as quoted in McDowell, *The New Evidence That Demands a Verdict*.

[29] See Romans 5:8: "But God demonstrates His own love toward us, in that while we were yet sinners, Christ died for us."

[30] During his lifetime the Buddha consistently denied being more than a man. See Chapter 9, "Buddhism (And Now For Something Completely Different)."

[31] In John 8:29, Jesus says, "I always do the things that are pleasing to Him [i.e., God]." See also Matthew 5:17 and John 17:4.

[32] See John 8:58, 17:5, and 17:24.

[33] The most explicit such statement is probably John 10:30: " 'I and the Father are one.' " For other examples, see: Matthew 14:33, 16:16-17, 26:63-64; Mark 8:29-30, 14:61-62; Luke 9:20-22, 10:22, 22:70; John 1:49-50, 5:17-18, 5:36-37, 8:18-19, 12:45, 14:6-9, 15:23.

[34] See, for example: Matthew 10:32-33, 10:37-40, 11:27-30, 19:29; Mark 8:34-38, 9:41, 10:29-30, 13:13; Luke 6:22-23, 7:23, 9:24-26, 12:8-9, 21:16-19, 22:28-30; John 3:14-18, 4:10, 4:14, 5:21-24, 6:27-29, 6:40, 8:12, 8:51, 10:9-10, 10:28, 11:25-26, 14:1.

[35] See, for example: Matthew 18:10, 22:29-30, 24:36, 26:53; Mark 12:25; Luke 20:35-36; John 3:13, 8:23, 14:2-3. And then there are verses in which Jesus implies that He knows what Heaven will be like, such as Matthew 5:3, 5:10, 5:12, 5:19-20, 6:1, 6:20, 7:21, 8:11, 11:11, 16:19, 18:1-4, 18:18, 19:21, 26:64; Mark 10:21, 13:24-27, 14:62; Luke 6:23, 10:18, 10:20, 12:33, 15:7, 18:22; John 6:38, 6:50-51.

[36] See Matthew 12:38-40, 16:21, 17:9-12, 17:22-23, 20:17-19, 26:1-2, 26:32, 27:62-63; Mark 8:31, 9:9-10, 9:31, 10:32-34, 14:28; Luke 9:21-22, 9:44, 17:25, 18:31-33. 24:6-7; John 2:18-22, 3:14-15, 10:11-18, 12:32-33, 14:28-29, 16:5-7, 16:16-22.

[37] See, for example: Matthew 16:21-23, 20:28, 26:28; Mark 8:31-33, 10:45, 14:24; Luke 22:19-20; John 6:51-58, 10:11, 10:15.

[38] See Matthew 9:2; Mark 2:5; Luke 5:20, 24; 7:47-48.

[39] See, for example: Matthew 6:14-15, 18:23-35; Mark 11:25-26; Ephesians 4:31-32, Colossians 3:13; and James 2:13.

[40] See, for example: Matthew 9:2; Mark 2:5; Luke 5:20, 7:47-48. In *Mere Christianity*, C.S. Lewis explained why this was so remarkable:

> One part of the claim tends to slip past us unnoticed because we have heard it so often that we no longer see what it amounts to. I mean the claim to forgive sins: any sins. Now unless the speaker

> is God, this is really so preposterous as to be comic. We can all understand how a man forgives offenses against himself. You tread on my toe and I forgive you; you steal my money and I forgive you. But what should we make of a man, himself unrobbed and untrodden on, who announced that he forgave you for treading on other men's toes and stealing other men's money?

Lewis, *Mere Christianity*, Book II, Chapter 3, p. 76.

[41] For other examples, see: Matthew 5:18, 5:20, 5:21-22, 5:26, 5:28, 5:31-32, 5:33-34, 5:38-39, 5:43-44, 6:2, 6:5, 6:16, 6:25, 8:11-12, 10:15, 10:23, 10:42, 11:1, 11:22, 11:24, 12:6, 12:31, 13:17, 17:12, 17:20, 18:3, 18:10, 18:13, 18:18-19, 18:21-22, 19:9, 19:23-24, 19:28, 21:21, 21:31, 21:43, 23:36, 24:2, 24:34, 26:13; Mark 3:28-29, 7:14-15, 8:12, 9:1, 9:13, 9:41, 10:15, 10:29-30, 11:23-24, 13:30, Luke 6:27-28, 7:26-28, 9:27, 10:12, 11:9, 12:4, 12:22, 18:17, 18:29, 21:3, 23:43; John 3:3, 3:5, 5:19, 5:24-25, 6:47, 6:53, 8:34, 8:51, 8:58, 10:1, 10:7, 12:24, 13:16, 13:20, 14:12, 16:23.

[42] See also Mark 1:22, Luke 4:32.

[43] See also Mark 11:28, Luke 20:1-2; and see John 2:18.

[44] Matthew 21:27; see also Mark 11:33, Luke 20:8

[45] See also John 6:37-40, 6:57, 17:1-8, 17:18, 17:21, 17:22-25.

[46] See Matthew 26:63-66 and Mark 14:61-64; see also, Luke 22:66-71.

Chapter 2
IS JESUS'S RESURRECTION FACT OR FAIRY TALE?
The Historical Evidence for the Resurrection of Jesus Christ

"This Jesus God raised up again, to which we are all witnesses."

—Acts 2:32

Christianity stands or falls on the answer to this question: did Jesus Christ die and then come back to life days later? If Christ's resurrection never happened, then Jesus's claims of divinity were nothing but the ravings of a lunatic or the inventions of a fraud—and Christianity is worthless. On the other hand, if Jesus truly rose from the dead, then Christianity is Truth itself and the hope of the world.

If you are skeptical of claims about a miracle that occurred almost 2,000 years ago, I quite understand. I grew up believing that miracles do not occur. Yet the alternative is truly startling, although it is seldom honestly confronted by the skeptics—if Jesus did not rise from the dead, then His followers *lied*. There is no middle ground, no other satisfactory explanation. But the idea that Jesus's followers made it all up is difficult to believe, because it would mean they were the best—and the worst—liars history has ever known. However, I'm getting ahead of myself. Let's begin by laying a good foundation.[1]

Laying the Foundation. We cannot discuss whether Jesus rose from the dead until we first establish three historical facts: (1) Jesus lived—that is, He was a real, historical person; (2) He was crucified by the Romans, was believed to be dead, and was buried in a known tomb which was found empty a few days later; and

(3) His followers said that He had been raised from the dead and ascended into heaven. By historical standards, these are well established facts, for which there is ample proof and virtually unanimous agreement among historians. Let's take a look.

Christian Sources

The New Testament Authors. We begin with the first-century witnesses: Peter, Matthew, Mark, Luke, John, Paul, James, and Jude—the authors of the books of the New Testament.

Peter, Matthew, and John were among Jesus's twelve apostles. Peter wrote the First Letter of Peter, and may have also written the Second Letter of Peter. Matthew probably wrote the Gospel that bears his name, although some believe a disciple of Matthew wrote it. Similarly, while John's authorship of the Gospel of John and the First Letter of John is doubted by some, the author of those books specifically claims to have been a disciple of Jesus and one who knew Him in the flesh, as well as an eyewitness to His teaching. [2] The author of Second Peter also claims to have been an eyewitness. [3] The apostle John is traditionally credited with being the author of Revelation and the other two Letters of John, although that is open to significant doubt.

Mark was Peter's interpreter in Rome, according to the fourth century historian Eusebius (who quotes Papias, second century Bishop of Hierapolis). Eusebius tells us that Mark based his Gospel on the speeches and recollections of Peter while they were together in Rome. Irenaeus, second century bishop of Lyons, says the same. Mark, who was also known as John Mark, travelled for awhile with Paul and Barnabas. [4]

Paul was a devoted Jew, religious scholar, and Pharisee, who had a miraculous vision of Christ on the road to Damascus. [5] He was the author of at least five—and as many as thirteen—letters in the New Testament. [6]

Luke, "the beloved physician" (Colossians 4:14), was one of Paul's early converts who became one of his travelling companions. [7] Luke wrote Acts and the Gospel of Luke, and he asserts that he did so after careful investigation. [8] James and Jude were brothers—or possibly half-brothers—of Jesus. [9] James—also known as "James the Just"—became the head of the Christians in Jerusalem. [10]

All of the books of the New Testament were written during the first century A.D. [11] Since Jesus is believed to have died around 30-33 A.D., this means that most of these books were circulating during the lifetimes of some who had witnessed His life and death.

Scholars believe the Gospel of Mark was completed *no later than* 70 A.D., Acts and the Gospels of Matthew and Luke by 85 A.D., [12] and John's writings (his Gospel, three letters, and Revelation) by 95 A.D. [13] Paul's letters were all written before 68 A.D., so they are even earlier than the Gospels. Most of his letters were written during the late 40's, 50's, and early 60's A.D. The letter of James probably predates even Paul's letters.

In addition, many scholars believe that portions of the New Testament—such as Romans 1:3b-4a, Luke 24:33-34, and 1 Corinthians 15:3-8—quote oral traditions that date to only a few years after Jesus's death. 1 Corinthians 15:3-8 says:

> For I delivered to you as of first importance what I also received, that Christ died for our sins according to the Scriptures, and that He was buried, and that He was raised on the third day according to the Scriptures, and that He appeared to Cephas, [14] then to the twelve. After that He appeared to more than five hundred brethren at one time, most of whom remain until now, but some have fallen asleep; then He appeared to James, then to all the apostles; and last of all, as to one untimely born, He appeared to me also. [15]

Paul was not an eyewitness to the resurrection, so his comment that he "delivered" what he also "received" implies that this is what he learned from conversations with the eyewitnesses.

Do We Really Have What They Wrote? Some people assume that writings that are 2,000 years old must have been corrupted along the way, through copying errors or intentional alterations, and thus what we have now is not at all what was written back then. But in the case of the New Testament, the facts are otherwise. The New Testament is actually the most reliable ancient historical document in existence.

Writers in the first century A.D. (when the New Testament books were written) wrote on papyrus, which decays rapidly except in arid climates. Because of this, *original* manuscripts for the New Testament books, or any other ancient writings, simply do not exist. Thus, we do not have samples of the handwriting of Paul or Julius Caesar or the Roman historian Tacitus.

And since the printing press would not be invented for another 1,400 years, [16] sharing and preserving these writings required that a person hand-copy them, word-for-word. This was a time-consuming process, so these copies—which I will henceforth refer to as "manuscripts"—were usually expensive. Most of them ended up in libraries or in the private collections of wealthy people, and later in churches and monasteries.

If a manuscript was not well cared for, or if its repository was destroyed by fire, war, or other calamity, it was simply lost. And any writing which was not deemed important enough to justify copying is of course gone forever. Perhaps we should be surprised that any writings from that time period survived. But manuscripts of the New Testament books did, and in amazing numbers.

Several manuscripts of portions of the New Testament have been found from the second century A.D. (In other words, those manuscripts were actually hand-copied by someone between 100 and 199 A.D.) The John Rylands manuscript, dating from about 100 – 130 A.D., has part of John's Gospel. It was found in Egypt, and is now in the John Rylands Library, Manchester, England. Other second century manuscripts include: the Bodmer Papyrus II, 150-200 A.D., which contains most of John's Gospel, and the *Diatessaron*, compiled by an Assyrian Christian named Tatian, which dates from about 160 A.D. The *Diatessaron* is a harmony of the four Gospels, although only a small portion of it still exists.

We have more complete manuscripts from later centuries. The Chester Beatty Papyri, which was hand-copied between 200 and 250 A.D., contains large portions of the New Testament. A manuscript containing the Gospels of Luke and John has been dated about 175-225 A.D. Manuscripts from as early as 325 to 350 A.D. include virtually the entire New Testament. [17] We also have many manuscripts from the fourth and fifth centuries which are written in various languages, such as Syriac (Christian Aramaic), Coptic (Egyptian), Latin, and of course Greek.

In addition, much of the New Testament could be reconstructed from the writings of Christians during those early centuries, [18] as well as from lectionaries [19] from the sixth and later centuries. Three Christian works that were written about 100 A.D.—the *Epistle of Barnabas*, the *Didache*, and Clement of Rome's *Letter to the Corinthians*—quote from books of the New Testament. [20] Ignatius, bishop of Syrian Antioch, writing in about 115 A.D., quotes from at least eleven New Testament books, [21] and probably alludes to eight more. Polycarp, bishop of Smyrna, wrote a *Letter to the Philippians*, ca. 110 A.D., which quotes from sixteen New Testament books. [22]

Compared to other ancient writings, there is simply no comparison. The earliest manuscripts for any of Plato's writings date from about 900 A.D., 1,300 years after Plato wrote them. For Aristotle, the date is even later—1,100 A.D. The Roman historian Tacitus wrote near the end of the first century A.D., yet the earliest copies of his two major works—*Annals* and *Histories*—are two partial manuscripts from the ninth and eleventh centuries A.D. [23] Similarly, the earliest manuscripts for Caesar's *Gallic Wars* (written 58-50 B.C.), Herodotus' *History* (ca. 488-428 B.C.), and Thucydides' *History* (ca. 460-400 B.C.)—aside from a few papyrus scraps—date from about 900 to 1,100 A.D. Of 142 books in Livy's *History of Rome,* 107 have been lost to history. The remaining 35 books are primarily contained in manuscripts dating from the 10th century A.D., although a manuscript from the fourth century A.D. contains portions of four of those 35 surviving books. Homer's *Iliad* fairs better, since the earliest partial manuscript is from about 400 B.C., but that is still 400 years after the *Iliad* was written. And the earliest complete manuscript of the *Iliad* is from the 13th century A.D.

When we talk about the number of manuscripts, the New Testament again compares favorably with other ancient literature. We have about 500 manuscripts of the New Testament that predate 500 A.D., and almost 25,000 total. Compare that to fifty copies of the *Iliad* that are dated within 500 years of the time it was written, and 643 total. We have 200 manuscripts for Demosthenes, only twenty for Livy's *History of Rome* and Tacitus' *Annals,* and ten or less for Plato, Caesar's *Gallic Wars,* Herodotus' *History,* Thucydides' *History,* and Pliny Secundus' *Natural History.* If we judge other ancient literature by the standard some wish to use for the New Testament, nothing would survive.

New Testament manuscripts are also remarkably consistent. If we set aside variations that do not affect meaning—like spelling errors and grammatical mistakes—the New Testament manuscripts agree with each other on 99.5% of the verses. Thus, only about one-half of one percent are in any doubt. [24] Compare this to about five percent of the *Iliad* and ten percent of India's *Mahabharata.* And these differences between New Testament manuscripts usually concern relatively unimportant matters. None impact basic Christian doctrines or beliefs. [25]

Thus, there are more and older copies of the New Testament in existence, with fewer discrepancies between manuscripts, than any other document of similar antiquity. A number of the manuscripts predate the rise of Christianity to a position of wealth and status, which did not even begin until the Roman persecutions ended in 323 A.D., under the Emperor Constantine. And the abundance, geographical dispersal, and varied languages of the manuscripts effectively preclude any systematic tampering.

Nor is there much doubt about the authenticity of most of the New Testament books. The Muratorian fragment [26] informs us that, as early as 180 A.D., Christians accepted all of the New Testament books as being authentic and sacred except Hebrews, James, first and second Peter, and third John. By the time of the church historian Eusibius, in the early fourth century A.D., all were accepted as genuine and scriptural except Hebrews, James, second Peter, second and third John, Jude, and Revelation.

Thus, the early Christians viewed all four Gospels, Acts, first John, and all of Paul's letters as authentic and scriptural from an early date.

And lest you think that the early Christians were credulous, many works failed to gain acceptance, including alleged letters from Paul to the Laodiceans and the Alexandrians, as well as the *Revelation of Peter, Letters of Barnabas, Institutions of the Apostles, Pastor, Gospel of Peter, Gospel of Thomas, Gospel of Judas, Gospel of the Hebrews, Acts of Andrew, Acts of Paul, Acts of John, Shepherd of Hermas, Apocalypse of Peter, Epistle of the Apostles, Treatise on the Resurrection, Apocryphon of James,* and others. Almost all of these rejected works were written in the second century A.D. or later, when the original eyewitnesses would have been deceased.

The first list of accepted books that corresponds to our current New Testament was set forth in a letter of Athanasius, the fourth century bishop of Alexandria, in about 367 A.D. This list was confirmed by the Synod of Hippo in 393 A.D.

The foregoing discussion demonstrates that, for most of the New Testament, we know that the books were written by people who knew Jesus, or by their close associates, that the books were written within the lifetimes of many of the people who knew Jesus, and that we have highly accurate versions of what they actually wrote. So what did they say?

The Early Christian Testimony. I'm sure you will not be surprised that each of the New Testament authors writes about Jesus as if he were a real, historical person, or that all four Gospel writers, along with Peter and Paul, mention his crucifixion at the hands of the Romans. [27]

But if you are not familiar with the New Testament, you might be surprised to learn that all except James and Jude mention Jesus's resurrection from the dead. [28] Luke describes His physical ascension into heaven, [29] while Peter and Paul place Him at the right hand of God in heaven. [30] The story of Christ's resurrection was thus central to the Christian message—and not only among the New Testament writers.

In other Christian writings of the first three centuries A.D., Christ's crucifixion, resurrection, and ascension feature prominently. Ignatius, the bishop of Syrian Antioch, who was martyred early in the second century A.D., mentions Christ's crucifixion and resurrection in his letters to the *Smyrnaeans* and the *Trallians*. Clement of Rome, in about 95 A.D., wrote that Christ's apostles were "fully assured through the Resurrection of our Lord Jesus Christ." [31]

Similarly, each of the following early Christian writings mentions Christ's resurrection and/or His ascension:

Source	Approximate Date of Writing	Mentions Christ's Resurrection	Mentions Christ's Ascension
Ignatius' Letter to the *Magnesians*	Prior to 108 A.D.	Yes	No
Letter of Barnabas	ca. 100-130 A.D.	Yes	No
Aristides' *Apology*	Between 138 and 161 A.D.	Yes	Yes
Polycarp's *Letter to the Philippians*	Probably written in about 110 A.D., and certainly prior to 155 A.D.	Yes	Portrays Jesus as sitting at God's right hand
Justin Martyr's *Apology*	150 A.D.	Yes	No
Justin Martyr's *Dialogue with Trypho*	Prior to 165 A.D.	Yes	Yes
Irenaeus' *Against Heresies*	Prior to 180 A.D.	Yes	Yes
Stromata, by Clement of Alexandria (as quoted by Eusibius)	195 A.D.	No	Yes
Acts of Thomas	160 – 200 A.D.	Yes	Yes
Various writings of Tertullian	Prior to 222 A.D.	Yes	Yes
The Apostolic Tradition of Hippolytus	225 A.D.	Yes	No

The crucifixion is also mentioned in many other Christian and Gnostic [32] sources, such as *Epistle of Barnabas, Martyrdom of Polycarp, Gospel of Peter, Epistle of the Apostles, Gospel of the Savior, Apocalypse of Peter,* and *The Second Treatise of the Great Seth.*

Both the resurrection and the ascension were part of the earliest Christian statements of belief, including the Creed of Caesarea (prior to 325 A.D.), the Creed of Nicaea (325 A.D.), the creed of Marcellus, Bishop of Ancyra (ca. 340 A.D.), the Dedication Creed (341 A.D.), and the Nicene Creed (451 A.D.).

While these sources do not prove that Jesus rose or ascended, they do demonstrate that the story of Christ's resurrection and ascension was proclaimed by His followers not long after His death, and continued to be circulated as a critical tenet of this new faith.

Secular Sources

Tacitus, Pliny, Suetonius, and Lucian. Jesus's death and the early Christian preaching about His resurrection are also mentioned in secular sources, most of them hostile to nascent Christianity.

Cornelius Tacitus was a Roman historian who wrote in about the year 115 A.D. In a passage of almost unquestioned authenticity, Tacitus mentions Christ's death while discussing the burning of Rome and Nero's persecution of Christians in 64 A.D.:

> No human endeavors, no princely generosity, no efforts to placate the gods were able to dispel the scandalous suspicion that the burning of the city was the result of an order. To silence this rumor, Nero pushed the Christians forward as the culprits and punished them with ingenious cruelty, as they were generally hated for their infamous deeds.
>
> *The one from whom this name originated, Christ, had been executed during the reign of Tiberius at the*

> *hands of the procurator, Pontius Pilate.* For a time this pernicious superstition was suppressed, but it broke out again, not only in Judea where this evil thing began, but even in the city itself where everything atrocious and shameful from all quarters flows together and finds adherents. [33]

Only a few years earlier, in 112 A.D., Plinius Secundus (also known as Pliny the Younger), Roman Governor of Bithynia in Asia Minor (modern Turkey), wrote a letter to the Roman Emperor Trajan, seeking advice about trials of Christians. In this letter, Pliny says that the *true* Christians of his day would not worship the Roman gods or revile Christ, even on pain of death, and he implies Christian worship of Jesus, noting that Christians sang hymns to Him "as to a god." [34]

Suetonius, another second century Roman historian and chief secretary to the Emperor Hadrian, mentions the Emperor Claudius' expulsion of the Jews from Rome in 49 A.D.: "He drove the Jews out of Rome who were rioting because of Chrestus." [35] Luke mentions this same expulsion, in Acts 18:2: "And he [Paul] found a Jew named Aquila, a native of Pontus, having recently come from Italy with his wife Priscilla, because Claudius had commanded all the Jews to leave Rome." We do not know the extent of the Christian presence in Rome at this time, but Suetonius' language shows that it was significant enough to upset the city's Jewish population, "who were rioting" because of the Christians.

These Romans—Tacitus, Pliny, and Suetonius—were all writing within 80 to 100 years after Christ's death, and all viewed Christianity as a superstition, a false religion. If doubt about Jesus's existence as a real, historical person had been prevalent, they surely would have mentioned it. But they accepted without question that Jesus was a real person. Tacitus mentions His execution by Pontius Pilate, while Pliny's letter shows that Christians worshiped Christ even at that early date.

We can also add the testimony of Lucian of Samosata, a Roman satirist from the mid- to late-second century A.D., who referred to Jesus as "the man who was crucified in Palestine because he introduced this new cult into the world. . . ." [36] And Lucian adds: " . . . and then it was impressed on them by their original lawgiver [an apparent reference to Jesus] that they are all brothers, from the moment that they are converted, and deny the gods of Greece, and worship the crucified sage, and live after his laws." [37] Thus, Lucian provides corroboration for Christ's death by crucifixion—a standard method of execution for non-Romans in the first-century Roman Empire—as well as for the fact that Christians worshipped Him.

Josephus. The Jewish historian, Flavius Josephus, also mentions Jesus. Josephus was born in Jerusalem in 37 A.D., only a few years after Christ's death, and by 94 A.D. he had written a history of the Jews—*Antiquities of the Jews*—which mentions Jesus and His crucifixion in a brief passage:

> Now there was about this time Jesus, a wise man, *if it be lawful to call him a man, for he was a doer of wonderful works*, a teacher of such men as receive the truth with pleasure. He drew over to him both many of the Jews, and many of the Gentiles. *He was the Christ*, and when Pilate, at the suggestion of the principal men among us, had condemned him to the cross, those that loved him at the first did not forsake him; *for he appeared to them alive again on the third day; as the divine prophets had foretold these and ten thousand other wonderful things concerning him.* And the tribe of Christians so named from him are not extinct at this day. [38]

The italicized portions are suspect, since they refer to Jesus as the Christ (i.e., the Messiah), and seem to accept His resurrection as fact. These would be odd comments for a Jewish historian to make. Yet most scholars regard the rest of the passage as authentic, in part because the style and vocabulary are typical of Josephus. These scholars contend that the italicized portions were added by a Christian who was copying the passage at a later date.

However questionable this passage may be, the authenticity of another reference to Jesus by Josephus is accepted by most historians. Josephus states that the high priest Ananias "convened the high council of judges and brought before them *James, the brother of Jesus (called the 'Messiah'),* and several others. He accused them of transgressing the laws and had them stoned." [39] This allusion to Jesus lends credibility to the earlier passage, since, as Josh McDowell points out, such a passing reference "does not make sense unless Josephus has provided a longer discussion about Jesus earlier in his *Antiquities*." [40]

Josephus also mentions John the Baptist and his death at the hands of King Herod, [41] which corroborates the Gospel accounts. [42]

Thallus, Celsus, Phlegon, and Julian. A Samaritan historian, Thallus, writing in about 52 A.D., wrote about Jesus and His crucifixion. Although we do not have Thallus' book, an early third century Christian, Julius Africanus, refers to it. Africanus' rebuttal to Thallus, written in about 221 A.D., says: "Thallus, in the third book of his histories, explains away this darkness [which accompanied Christ's crucifixion] [43] as an eclipse of the sun—unreasonably, as it seems to me (unreasonably, of course, because a solar eclipse could not take place at the time of the full moon, and it was at the season of the Paschal full moon that Christ died)." [44]

Africanus also quotes a history written by Phlegon which made the same argument as Thallus—i.e., that the darkness at the time of Christ's crucifixion resulted from a solar eclipse. Note that both Phlegon and Thallus accepted as fact that Jesus was a real person who had been crucified, as well as the darkness which descended upon Jerusalem at the same time, and sought to explain this darkness naturally.

Another pagan author, Celsus, wrote in the late second century A.D. As with Thallus, Celsus' writings have been lost to history. However, his works are quoted extensively by the Christian writer, Origen, who wrote a refutation of Celsus in the mid-third century. From Origen's quotations, we know that Celsus mentioned Jesus's crucifixion, as well as His resurrection.

Even Julian "the Apostate," Roman Emperor 361-363 A.D., writing against Christianity more than 300 years after Christ's death, did not question the fact that Jesus was a real person:

> Jesus . . . has now been celebrated about three hundred years; having done nothing in his lifetime worthy of fame, unless anyone thinks it a very great work to heal lame and blind people and exorcise demoniacs in the villages of Bethsaida and Bethany. [45]

Each of these men—Tacitus, Suetonius, Pliny, Josephus, Lucian, Thallus, Phlegon, and Julian—lived much closer in time to the actual events, had access to documents and sources now lost to us, and were no friends of early Christianity. The fact that none of them questioned Jesus's existence should satisfy all but the most closed-minded skeptics.

In addition, Tacitus, Lucian, Phlegon, and Thallus—and perhaps Josephus—provide strong corroboration for the Christian testimony that Jesus was crucified by the Romans, and the writings of Lucian and Pliny show that Jesus was worshiped as God by His disciples. Finally, it is worth noting that no ancient writing says Jesus died in a manner other than crucifixion.

The Empty Tomb

Each of the Gospel writers tells the story of Jesus's body being placed in a tomb belonging to Joseph of Arimathea and then disappearing by Sunday morning. [46] Matthew says the Jewish authorities, in order to explain the body's disappearance, spread a story that His disciples had stolen the body. [47] Whatever the cause of the disappearance, the fact of the empty tomb is not challenged or questioned by any ancient source, Christian or otherwise.

From the foregoing, we see that Jesus's existence and His death by crucifixion, as well as the disappearance of His body, are accepted facts of history, by both Christianity's adherents and its enemies. We have also seen that the story of Jesus's resurrection, and to a lesser extent His ascension, was central to the Christian narrative, in both the books of the New Testament and the writings of early Christians. Of course, none of this proves that He rose from the dead. But what are the realistic alternatives?

Explanations for the Resurrection Story

A variety of explanations have been put forward for why Jesus's followers claimed that He had risen from the dead:

1. The disciples stole Jesus's body so they could claim that he had risen from the dead.
2. The disciples went to the wrong tomb, found it empty, and assumed Jesus had risen from the dead.
3. The Jews or the Romans moved the body, perhaps from fear that Jesus's disciples would steal it, so when the disciples went to the tomb and found it empty they assumed Jesus had risen from the dead.
4. Joseph of Arimathea, the man who took custody of Jesus's body after He died and laid it in a tomb, [48] moved the body, so the disciples found an empty tomb and assumed Jesus had risen from the dead.
5. Jesus did not actually die on the cross, but merely passed out. The Romans, thinking Him dead, allowed

Joseph of Arimathea to take the body and entomb it, where Jesus revived.

6. The disciples had a hallucination. In other words, they did not really see Jesus alive again, but merely thought they did.
7. Jesus's disciples lied.
8. They told the truth, because the resurrection actually happened.

Let's look at these explanations one at a time.

The Disciple Stole the Body. The story that the disciples stole Jesus's body was apparently one of the earliest explanations for the resurrection story—so early in fact that Matthew mentions it, and feels the need to explain its genesis:

> Now on the next day, the day after the preparation, the chief priests and the Pharisees gathered together with Pilate, and said, "Sir, we remember that when He was still alive that deceiver said, 'After three days I *am to* rise again.' Therefore, give orders for the grave to be made secure until the third day, otherwise His disciples may come and steal Him away and say to the people, 'He has risen from the dead,' and the last deception will be worse than the first." Pilate said to them, "You have a guard; go, make it *as* secure as you know how." And they went and made the grave secure, and along with the guard they set a seal on the stone.
>
> —Matthew 27:62-66 [49]

> . . . some of the guard came into the city and reported to the chief priests all that had happened. And when they had assembled with the elders and consulted together, they gave a large sum of money to the soldiers, and said, "You are to say, 'His disciples came by night and stole Him away while we

> were asleep.' And if this should come to the governor's ears, we will win him over and keep you out of trouble." And they took the money and did as they had been instructed; and this story was widely spread among the Jews, *and is* to this day.
>
> —Matthew 28:11-15

This story that the disciples had stolen the body continued to circulate for many centuries after Jesus's death, as evidenced by the writings of early Christians such as Justin Martyr, Tertullian, Origen, and John Chrysostom, who wrote rebuttals against it.

This theory has some obvious problems, such as the fact that the guards could not have known what happened if they were asleep, or the presence of Jesus's grave clothes in the tomb, with the face cloth rolled up. [50] No thieves would have bothered to remove those clothes, much less roll them up. And no one seems to have arrested, or even investigated, Jesus's followers for this alleged grave robbing.

But more importantly, if Jesus's disciples stole the body, then they must have lied about His resurrection. After all, they did not merely claim that His tomb was empty—which seems to have been an accepted fact by all involved, including the Jewish leaders—but that He had come back to life and later ascended into Heaven. So this first explanation turns out to be the same as explanation #7: Jesus's followers simply lied.

Wrong Tomb. According to theory #2, Mary Magdalene and another woman named Mary [51] watched Joseph bury Jesus's body from a distance, and then went to the wrong tomb when they returned on Sunday morning, naturally finding it open and empty. The women then told the other disciples, who assumed Jesus must have risen from the dead.

Of course, this theory fails to explain why the Jewish or Roman authorities didn't simply produce Jesus's body from the correct tomb and kill the resurrection story in its infancy. The Jewish leaders in particular had every reason to do so, since they viewed the Christians as false prophets and blasphemers who were misleading the Jewish people and insulting the Jewish leaders (saying that they had killed God's Messiah). [52]

But again, this explanation is really no different from theory #7, that the disciples lied. Jesus's followers did not merely preach an empty tomb. They insisted that they had seen Jesus alive and well after His crucifixion, and that they walked with Him, [53] ate with Him, [54] talked with Him, [55] and even saw and touched His wounds. [56] Paul proclaimed that Jesus appeared to Peter and James, to the twelve apostles, and even to 500 people at one time. [57] And Luke adds that Jesus "presented Himself alive after His suffering, by many convincing proofs, appearing to them over *a period of* forty days and speaking of the things concerning the kingdom of God." (Acts 1:3) If none of these stories was true, then the disciples lied.

Someone Moved the Body. Theory #3 is that the Romans or the Jews moved the body, perhaps to frustrate any attempt by Jesus's disciples to try to steal it. But this theory gets us no further than #2, for it suffers from the same infirmities. If the Jews or the Romans were in possession of Jesus's body, they could have easily produced it as soon as the Christians began proclaiming the resurrection. And as with #2, if this theory is true then the story told by Jesus's followers *cannot* be true—they cannot have seen Him, eaten with Him, or touched Him. In other words, they lied.

Theory #4—that Joseph of Arimathea moved the body—is a bit more intriguing, but only a bit. On the evening of the crucifixion, Joseph laid the body in his own new tomb. [58] This was probably done in haste, since the Sabbath, which began at sundown, was fast approaching. [59] According to this theory, Joseph later decided to move the body to a more suitable or convenient location. So when the women arrived at the grave Sunday morning, they found it empty and everyone assumed Jesus had risen. Joseph, himself a Christian, knew the truth, but did not want to embarrass his friends, so he kept quiet and did not reveal the location of the body.

However, we now run into the same problem as before—theory #4 does not explain why Jesus's followers claimed that He appeared to them alive, unless of course they lied, which is theory #7. The next two theories seek to explain these appearances.

Jesus Did Not Really Die on the Cross. In more recent times, theory #5 came into vogue—that Jesus did not actually die on the cross. Unlike the two men who were crucified with Him, Jesus's legs were not broken in order to hasten death, because He was already believed to be dead. [60] And when Joseph asked for Jesus's body, Pilate was surprised to hear that Jesus had died so quickly. [61]

So theory #5 speculates that the Romans erred in pronouncing Jesus dead, and that He was in fact still alive when He was taken down from the cross. He then revived in the tomb and came out to appear to His disciples. What recommends this theory is that it accounts for the insistence of Jesus's followers that they had seen a real, living person. But it fails on almost every other level.

The first problem is that no one associated with the event—the Romans, the Jewish leaders, the various onlookers—doubted that Jesus was dead. Only Pilate questioned it, and he received assurances of Jesus's demise from a Roman centurion—presumably the same centurion who had overseen the crucifixion. [62] Furthermore, no one apparently questioned it later, for no ancient document claims that Jesus did not actually die on the cross. This theory was an invention of the eighteenth century.

Furthermore, if Jesus simply revived in the tomb, how was He able to roll away the heavy stone which blocked the entrance, [63] and then slip past the guards who would have arrested Him? And what became of Him after He had appeared to His followers for forty days? While there are many stories about what happened to Jesus's disciples in the years following His death, some more reliable than others, history does not give us even one story or legend that hints that Jesus lived on and died somewhere else.

But the greatest flaw in this theory is that it ignores the evidence regarding what Jesus suffered, and what was said about Him afterward. The Romans beat and scourged Him to the point that He needed help carrying His cross to His own death. [64] Scourging was a brutal form of torture in itself. The victim was flogged with a whip imbedded with pieces of metal that tore into the flesh, sometimes cutting even to the bone.

The Romans then subjected Jesus to one of the cruelest forms of execution known to mankind—crucifixion. The victim's wrists and feet were nailed to a cross, with the arms outstretched. While hanging in that position, breathing became difficult unless the victim used his legs to push himself up. The nailed feet must have made such exertions excruciatingly painful. Eventually the victim became too exhausted to push himself up and died from asphyxiation.

Josephus gives us an idea of how unlikely survival of crucifixion truly is. Three of his friends were subjected to crucifixion for a relatively short time until he managed to intervene on their behalf with the Roman commander, Titus, who ordered that they be taken down. Despite the best medical care Rome could provide, two of the three ultimately died. In contrast, Jesus hung on the cross for more than three hours. [65] And according to John's Gospel, death was further ensured when a Roman soldier pierced Jesus's body with a spear as it hung limply on the cross. [66]

Yet only a few days later He walked seven miles from Jerusalem to the village of Emmaus. [67] He walked around Jerusalem, appearing to His followers near the tomb [68] and in Jerusalem itself, [69] and later walked with them to Bethany. [70] He met them by the Sea of Tiberias [71] (also known as the Sea of Galilee)—a distance of more than sixty miles from Jerusalem—and even cooked them breakfast. [72] He offered to let them touch His wounds. [73]

The Gospels and Acts present the risen Jesus as vibrant and healthy, not at all like a man in desperate need of a lengthy convalescence. Of course, Jesus's followers might have lied about His post-crucifixion condition, but that is theory #7 again. And in any event, they must have lied about His ascension. [74] So even if Jesus didn't really die on the cross—which seems ludicrous—the disciples still lied.

Hallucinations. According to theory #6, the disciples didn't really see Jesus alive after the crucifixion—they just *thought* they did. The appeal of this theory lies in the fact that it provides an explanation for the disciples' remarkable devotion to the resurrection story. This version of the story concedes that they really, truly *believed* Jesus had been resurrected. This theory also explains the ascension, for it too was just a hallucination. Yet this theory falls short when we examine what science tells us about hallucinations. [75]

Hallucinations do not just happen. They are almost always the result of drug use, mental or physical illness, or extreme fatigue or emotional instability. Often the person is highly imaginative, and wants to see someone or something so badly that they subconsciously attach reality to imagination—such as when a person "sees" a loved one who is deceased. Furthermore, hallucinations are usually prompted by familiar times or places that bring to mind memories the person may wish to relive.

Most hallucinations involve only one of the senses—for example, sight or hearing. Only rarely do they involve multiple senses. Hallucinations are also individualistic and subjective, and are more common among females than males. As far as scientists have been able to tell, *group* hallucinations simply do not happen, just as group dreams do not occur.

Now compare this with the story told by Jesus's followers. First, Jesus's resurrection appearances were not merely to individuals, but to multiple persons on several occasions—such as the two disciples on the road to Emmaus; [76] or groups that included some or all of the eleven remaining apostles. [77] In 1 Corinthians, written about 55 A.D., Paul says Jesus appeared to more than 500 people at one time. [78]

Nor did His followers just *see* Him. He talked with them. [79] He manipulated real objects, such as food, [80] and they physically touched Him. [81]

And unlike normal hallucinations, Jesus's appearances lasted for extended periods of time. He held a lengthy conversation with Cleopas and his companion along the road to Emmaus, explaining the Scriptures, before briefly joining them for supper. [82] He cooked and ate breakfast with several disciples by the Sea of Galilee, then had a conversation with them. [83] And of course, He continued to appear to His disciples for forty days. [84]

Then the appearances abruptly stopped—unless we count Paul's vision. [85] Hallucinations, like insanity, do not normally vanish so abruptly.

Nor were Jesus's appearances limited in time or place—they occurred in both the morning and the evening, and took place in Jerusalem, Galilee, and elsewhere. [86]

Finally, Jesus's followers were hardly predisposed to "see" a resurrected Jesus—they were instead quite skeptical when they heard of it and were hard to convince. [87] In fact, Jesus's resurrection was so unexpected that on three occasions He was not even recognized when He initially appeared. [88] The hallucination theory also does not account for Jesus's appearance to Paul, [89] who was an enemy of the Christians at the time.

However, the strongest argument against this explanation has yet to be made: if Jesus's resurrection appearances were just a hallucination, why didn't the Jewish leaders or the Roman authorities produce the body and discredit the story? They were certainly motivated to do so. The Romans were interested in civil order, and the Christians were upsetting that order. (We know this from the book of Acts, [90] as well as Claudius' decree expelling the Jews from Rome "who were rioting because of Chrestus.")

The Jewish leaders had an even stronger motive for disproving the resurrection story, because it portrayed those leaders as murderers of the long-awaited Messiah. Furthermore, this preaching was going on right under their noses, in Jerusalem itself. Yet neither the Romans nor the Jews produced the body. Instead they tried to suppress the story through intimidation and persecution, [91] and spread the story that the disciples had stolen the body. [92]

While Luke attributes the Jewish leaders' persecution to jealousy, [93] I believe they saw what we seem to have lost sight of: if the disciples' story about the resurrection was not true, then they were liars and scoundrels, deliberately deceiving people and leading them to their ruin. [94] Saul of Tarsus understood this, which is why he persecuted the early Christians without mercy. [95] He knew there were only two possible alternatives: either Jesus's resurrection really happened and the disciples honestly reported what they saw, or it was all a hoax, a sham, a lie. Saul was certain the disciples were frauds, until his experience on the road to Damascus convinced him otherwise. [96]

So which explanation—truth or lie—is more credible?

The Credibility of the New Testament

The Portrait of Jesus. If you are evaluating whether or not someone is telling you the truth, a good starting point is to consider what they say. And so we start with what the New Testament writers actually say about Jesus.

As we saw in Chapter One, Jesus is unique among religious figures. In everything He says and does, He is nothing like the gods that men dream up, for He doesn't think like men, react like men, or value the things that men value. Perhaps nothing demonstrates Jesus's uniqueness better than His forgiveness toward those who were crucifying Him [97] and toward Peter who had denied Him. [98]

Yet Jesus also has real human qualities that we seldom see in stories about mythical gods: He weeps; [99] He anguishes in the Garden of Gethsemane as His death approaches; [100] He cares deeply about people. [101] The Jesus we see in the Gospels seems true to life, rather than a fantasy concocted by men. As the famous historian, Will Durant, said: "That a few simple men should in one generation have invented so powerful and appealing a personality, so lofty an ethic and so inspiring a vision of human brotherhood, would be a miracle far more incredible than any recorded in the Gospels." [102]

Perhaps Durant overstates the case. Nevertheless, the portrait of Jesus in the New Testament is exceptional among religious figures, for He displays not only power, eloquence, and wisdom, but also compassion and human frailty. Among the gods and the founders of religions, only the Buddha can rival Jesus's appeal. But the Buddha never claimed to be divine, nor did his followers assert that he had been bodily resurrected. [103]

Next we consider what the New Testament authors say about themselves and others.

A High Regard for Truth. Liars often try to hide their flaws, mistakes, and poor decisions, or at least minimize them. The New Testament writers do not. They display a remarkable level of honesty, for they include details that are potentially embarrassing or counter-productive. Just look at what they say about Peter.

Peter became one of the prominent leaders of the Christians after Jesus's death. Peter made the first public speech about Christ's resurrection, [104] and was the first of the disciples to perform a miraculous healing in Jesus's name. [105] When the disciples were arrested for preaching about Jesus, Peter spoke for all of them. [106] He confronted the dishonest Ananias and Sapphira, [107] and the greedy Simon. [108] Peter was the first disciple to extend Christianity and Christian baptism to the Gentiles, [109] and then bravely defended what he had done, winning over those who believed that Christ had come only for the Jews. [110]

If our witnesses were inventing a new religion—a religion based on a lie—we would expect them to exalt this early leader into heroic, larger-than-life status, like a Greek hero or a Roman god. Yet the Gospel writers tell embarrassing stories about Peter that make him look dense, foolish, and cowardly.

All four Gospels admit that Peter denied knowing Jesus three times after His arrest, [111] after vehemently pledging to remain faithful to the point of death. [112] Matthew and Mark tell us that Jesus once rebuked Peter in harsh terms: "Get behind Me, Satan." (Matthew 16:23) [113] When Jesus walked on water, Peter bravely tried it himself—but quickly failed. [114] At Jesus's miraculous transfiguration, where He is met by the supernatural Moses and Elijah, Peter foolishly asked if he should make tents for the three of them. [115] When Jesus stooped to wash the apostles' feet on the night He would be arrested, Peter objected, and was once again rebuked by Jesus. [116] Peter was even criticized by Paul for hypocrisy regarding eating with Gentiles. [117]

Nor is Peter the only disciple to receive this humiliating treatment. The Gospel writers tell us that on the night Jesus was betrayed and arrested—during His hour of greatest need—His closest followers fell asleep when He went off to pray. [118] Indeed, Matthew and Mark tell us that this happened more than once. Then when Jesus was arrested, His followers all ran away and deserted Him. [119]

The Gospels also frequently present Jesus's disciples as obtuse, such as when they failed to grasp the real meaning of what He said and did, [120] or when they were slow to understand who and what He was. [121] When the women reported that Jesus had risen, the men refused to believe it. [122] The apostle Thomas would not believe Jesus was alive even when the other apostles corroborated the women's story. [123]

The New Testament writers provide other examples of the disciples' weaknesses and failings: their inability to cast out a demon; [124] their argument about which of them was the greatest; [125]

their terror at seeing Jesus walking on water, [126] at His transfiguration, [127] and at the prospect of going to Jerusalem where Jesus would be condemned. [128]

Even Paul, the great Christian missionary, does not escape. His persecution of the church is prominently mentioned, [129] and he calls himself the foremost of sinners. [130] He talks openly about his own weaknesses and deficiencies, [131] and reveals problems within the churches that he had helped to plant. [132]

Jesus's disciples must have told these stories for many years before the New Testament writers finally recorded them. If you were fabricating a myth to make yourself look good, you would not include—much less *invent*—stories that made you and your co-conspirators look foolish, especially many years after the fact. For this reason alone, the New Testament exudes honesty and frankness. But there is more.

Matthew addressed his Gospel to a Jewish audience, as shown by his eagerness to prove that Jesus was their long-awaited Messiah who fulfilled many of the Messianic prophecies. [133] So we are not surprised that in Matthew's Gospel Jesus refers to Himself thirty times as the "Son of Man," [134] the Messianic reference from the prophet Daniel. [135] But Mark and Luke wrote for Gentiles, [136] who were unfamiliar with the Jewish scriptures, and for whom "Son of Man" would seem to contradict Jesus's claims of divinity. So if Mark and Luke were merely inventing a deity, we would expect them to drop this inconvenient moniker. Yet we find Jesus referring to Himself as the Son of Man fourteen times in Mark's relatively short Gospel, and twenty-five times in Luke. [137] This is a striking illustration of honesty solely for the sake of honesty.

The seven-weeks gap is another. Jesus's resurrection, according to all of the accounts, occurred mere days after his death. Yet Acts says that His followers did not proclaim this to the world until about seven weeks later, on the day of Pentecost. [138] Even if we assume this was what actually happened, why wouldn't liars change the script to make the story more believable? After all, if the resurrection story was a lie, what's one more lie?

Admitting that they waited almost fifty days would make people wonder why they had delayed so long and invite speculation that they had used that time to fabricate the story. If the resurrection story was mere falsehood, this gap of seven weeks would never have become part of the story—or it would have been quickly discarded as unhelpful. It certainly would not have been included in a pro-Christian writing some thirty years after the fact. Its presence in Acts lends great weight to both the authenticity of the story and the author's credibility.

An often overlooked example of the New Testament authors' brutal honesty is the fact that, in each of the four Gospels, *women* discovered the empty tomb. [139] In Greco-Roman society of Jesus's day, as in many societies throughout history, the testimony of women was much more suspect than that of men, if not completely worthless. [140] If this story was merely a lie, the authors would have had a man discover the empty tomb and witness the accompanying angelic appearances—a man such as Joseph of Arimathea or Nicodemus, both of whom knew where Jesus's tomb was located. [141] But if the writers were telling the truth, they had to tell the story as it actually happened, however inconvenient that may have been.

In my experience as an attorney, liars frequently change or omit details that they believe are detrimental to their purposes. The New Testament authors did not do that, presumably because they were either obtuse or scrupulously truthful.

Stories that Mesh. Any judge, attorney, or psychologist will tell you that people see and remember events differently, because we all have unique perspectives and filters. A person witnessing an armed robbery from a hundred feet away might remember many details about the robber's clothing and appearance, whereas the person actually being robbed may remember only what the gun looked like. In this scenario, the disparity is simply the result of where their attention is focused. But perceptions and memories can also be influenced by many other factors, such as background, prior experiences, biases, expectations, etc.

For this reason, witnesses often perceive and remember distinct aspects of the same event, and the complete truth becomes apparent only by piecing together their stories like a jigsaw puzzle, to make sense of what is otherwise unclear. We see this in the New Testament.

Luke, the author of Acts and a friend of Paul, mentions a dispute between Paul and Barnabas that was so serious that it split them up as a missionary team. [142] They argued over whether to take Mark along on their second missionary journey, after he had deserted them during their first trip. [143] As a result, Barnabas returned to Cyprus (Barnabas' home [144]) with Mark, while Paul took Silas and went back to Asia Minor. [145] Luke doesn't tell us why Barnabas was so adamant that Mark should go with them, but we can discern the likely answer from one of Paul's letters. Colossians 4:10 tells us that Mark and Barnabas were cousins. [146] Thus, Barnabas was tied to Mark by family loyalty. Neither Luke nor Paul calls attention to this consonance between their respective writings, but together they explain much.

This is but one of many examples. In 1 Thessalonians 2:2, Paul mentions in passing that he suffered persecution in Philippi and faced much opposition in Thessalonica. Luke corroborates this story in Acts 16:12 – 17:9, where he describes these events in great detail. Further, Luke tells us that Paul stayed with a man named Jason while in Thessalonica, but doesn't tell us why. [147] Another of Paul's letters fills in the gap by informing us that Jason was Paul's kinsman. [148]

When Jesus was crucified, Mark's Gospel says three women were watching: Mary Magdalene, Mary the mother of James the Less and Joses, and Salome. [149] But later, when His body was buried, only the two Mary's were present to see where he was laid. [150] What happened to Salome? Matthew provides our first clue, since he tells us that among the women watching Jesus's crucifixion were Mary Magdalene, Mary the mother of James and Joseph, and "the mother of the sons of Zebedee." [151] If the last is Salome—which seems logical—then she is the mother of James and John, the sons of Zebedee. [152] This becomes important when we read the account of Jesus's crucifixion in John's Gospel, in which Jesus instructs John to look after Jesus's mother, Mary. [153] That helps to explain why Salome was not at the burial—she was probably helping her son John take care of Jesus's grieving mother after His death. This explanation is admittedly a bit speculative, but it makes sense, and it illustrates how three different Gospel accounts, each incomplete in itself, fit together to explain what is otherwise mysterious.

All four Gospels tell the story of the miracle of the feeding of the 5,000. [154] Only Luke tells us where this miracle occurred—near the town of Bethsaida. [155] But John adds an interesting detail to the story: before performing the miracle, Jesus turns to Philip and asks, "Where are we to buy bread?" (John 6:5) Why ask Philip? Perhaps because Philip was from Bethsaida, as John tells us elsewhere in his Gospel. [156] The subtle agreement between Luke and John on this matter is impressive, and gives credence to both the story and the miracle.

In Chapter 4 of *Who Moved the Stone?* ("A Psychological Parallelogram of Forces"), Frank Morison weaves together the Gospel accounts of Jesus's trial before Pontius Pilate, [157] discussing how they explain and corroborate each other.

Mark and Matthew seem to begin the trial with Pilate's question to Jesus, "Are You the King of the Jews?" (Matthew 27:11) [158] This odd beginning suggests that something must have been omitted. Luke fills in the gap by explaining that this question was preceded by the Jewish leaders' accusations that Jesus was "misleading our nation and forbidding to pay taxes to Caesar, and saying that He Himself is Christ, a King." (Luke 23:2)

John's Gospel begins even earlier, recounting Pilate's question to the Jewish leaders: "What accusation do you bring against this Man?," and the Jews' surprising response, "If this Man were not an evildoer, we would not have delivered Him to you." (John 18:29-30) Furthermore, Morison speculates that the Jews would not have uttered such an insolent response unless they had been led to expect that no trial would be necessary, and that Pilate would simply rubber-stamp the Sanhedrin's earlier decision that Jesus should die. [159] John gives us no clue as to what might have induced Pilate to suddenly insist on proper Roman procedure, but perhaps Matthew does, for he tells us that Pilate's wife sent him a message, "Have nothing to do with that righteous Man; for last night I suffered greatly in a dream because of Him." (Matthew 27:19) [160]

While the foregoing examples involve some degree of speculation or assumption, we are on rock-solid ground when we consider references to people in the New Testament. As you might expect, Jesus, Peter, and the other apostles are mentioned by multiple New Testament authors. But so are many other individuals. We have already seen that John Mark is named in both Acts and Colossians. [161] He is also mentioned in two of Paul's other letters, as well as 1 Peter. [162] Paul, whose adventures are the subject of chapters eight, nine, and thirteen through twenty-eight of Acts, is also the author of thirteen books of the New Testament, [163] and is mentioned in Second Peter 3:15.

Other examples include such prominent Christians as Apollos; [164] Aquila and his wife Priscilla; [165] Barnabas (a/k/a Joses or Joseph); [166] James, brother of Jesus and head of the Jerusalem church after Christ's death; [167] Joseph of Arimathea; [168] Luke, "the beloved physician"; [169] Martha and her sister Mary; [170] Mary Magdalene; [171] Silas (also called Silvanus); [172] Timothy; [173] and Titus. [174]

Many otherwise obscure persons also show up in multiple books, such as Alexander the coppersmith; [175] Archippus; [176] Aristarchus, a traveling companion of Paul; [177] Crispus, a Corinthian;[178] Demas;[179] Epaphras;[180] Erastus;[181] Gaius, another of Paul's traveling companions;[182] Jason;[183] Lucius of Cyrene;[184] Onesimus;[185] Rufus;[186] Sosthenes,[187] Trophimus the Ephesian;[188] and Tychicus.[189] On the other hand, many other persons are mentioned only in a single book.[190]

These are but a few instances of the seemingly unintentional agreement among different New Testament writers. Of course, this does not prove they are truthful in all that they wrote. However, such agreement demonstrates that we are not dealing with pure fiction here. The writers were discussing people and events with which they were familiar. And the agreement among different writers certainly adds significantly to their credibility. But let us delve even deeper.

Archaeology and Secular History. It's not enough for a person to *seem* credible, because some people are good liars. One of the best ways to determine if someone is telling the truth is to see if other evidence corroborates or refutes their story. We have seen that the New Testament books have a lot of apparent credibility and internal consistency, but what does history and archaeology say about them?

The book of Acts has been repeatedly shown to be historically accurate. Indeed, the famous British archaeologist, Sir William Ramsay, who was taught that Acts was a historically inaccurate product of the second century A.D., learned differently later in life: "I gradually came to find it a useful ally in some obscure and difficult investigations."[191] Most of the 54 cities named in Acts, once lost to history, have now been found by archaeologists. And we have already seen how Luke's passing mention of Claudius' expulsion of the Jews from Rome[192] is corroborated by the Roman historian, Suetonius.

Chapter 19 of Acts discusses one of Paul's visits to the city of Ephesus, in western Asia Minor (now Turkey), during which the people rioted over the economic and religious impact of Christianity on the city's cult worship of the goddess Artemis (Roman name, Diana), twin sister of the god Apollo. Acts mentions the temple of Artemis, [193] and quotes the people as crying out, "Great is Artemis of the Ephesians." (Acts 19:28, 34)

We know from history that Ephesus had a special relationship with this particular goddess, and the city's Temple of Artemis was one of the Seven Wonders of the Ancient World. The Temple was destroyed in the fifth century A.D., but archaeologists found its remains in the late nineteenth century. Archaeologists also uncovered the theater where, according to Acts, the rioting Ephesians dragged several Christians. [194] The theater could hold 25,000 people. Luke's account is therefore entirely consistent with what history says about Ephesus.

Luke's terminology in Acts was once thought to be inaccurate, but no more. In Acts 13:7, Luke refers to Sergius Paulus as the "proconsul" of Cyprus. A Roman province under the jurisdiction of the Roman Senate was ruled by a proconsul, but a province under the jurisdiction of the emperor was ruled by a procurator—like Pontius Pilate in Judea. Cyprus was thought to have been an imperial province, until historians discovered that it was changed to a senatorial province in 22 B.C., confirming that Luke was right.

Luke's description of Gallio as "proconsul of Achaia" has been verified by an inscription at Delphi which refers to Gallio by the same title. Similarly, Luke's reference to Publius as "leading [or first] man of the island" of Malta in Acts 28:7 matches Maltese inscriptions that give him that identical appellation. Luke's use of the Greek word *politarchs* for the authorities in Thessalonica [195] and *meris* to refer to a "district" of Macedonia [196] were once thought to be wrong, but in each case his terminology has proven to be accurate.

Romans 16:23 is one of those verses that most of us gloss over. In it, Paul conveys greetings from those who were with him, one of whom is "Erastus, the city treasurer." Paul's letter to the Romans was probably written from the Greek city of Corinth, [197] in about 55-56 A.D. Thus, we may surmise from Paul's letter that

Erastus was the city treasurer for Corinth. This is further corroborated by 2 Timothy 4:20, where Paul says, "Erastus remained at Corinth."

Excavations of Corinth in 1929 uncovered a first-century pavement inscribed: "Erastus, curator of public buildings, laid this pavement at his own expense." If this does not refer to Paul's Erastus, then it is an astonishing coincidence. But I believe it is yet another confirmation of the accuracy and reliability of the New Testament writers.

So far we have seen that the New Testament writers were brutally and embarrassingly honest about their own shortcomings; they were consistent with each other, even about seemingly minor details; and they have been confirmed by history and archeology in many of their facts. Although history was not their purpose, the New Testament writers appear to have been excellent historians. Yet even excellent historians are capable of lying. And so we turn to the most convincing proof of all.

The Most Convincing Proof of All. What would you regard as conclusive proof that Jesus rose from the dead? We have eyewitness testimony, from John, Peter, and Paul, [198] and perhaps Matthew, and we have second-hand reports from Mark and Luke. We can be confident that we have what they actually said and wrote, at least in substance, since the New Testament books are among the most reliable ancient documents in existence, with more and older copies, and fewer discrepancies between manuscripts, than any comparable writings. But did the eyewitnesses and their close associates lie?

The skeptic will point out that the witnesses are biased. Yet how could they not be? Witnessing a dead person come back to life would be a life-changing experience. No one could remain neutral. So perhaps the key to deciding where the truth lies is not what these witnesses said, but what they did.

As an attorney, I have seen many people who were accused of crimes deny guilt when questioned by the police, only to later admit guilt. They lied because they thought it would make their situation better, but when they learned otherwise they changed their story. Some people have even admitted guilt to crimes they did not commit, because they believed, rightly or wrongly, that they would be better off by doing so.

Call me a cynic, but I believe most of us would lie under the right circumstances, such as to avoid death or severe suffering. On the other hand, how many of us would be willing to suffer or die *for a lie*?

Make no mistake, Jesus's followers suffered a great deal. Recall Tacitus, the Roman historian, who discusses the persecution and executions of Christians by the Emperor Nero in 64 A.D., some 30 years after Christ's death. Suetonius also mentions this persecution by Nero: "punishment was inflicted on the Christians, a set of men adhering to a novel and mischievous superstition." [199] And the letter of Pliny the Younger talks of his execution of obstinate Christians in the early second century A.D.

The Romans carried out ten major persecutions of Christians in the first 300 years after Christ's death, [200] and many lesser persecutions. In Acts we read that the Romans beat and imprisoned Paul and Silas when they were in Philippi. [201] Christian preaching in Ephesus caused a riot, [202] and such preaching was the likely cause of Emperor Claudius' order expelling the Jews from Rome, as reported by Suetonius and Acts. [203] Clement of Rome and Polycarp both wrote of the sufferings of Jesus's followers in the decades following His death.

For three centuries Christians frequently lost property and position, and faced slavery, torture, and death because of their faith. Yet until the destruction of Jerusalem in 70 A.D., Christians often suffered the most zealous persecution from their monotheistic cousins, the Jews.

In the days after Pentecost the Jewish leaders ordered that Peter and the apostles be jailed and flogged to dissuade them from preaching about Christ's resurrection. [204] To please the Jews, King

Herod had Peter arrested and jailed—likely to await execution—until he miraculously escaped. [205] Paul faced opposition from the Jews in many of the cities he visited, [206] even though he had previously been the chief persecutor of the Christians. [207] In Lystra, a mob, incited by Jews from nearby towns, tried to kill Paul by stoning him, [208] and Acts tells us about at least two plots against his life. [209]

Paul, while defending himself against some of his critics, lists his many difficulties in 2 Corinthians 11:23-27:

> Are they servants of Christ?—I speak as if insane—I more so; in far more labors, in far more imprisonments, beaten times without number, often in danger of death. Five times I received from the Jews thirty-nine *lashes*. Three times I was beaten with rods, once I was stoned, three times I was shipwrecked, a night and a day I have spent in the deep. *I have been* on frequent journeys, in dangers from rivers, dangers from robbers, dangers from *my* countrymen, dangers from the Gentiles, dangers in the city, dangers in the wilderness, dangers on the sea, dangers among false brethren; *I have been* in labor and hardship, through many sleepless nights, in hunger and thirst, often without food, in cold and exposure.

Paul also mentions that he and the other apostles are "both hungry and thirsty, and are poorly clothed, and are roughly treated, and are homeless"; furthermore, they are "without honor," persecuted, slandered, and like "the scum of the world, the dregs of all things." (1 Corinthians 4:9-13)

Such maltreatment was not limited to the Christian leaders. Persecution, suffering, and insults were the lot of many early Christians, as discussed by several New Testament writers who encouraged Christians to bear these difficulties with patience and endurance. [210]

Yet despite their sufferings, Jesus's followers traveled throughout the Roman Empire, and beyond, to spread their message. We know from Acts that Philip went to Samaria, Gaza, and Caesarea; [211] that Peter traveled to Samaria and several cities in Palestine; [212] and that Paul—accompanied at times by Barnabas, Mark, Silas, and others—went to Syria, Cyprus, Asia Minor (Turkey), Macedonia, and Greece. [213] The reference to "Babylon" in 1 Peter 5:13 [214] probably means that Peter wrote the letter from Rome (which Christians considered to be a center of evil, like the Babylon of Old Testament times). Peter's presence in Rome is confirmed by early Christian writers such as Jerome and Eusebius.

Christian writers of the first three centuries after Christ's death tell us that one or more of the apostles, or their close associates, traveled to Asia Minor, Greece and Macedonia, Syria and Lebanon, Spain, France, Egypt, Libya, Armenia and other areas near the Black Sea, Mesopotamia, Iran, India, and other locations. Even if we did not have these sources, or the New Testament, the rapid spread of Christianity in its early years would necessarily imply extensive travel by the early Christians.

We have already seen that the Christian presence in Rome by 49 A.D.—less than 20 years after Jesus's death—was significant enough to produce an uproar among the Jews that resulted in an imperial decree expelling them from Rome. Fifteen years later the Christians in Rome were so numerous that the Emperor Nero was able to use them as a scapegoat for the burning of Rome and make their systematic execution part of the Roman Games.

Nero's persecution of Christians is believed to have claimed the lives of both Peter and Paul. Clement of Rome, a first century Christian bishop, wrote a letter to the Corinthians in which he strongly implies that both suffered martyrdom. Clement's letter was probably written about 95-97 A.D., but may have been written as early as 68-70 A.D. Later Christian writers tell us that Paul was beheaded and Peter was crucified, both in Rome. Their fate was similar to that of many of Jesus's closest followers.

As we saw earlier, Josephus reported that Jesus's brother, James, [215] was stoned to death along with some fellow Christians. Acts records the deaths of two Christians—James the son of Zebedee, who was executed on the orders of King Herod, [216] and Stephen, who was stoned to death by the Jews. [217] Early Christian writings unanimously record the martyrdoms of the apostles Thomas and Philip, as well as Barnabas' cousin John Mark. (On the other hand, all agree that John, the son of Zebedee, died of old age, as did Barnabas.)

The fate of some of Jesus's other followers is less clear. Christian sources agree that the apostles Andrew, Bartholomew, Jude, Simon the Zealot, and Matthias [218] were all martyred, but stories conflict about the methods and locations of their individual martyrdoms. Luke and Matthew may have died natural deaths, although some traditions say that they too were martyred. And the fate of the apostle James the Less is unclear, because he is too often confused with the other two men of the same name: James the Greater, the son of Zebedee, and James the Just, the brother of Jesus.

Thus, we have strong evidence that many of Jesus's followers traveled, suffered, and ultimately died because of their insistence that this story of Jesus's resurrection was true. And so far as we know, none of them ever recanted or disavowed this story, nor did they renounce Christianity or the Christian community.

Furthermore, these were not the type of men you would expect to suffer and die for *anything*. Three times Peter denied even knowing Jesus because he feared what might happen if he were discovered. All of Jesus's closest followers deserted Him when He was arrested, and only John and a few women showed up to watch Him die on the cross. When Jesus returned alive, He found them huddled behind locked doors, hiding from the Jewish authorities.[219] Yet something changed each of them into an impregnable fortress of courage, strength, and determination—many to the point of death.

Something even changed people who were initially opposed to Christianity. Most prominent among these is Paul, also known as Saul, who was one of the early church's most passionate enemies.[220] He later became its greatest missionary after receiving a vision of the risen Christ.[221]

But often overlooked in this regard are the members of Jesus's own family. While He was alive, Jesus's family members were not among His followers, and may have thought He had lost His mind.[222] Yet sometime after His death Jesus's mother and brothers joined the ranks of the Christians.[223] His brothers, Jude and James "the Just," both wrote letters which became part of our New Testament,[224] and James became one of the leaders of the Christians in Jerusalem.[225] Perhaps Jesus's post-resurrection appearance to his brother James[226] convinced them that Jesus's claims of divinity were actually true.

Two Inescapable Conclusions

As we have seen, there are really only two alternatives to explain what Jesus's followers claimed to have seen after His death—either they told the truth about what they witnessed, in which case the resurrection is a fact of history, or they lied. Anyone who prefers the second alternative must face two difficult, but inescapable, conclusions.

If we assume for the moment that the disciples lied, then they were the worst liars history has ever seen. First, they were absurdly foolish, because they seem to have gained *nothing* that the world considers valuable. None achieved a position of power or accumulated wealth—indeed, they were suspicious of the latter, considering the love of money to be "a root of all sorts of evil." (1 Timothy 6:10)[227]

If they hoped to exact revenge against those who had murdered Jesus, that effort was a colossal failure, too. However, revenge seems an unlikely motive. Like Jesus Himself, His followers renounced violence and revenge, while advocating kindness and forgiveness.[228] And they excused the ruling authorities for executing their Master, while instructing Christians to obey the government.[229]

On the other hand, if the disciples' purpose was merely to avoid the kind of trouble that resulted in the death of their leader, that also failed miserably. Their story actually brought more trouble than they probably imagined: hardship, suffering, imprisonment, exile,[230] and for many, an early and painful death. To continue telling a lie that brings only suffering, hardship, and death is just stupid—as well as immensely unlikely. And let us not pretend that they were somehow motivated by the hope of recompense in the next life, because if the resurrection was a lie, then so too was the promise of eternal life.

Yet if Jesus's followers held out any hope for another life, they must have known that they were hopelessly unworthy of it, because they were also the "worst" liars in history from a moral perspective. This lie they fabricated was unspeakably despicable. They led countless others into persecution and death, *knowing* Christianity was based on a lie. And they did so while strongly advocating honesty, truthfulness, and sincerity—and insistently affirming their own.[231] Could there be greater evil and hypocrisy than this?

The second inescapable conclusion is that these men and women were also the *best* liars history has ever seen, because they told an incredible whopper and actually convinced huge numbers of people that it was true.

However gullible and ignorant our ancestors may have been about some things, they were no fools. They knew from long and repeated experience that dead people don't come back to life. They laughed at Jesus when He told them that a dead girl was merely "asleep." [232] People in the first century A.D. must have been no less skeptical than we would be when the Christians told them Jesus had been crucified and then come back to life. Such things just don't happen, then or now.

Yet many people who had never even known Jesus in the flesh became so convinced that the resurrection was a fact that they too willingly suffered loss of property, imprisonment, enslavement, and even death—as Pliny's letter shows us—rather than renounce it.

And we must not overlook the fact that this resurrection tale originated in Jerusalem—the city that also housed the Jewish religious leaders who had the most to gain by discrediting the disciples' story, and the most to lose by its continued success.

But the Christians were successful, as even the most determined skeptic must concede. Despite threats and persecution by the Jewish leaders and the Romans, Jesus's followers were able to spread this new religion like wildfire all over the Roman Empire and beyond. And so you may ask, why did they succeed?

Simply put, they succeeded because Jesus's followers were changed. Before His crucifixion they were foolish and dense. Seven weeks later, they were unshakable advocates for faith in Jesus, instructing others about His life, teachings, death, and resurrection.

The cowardly Peter now boldly preached the gospel despite opposition, threats, and beatings. The enemy of the faith, Paul, turned into its greatest missionary. Thomas, the stubborn skeptic, became a confident believer. James and Jude, once concerned about their brother's sanity, now assumed leadership roles among His followers. All of Jesus's disciples were changed from frightened rabbits, hiding behind locked doors, into fearless lions carrying the Gospel all over the Roman Empire and beyond—willing to suffer any adversity, including death, to spread their message. As one pastor said, "Men are changed by lies, but seldom for the better." [233]

The contemporaries of Jesus's followers had an opportunity to personally observe their demeanor, their credibility, and the way they lived their lives. The slightest hint of prevarication or hypocrisy, or even self-delusion, would have permanently crippled the credibility of the resurrection story and this infant Christian movement. Instead, the movement grew exponentially, despite everything Judaism and the Roman Empire tried to do to stop it.

Anyone who claims that Jesus's resurrection was a fairy tale must satisfactorily answer two questions: ***How*** were Jesus's followers able to fool so many people into believing this fantastic story? And ***why*** did they bother? It may be hard to believe that Christ's resurrection really happened, but after you have looked at the evidence it is even harder to believe that it didn't.

For Further Study. If you want to conduct your own study, a good place to begin is with Frank Morison's *Who Moved the Stone?*, an easy read that is nonetheless compelling. Other excellent sources include Josh McDowell's *Evidence that Demands a Verdict* (especially Section II) and *More Than a Carpenter*; Lee Strobel's *The Case for Christ*; and C.S. Lewis' *The Case for Christianity*. William Steuart McBirnie's well-written and painstakingly researched *The Search for the Twelve Apostles* documents the historical evidence regarding the lives and deaths of Jesus's followers. And for an exhaustive treatment of the evidence, read Michael R. Licona's *The Resurrection of Jesus: A New Historiographical Approach.* [234] These are only a start. The resources are almost endless.

Endnotes for Chapter Two, "Is Jesus's Resurrection Fact or Fairy Tale?"

1 The general outline of this proof is based on the sermons of the late Dr. Gene Scott, former pastor of Faith Center in Glendale, California.

2 See John 21:20-24 and 1 John 1:1-5.

3 2 Peter 1:16

4 Mark is specifically mentioned in Acts 12:25, 13:13, and 15:37-39; Colossians 4:10; Philemon 24; and 1 Peter 5:13.

5 Acts 9:3-9, 22:5-11, and 26:12-18

6 Virtually no one questions Paul's authorship of Romans, First Corinthians, Second Corinthians, Galatians, and Philippians, and few doubt his authorship of First Thessalonians and Philemon. The other letters commonly attributed to Paul are Ephesians, Colossians, Second Thessalonians, First Timothy, Second Timothy, and Titus.

7 See Philemon 24; 2 Timothy 4:11; and compare Acts 16:8 and 16:10, where "they" becomes "we."

8 See Luke 1:1-4 and Acts 1:1.

9 Galatians 1:19 and Jude 1:1

10 See Acts 12:17, 15:13, 21:18; Galatians 2:9 and 2:12.

11 The estimated dates for the writing of the New Testament books are as follows (all dates are A.D.):

Matthew	ca. 70-85	1 Timothy	ca. 61-63
Mark	ca. 50-70	2 Timothy	ca. 64-68
Luke	ca. 60-85	Titus	ca. 61-63
John	ca. 80-95	Philemon	before 68
Acts	ca. 64-80	Hebrews	ca. 80-95
Romans	ca. 55-58	James	ca. 44-48
1 Corinthians	ca. 53-57	1 Peter	ca. 64
2 Corinthians	ca. 57	2 Peter	ca. 67
Galatians	ca. 47-58	1 John	ca. 90-95
Ephesians	ca. 57-63	2 John	ca. 90-95
Philippians	ca. 61-64	3 John	ca. 90-95
Colossians	ca. 58-63	Jude	ca. 95

1 Thessalonians	ca. 50	Revelation	ca. 95
2 Thessalonians	ca. 50	1 Timothy	ca. 61-63

[12] Acts was probably written no later than about 68 A.D. because of what it leaves out. Acts ends with Paul under house arrest in Rome, awaiting a hearing on his appeal to the Emperor. (See Acts 25:11-12 and 28:16-31.) Early Christian writings tell us that Paul was subsequently released and traveled to Spain before later being imprisoned a second time in Rome and beheaded in about 64-68 A.D. Since Acts omits these later events, I believe it was completed before Paul's release from house arrest. Acts also says nothing about the Roman destruction of Jerusalem, which occurred in 70 A.D. This also favors an early date for Acts, since it seems unlikely Luke would have failed to mention such a significant event, at least in passing. Luke says he wrote Acts after writing his Gospel (see Acts 1:1-2), and Mark almost certainly wrote his Gospel before Luke's, so those two Gospels were also probably written prior to 68 A.D.

[13] Luke and Matthew appear to borrow heavily from Mark's Gospel, which is why most scholars believe Mark's Gospel was written first. But all three of these Gospels have passages that are not in the others, leading to speculation that one or more may have used another Gospel, now lost, which has been given the moniker, "Q document." The existence of such a document cannot be proven or disproven.

[14] "Cephas" is Aramaic for "rock," just as "Petras"—from which we get "Peter"—is Greek for "rock."

[15] While the Gospels do not perfectly parallel the list of post-resurrection appearances in 1 Corinthians 15:3-8, there are many similarities and parallels, such as: the appearance to Peter (Cephas) is implied in Mark 16:7 and mentioned in Luke 24:34; the appearance to The Twelve (which were only eleven, due to Judas' suicide) is mentioned in Matthew 28:16-17, Luke 24:33-50, John 20:19-29, as well as Acts 1:2-3; the appearance to more than 500 might refer to the appearance in Galilee in Matthew 28:16-18. Of course the appearance to Paul is specifically mentioned in Acts 9:1-6, 22:6-10, and 26:12-18, as well as 1 Corinthians 9:1.

[16] Gutenberg invented the printing press in 1439 A.D.

[17] For example, the *Codex Vaticanus* dates from about 325-350 A.D., and the *Codex Sinaiticus* is from about 350 A.D.

[18] The seven epistles of Ignatius, who was martyred in about 110 A.D., contain quotations from 17 of the 27 New Testament books, including the Gospels of Matthew and John. Clement of Alexandria (ca. 150-212 A.D.) quotes the New Testament about 2,400 times, and quotes from 24 of the 27 books. The writings of Irenaeus, the second century Bishop of Lyons, contain 1,038 quotations from the Gospels and 781 quotations from other New Testament books. Justin Martyr, who died in 166 A.D., quotes the Gospels 268 times and other N.T. books 62 times. Origen, who lived in the 3rd century A.D., quotes the Gospels 9,231 times and other N.T. books 8,761 times. Other early Christian writers that quote the New Testament include Barnabas (ca. 70 A.D.); Hermas (ca. 95 A.D.); Tertullian (ca. 160-220 A.D.); Tatian (ca. 170 A.D.); Hippolytus (ca. 170-235 A.D.); and Cyprian (died 258 A.D.).

[19] Lectionaries were Scriptural lessons intended to be read during Christian worship services.

[20] In all, these three works include quotations from ten of the twenty-seven New Testament books: Matthew, Mark, Luke, Acts, Romans, 1 Corinthians, Ephesians, Titus, Hebrews, and 1 Peter.

[21] Matthew, John, Romans, 1 Corinthians, 2 Corinthians, Galatians, Ephesians, Philippians, 1 Timothy, 2 Timothy, and Titus

[22] Matthew, Mark, Luke, Acts, Romans, 1 Corinthians, 2 Corinthians, Galatians, Ephesians, Philippians, 2 Thessalonians, 1 Timothy, 2 Timothy, Hebrews, 1 Peter, and 1 John

[23] Tacitus' *Histories* originally contained 14 volumes, but only four and a half have survived. Of the 16 volumes of his *Annals*, we have ten, as well as parts of two more.

[24] The most significant differences between manuscripts, by far, are John 7:53 – 8:11 (the woman caught in adultery), Mark 16:9-20 (Jesus' resurrection appearances), and 1 John 5:7-8. These verses are not in the oldest New Testament manuscripts, and are presumably later additions.

[25] An excellent, detailed discussion of the nature and impact of these differences can be found in Chapter 2 of Lee Strobel's book, *The Case for the Real Jesus*.

[26] The Muratorian fragment is named after an Italian archeologist, Ludovico Antonio Muratori (1672-1750), who discovered it in 1740 A.D.

[27] See, for example, Matthew 27:33-50; Mark 15:22-37; Luke 23:33-46; John 19:17-30; Acts 2:22-23, 2:36, and 4:10; Romans 6:6; 1 Corinthians 1:13, 1:23, 2:2, 2:8, and 15:3-4; 2 Corinthians 13:4; Galatians 2:20 and 3:1; 1 Peter 2:23-24 and 3:18; and Revelation 11:8.

[28]**Peter**: See 1 Peter 1:3, 1:21, and 3:21-22; see also the following verses in Acts, which talk about Peter (as well as Jesus' other disciples) proclaiming Christ's resurrection: Acts 2:24, 2:32, 3:15, 4:2, 4:10, 4:33, 5:30, and 10:40-41

Luke: Luke 24:1-51; Acts 1:1-3

Paul: Romans 1:4, 7:4, 10:9, 14:9; 1 Corinthians 15:3-8, 15:12-20; 2 Corinthians 4:14, 5:15; Galatians 1:1; Ephesians 1:20, 2:6; Philippians 3:10; Colossians 1:18, 2:12; 1 Thessalonians 1:10; 2 Timothy 2:8; see also the following verses in Acts, which talk about Paul preaching Jesus' resurrection: Acts 13:30-31, 17:3, 17:18, 17:31, and 26:23

John: John 20:1-21:24

Matthew: Matthew 28:1-10, 16-20

Mark: 16:1-7 (I do not include Mark 16:9-19, because scholars generally agree that these verses were not part of the Mark's original Gospel, since they are not found in some of the oldest manuscripts)

[29]**Luke**: Luke 24:51; Acts 1:2 and 1:9

[30]**Peter**: 1 Peter 3:22

Paul: Ephesians 1:20 and 2:6

[31] Clement of Rome, *Epistle to the Corinthians*, xl. sqq., quoted in Bettenson, *Documents of the Christian Church*, pp. 62-63.

[32] Gnostics believed in a secret truth, or "Gnosis," which was revealed only to believers. Gnosticism taught that flesh is evil, and that salvation is the freeing of spirit from the flesh. Since they believed flesh is evil, Gnostic Christians taught that Jesus was pure spirit, and therefore His earthly body was merely an illusion, as were His death and resurrection.

[33] Tacitus' Annals, XV.44, as quoted in *The Early Christians*, p. 61 (emphasis added).

[34] As quoted in *The Early Christians*, pp. 63-65 (emphasis added).

[35] Suetonius' *The Twelve Caesars*, "Claudius," 25, as quoted in Keller's *The Bible as History*, p. 379. See also, Durant's *The Story of Civilization*, p. 554, which says: "Suetonius . . . reports Claudius' banishment (*ca.* 52) of 'Jews

who, stirred up by Christ [*impulsore Chresto*], were causing public disturbances. . . .' " Claudius was Emperor of Rome from 41 to 54 A.D.

[36] Quoted from Lucian's *The Death of Peregrine*, 11-13, as quoted in McDowell, *The New Evidence That Demands a Verdict*, p. 121.

[37]*The Passing Peregruis*, by Lucian, quoted in McDowell, *Evidence That Demands a Verdict*, p. 84.

[38] Josephus, *Antiquities of the Jews*, XVIII, 33, as quoted in McDowell, *The New Evidence That Demands a Verdict*, p. 125 (italics added by the latter). This passage is also known as the "Testimonium."

[39]*Antiquities of the Jews*, xx.9:1, by Flavius Josephus (emphasis added), as quoted in *The Early Christians*, p.62

[40]McDowell, *The New Evidence That Demands a Verdict*, p. 126

[41]*Antiquities of the Jews*, xviii.5.2, as quoted in McDowell, *The New Evidence That Demands a Verdict*, p. 56.

[42] The New Testament contains many references to John the Baptist, such as: Matthew 3:1-14, 4:12, 9:14, 11:2-14, 11:18, 14:2-12, 16:14, 17:13, 21:25-26, 21:32; Mark 1:2-9, 1:14, 2:18, 6:14-29, 8:28, 11:30-32; Luke 1:13-17, 1:60, 1:63, 3:2-20, 5:33, 7:18-28-30, 7:33, 9:7-9, 9:19, 11:1, 16:16, 20:4-6; John 1:6-8, 1:15, 1:19-36, 1:40, 3:23-30, 4:1, 5:33, 10:41-42; Acts 1:5, 1:22, 10:37, 11:16, 13:24-25, 18:25 19:3-4.

[43] See for example Matthew 27:45: "Now from the sixth hour [noon] darkness fell upon all the land until the ninth hour [3:00 p.m.]." See also Mark 15:33, and Luke 23:44.

[44] As quoted in McDowell, *Evidence That Demands a Verdict*, p. 86

[45] Philip Schaff, *The Person of Christ* (New York: American Tract Society, 1913), p. 133, as quoted in McDowell, *Evidence That Demands a Verdict*, p. 130.

[46] See Matthew 27:57-61, 28:1-6; Mark 15:42-47, 16:1-6; Luke 23:50-53, 24:1-12; John 19:38-42, 20:1-15.

[47] Matthew 28:11-15

[48] See Matthew 27:57-60, Mark 15:42-46, Luke 23:50-53, John 19:38-42.

[49] This "guard" posted at Jesus' tomb has traditionally been viewed as a small group of Roman soldiers. However, Matthew is ambiguous on this

point. And as Frank Morison points out in *Who Moved the Stone?*, Pilate's comment, "You have a guard; go, make it as secure as you know how" (Matthew 27:65), could mean that he declined the Jewish leaders' request for a Roman guard. Morison argues that the Jewish leaders posted Jewish Temple guards around the tomb. (See Morison, *Who Moved the Stone?*, pp. 152-159. For a contrary view, see McDowell, *The New Evidence That Demands a Verdict*, pp. 235-237.)

[50] See Luke 24:12 and John 20:5-7. See also, Matthew 27:59, Mark 15:46, Luke 23:53, and John 19:40.

[51] See Matthew 27:61, Mark 15:47, Luke 23:55

[52] The persecution of early Christianity by the Jews is well documented in the book of Acts. See, for example, Acts 4:1-3, 18; 5:17-18, 26-28, 40; 6:8-14; 7:57-60; 8:1-3; 9:1-2; 12:1-5; 13:45, 50; 14:2, 5, 19; 17:5-9, 13; 18:12-17; 20:3; 21:27-36; 22:22; 23:2, 12-15. Christians also suffered persecution from the Romans. See Acts 16:19-24; 19:23-40; 22:24-25.

[53] Luke 24:13-28

[54] Luke 24:42-43; John 21:9-13

[55] Matthew 28:9-10, 28:18-20; Luke 24:15-32, 24:36-50; John 20:15-17, 20:19-23, 20:26-29; John 21:5-6, 21:9-12, 21:15-22; Acts 1:4-8

[56] Luke 24:39; John 20:27-29

[57] See 1 Corinthians 15:5-8. The twelve to whom Paul refers would not have included Judas, who committed suicide the night he betrayed Jesus (Matthew 27:3-5), but would have included Matthias, who replaced Judas (Acts 1:15-26).

[58] See Matthew 27:59-60, Luke 23:53, and John 19:41. See also, Mark 15:46.

[59] See Luke 23:54 and John 19:42.

[60] See John 19:32-33.

[61] See Mark 15:43-45.

[62] See Matthew 27:54; Mark 15:39, 15:44-45; and Luke 23:47.

[63] See Matthew 27:60, 27:66, 28:2; Mark 15:46, 16:3-4; Luke 24:2; John 20:1

[64] Matthew 27:32; Mark 15:21; Luke 23:26

[65] We know Jesus was on the cross before noon and remained there until at least 3:00 p.m. See Matthew 27:45-46; Mark 15:33-34; Luke 23:44-46.

[66] John 19:34

[67] See Luke 24:13-31.

[68] Matthew 28:8-10, John 20:11-17

[69] Luke 24:33-36, John 20:19

[70] Luke 24:50

[71] Matthew 28:16-18; John 21:1-8; and see Matthew 28:7-10, Mark 15:6-7.

[72] John 21:9-13

[73] Luke 24:39, John 20:26-27

[74] See Luke 24:51 and Acts 1:9.

[75] Many of the facts which make the hallucination theory implausible would similarly discredit the contention that the resurrection story was the result of a dream, vision, or trance.

[76] Luke 24:13-15

[77] Matthew 28:8-9, 16-18; Luke 24:33-36; John 20:19, 26, 21:1-12; Acts 1:2-4; 1 Corinthians 15:5, 7

[78] 1 Corinthians 15:6

[79] Matthew 28:10, 28:18-20; Luke 24:17, 24:19, 24;25-27, 24:36, 24:38-39, 24;41, 24:44-49; John 20:15-17, 20:19, 20:21-23, 20:26-27, 20:29, 21:5-6, 21:10, 21:12, 21:15-18, 21:22; Acts 1:4-5, 1:7-8.

[80] Luke 24:30, 41-43; John 21:12-13

[81] Matthew 28:9; Luke 24:39-40; John 20:16-17, 25-28

[82] See Luke 24:13-32.

[83] See John 21:1-22.

[84] Acts 1:3

[85] Acts 9:1-6

[86] Morning appearances: Matthew 28:1-10; John 20:1-18; John 21:1-23
Evening appearances: Luke 24:13-31; John 20:19-29
Appearances in Jerusalem: Matthew 28:1-10; John 20:1-29; Acts 1:4-8
Appearances in Galilee: John 21:1-23
Other appearances: Luke 24:13-31 (on the road to Emmaus)

[87] See, for example, Matthew 28:17; Luke 24:8-11, 36-42; John 20:24-29. And of course, Saul (Paul) was an enemy of Christianity until he had his

vision of the risen Christ. See, for example, Acts 8:1-3, 1 Corinthians 15:9, and Galatians 1:13. Jesus' followers believed that Jesus had actually been resurrected, but like Thomas, they believed it only when confronted by the reality of it. Matthew 28:17—which says that "some were doubtful"—does not say otherwise. As discussed by Licona at pages 358-362 of his book *The Resurrection of Jesus,* the Greek in Matthew 28:17 has a similar meaning as in Mark 9:24: "I do believe; help my unbelief." The word means to have conflicting thoughts about something, so in Matthew 28:17 it means that some could hardly believe what they were seeing because it seemed too wonderful to be true.

[88] See Luke 24:15-16, John 20:14-16, and John 21:4-7.

[89] See Acts 9:1-9.

[90] See, for example, Acts 8:57-59, 14:4-5, 14:19, 16:19-21, 17:5-8, 17:13, 18:12-17, 19:23-41, 21:27-36, 22:22, 23:10, 23:12-21.

[91] See, for example, Acts 4:15-18, 5:18, 5:26-28, 5:40, 6:8-14, 7:57-60, and 8:1-3.

[92] Matthew 28:11-15

[93] Acts 5:17

[94] The Jewish leaders viewed Jesus as a deceiver. See Matthew 27:63.

[95] Acts 8:1, 8:3, 9:1-2, 9:21, 22:3-5, 26:9-11; 1 Corinthians 15:9; Galatians 1:13

[96] Acts 9:3-9, 22:5-11, and 26:12-18

[97] Luke 23:34

[98] See, for example, John 21:15-19.

[99] Luke 19:41; John 11:35

[100] See Matthew 26:37-39; Mark 14:33-36; Luke 22:42-44

[101] See, for example, Matthew 9:36, 14:14, 15:32, 20:34; Mark 1:41, 6:34, 8:2-3; Luke 7:13.

[102] Durant's *The Story of Civilization,* Vol. III ("Caesar and Christ"), p. 557

[103] See Chapter 9, "Buddhism (And Now For Something Completely Different)."

[104] See Acts 2:14-40.

[105] See Acts 3:1-8.

[106] See Acts 4:1-12 and 19-20, and Acts 5:29-32.

[107] Acts 5:1-10

[108] Acts 8:18-23

[109] Acts 10:1-48

[110] See Acts 11:1-18.

[111]Matthew 26:69-75; Mark 14:66-72; Luke 22:54-62; John 18:15-18, 25-27

[112]Matthew 26:33-35; Mark 14:29-31; Luke 22:33; John 13:37

[113] Matthew 16:21-23; see also Mark 8:31-33.

[114]Matthew 14:22-33

[115]Luke 9:28-36; Mark 9:2-10; Matthew 17:1-9

[116] John 13:3-10

[117] See Galatians 2:11-14.

[118]Matthew 26:40-45; Mark 14:37-41; Luke 22:45-46

[119] Matthew 26:56; Mark 14:50-52

[120] For example, see Matthew 16:5-12 and Mark 8:14-21 (the disciples misunderstood Jesus' meaning regarding the "leaven" of the Jewish leaders); Mark 4:13 (the disciples did not understand the meaning of Jesus' parable of the sower); Mark 9:31-32, Luke 9:44-45, and Luke 18:31-34 (the disciples did not understand Jesus' prediction of His own death and resurrection). See also, Matthew 13:36, 15:15-17; Mark 4:10, 7:17-18; Luke 8:9; John 3:1-10, 11:11-14, 12:16, 16:17-18.

[121] See, for example, Matthew 8:24-27 and Luke 8:23-25 (Luke 8:25: "Who then is this, that He commands even the winds and the water, and they obey Him?"). See also Matthew 14:25-26

[122] Luke 24:8-11

[123] John 20:24-29

[124] See Matthew 17:14-16, Mark 9:17-18, and Luke 9:38-40.

[125] See Mark 9:33-34, Luke 9:46, and Luke 22:24.

[126] Matthew 14:26; Mark 6:49-50; John 6:19

[127] Matthew 17:6; Mark 9:6

[128] Mark 10:32

[129] Acts 8:1-3, 9:1-2; 1 Corinthians 15:9, Galatians 1:13-14; Philippians 3:6; 1 Timothy 1:13

[130] 1 Timothy 1:15

[131] See 1 Corinthians 1:17, 2:1-5, 4:10, 9:22; 2 Corinthians 10:10, 11:30, 12:7-10, 13:4, 13:9

[132] For example, he criticizes the Corinthians for, among other things, their divisions and disunity (1 Corinthians 1:11-12), sexual immorality (1 Corinthians 5:1—i.e., a man sleeping with his step-mother), and lawsuits against one another (1 Corinthians 6:1-6). Paul was critical of the Galatian Christians for adopting the Jewish law and customs. (See Galatians 3:1-3, 4:21, and 5:2-4.) And he warned those among the Thessalonians who had become lazy busybodies. (2 Thessalonians 3:11)

[133] For example, see Matthew 1:22-23, 2:1-6, 2:14-18, 3:1-3, 4:12-16, 8:16-17, 12:15-21, 13:34-35, 21:1-5, 27:3-10.

[134] See Matthew 8:20, 9:6, 10:23, 11:19, 12:8, 12:32, 12:40, 13:37, 13:41, 16:13, 16:27, 16:28, 17:9, 17:12, 17:22, 18:11, 19:28, 20:18, 20:28, 24:30 (2 times), 24:37, 24:39, 24:44, 25:31, 26:2, 26:24 (2 times), 26:45, and 26:64.

[135] See Daniel 7:13-14.

[136] We know this about Mark because of his explanations of Jewish terminology and customs, which would not have been necessary for a Jewish audience. For example, see Mark 5:41, 7:3-4, 7:11, 7:34. Luke was himself a Gentile, a Greek physician, and he wrote his Gospel for Theophilus, Greek for "lover of God." See Luke 1:3.

[137]**Mark**: Mark 2:10, 2:28, 8:31, 8:38, 9:9, 9:12, 9:31, 10:33, 10:45, 13:26, 14:21 (2 times), 14:41, and 14:62

Luke: Luke 5:24, 6:5, 6:22, 7:34, 9:22, 9:26, 9:44, 9:58, 11:30, 12:8, 12:10, 12:40, 17:22, 17:24, 17:26, 17:30, 18:8, 18:31, 19:10, 21:27, 21:36, 22:22, 22:48, 22:69, and 24:7.

The Gospel of John, the last of the four Gospels to be written, has eleven such references: John 1:51, 3:13, 3:14, 5:27, 6:27, 6:53, 6:62, 8:28, 9:35, 12:23, 13:31 (and see John 12:34).

[138] Acts 2:1 *et. seq.*

[139] See Matthew 28:1-10; Mark 16:1-8; Luke 23:55 - 24:10; John 20:1-2. Some critics point to Mark 16:8, which says that the women "said noth-

ing" about what they had seen at Jesus' tomb. However, as Licona points out at pages 343-347 of his book, *The Resurrection of Jesus*, this simply means that the women went directly to the disciples to report what they had seen and heard, without stopping or being distracted along the way. Mark 1:44 uses a similar phrase, with similar meaning, where Jesus tells a healed leper to "say nothing to no one," but to go show himself to the priest.

[140] See, for example, Luke 24:11, which says that the apostles and the other disciples regarded the women's report of the empty tomb and the angelic appearance as nonsense.

[141] See Matthew 27:57-60, Mark 15:43-46, Luke 23:50-53, and John 19:38-42.

[142] Acts 15:36-39

[143] Acts 15:36-39 and 13:13

[144] Acts 4:36

[145] Acts 15:39-41

[146] The same verse implies that Paul and Mark had been reconciled by the time Paul wrote his letter to the Colossians.

[147] Acts 17:5-7

[148] Romans 16:21

[149] Mark 15:40

[150] Mark 15:47

[151] Matthew 27:55-56

[152] See Matthew 4:21, 10:2; Mark 1:19, 3:17, 10:35; Luke 5:10.

[153] John 19:26-27

[154] See Matthew 14:15-21; Mark 6:35-44; Luke 9:12-17; John 6:1-13. Actually, 5,000 *men*, plus women and children, were fed. The total number of people fed probably numbered between 10,000 and 15,000.

[155] Luke 9:10; Matthew and Mark only tell us that it was a "secluded place" which Jesus and His disciples reached by boat. See Matthew 14:13 and Mark 6:32.

[156] John 1:44

[157] Matthew 27:11-26; Mark 15:1-15; Luke 23:1-25; John 18:28-19:16

[158] See also Mark 15:1-2.

[159] See Matthew 26:65, 27:1; Mark 14:64

[160] To accept this explanation, we must assume that Matthew's account does not proceed in chronological order, since the message seems to come *during* the trial, or even near the end of the trial, rather than prior to it. However, this is not an unreasonable assumption. In Matthew, Pilate's question to Jesus, "Are you the King of the Jews?," ***precedes*** the Jewish leaders' accusations, which also seems out of chronological, and logical, sequence. See Matthew 27:11-13.

[161] Acts 12:12, 12:25, 13:5, 13:13, 15:37-39; Colossians 4:10

[162] See 2 Timothy 4:11; Philemon 24; and 1 Peter 5:13.

[163] Romans, 1 Corinthians, 2 Corinthians, Galatians, Ephesians, Philippians, Colossians, 1 Thessalonians, 2 Thessalonians, 1 Timothy, 2 Timothy, Titus, and Philemon

[164] See Acts 18:24, 19:1; 1 Corinthians 1:12, 3:4-6, 3:22, 4:6, 16:12; Titus 3:13

[165] See Acts 18:2, 18:18, and 18:26; Romans 16:3; 1 Corinthians 16:19; and 2 Timothy 4:19.

[166] Acts 4:36, 9:27, 11:22, 11:30, 12:25, 13:1-2, 13:7, 13:43, 13:46, 13:50, 14:12, 14:14, 14:20, 15:2, 15:12, 15:22, 15:25, 15:35-37, 15:39; 1 Corinthians 9:6; Galatians 2:1, 2:9, 2:13; Colossians 4:10

[167] Two of Jesus' twelve apostles were also named James, but James the brother of Jesus was not one of those. He is referred to in Matthew 13:55; Mark 6:3; Acts 12:17, 15:13, 21:18; 1 Corinthians 15:7; Galatians 1:19, 2:9, 2:12; James 1:1; Jude 1.

[168] Matthew 27:57-59; Mark 15:43-45; Luke 23:50-51; John 19:38

[169] Luke is believed to be the author of both the Gospel that bears his name and Acts, but he is also mentioned by Paul in Colossians 4:14, 2 Timothy 4:11, and Philemon 24.

[170] Luke 10:38-41; John 11:1-2, 11:5, 11:19-21, 11:24, 11:28, 11:30-32, 11:39, 11:45, 12:2-3; see also Luke 7:38-39, which appears to parallel John 12:2-3

[171] Matthew 27:56, 27:61, 28:1; Mark 15:40, 15:47, 16:1, [16:9 – but this verse is not in the oldest manuscripts]; Luke 8:2, 24:10; John 19:25, 20:1, 20:18

[172] Acts 15:22, 15:27, 15:32, 15:34, 15:40, 16:19, 16:25, 16:29, 17:4, 17:10, 17:14-15, 18:5; 2 Corinthians 1:19; 1 Thessalonians 1:1; 2 Thessalonians 1:1; 1 Peter 5:12

[173] Acts 16:1, 17:14-15, 18:5, 19:22, 20:4; Romans 16:21; 1 Corinthians 4:17, 16:10; 2 Corinthians 1:1, 1:19; Philippians 1:1, 2:19; Colossians 1:1; 1 Thessalonians 1:1, 3:2, 3:6; 2 Thessalonians 1:1; 1 Timothy 1:2, 1:18, 6:20; 2 Timothy 1:2; Philemon 1; Hebrews 13:23

[174] 2 Corinthians 2:13, 7:6, 7:13-14, 8:6, 8:16. 8:23, 12:18; Galatians 2:1, 2:3; 2 Timothy 4:10; Titus 1:4

[175] Mark 15:21; Acts 19:33; 1 Timothy 1:20; 2 Timothy 4:14

[176] Colossians 4:17; Philemon 2

[177] Acts 19:29, 20:4, 27:2; Colossians 4:10; and Philemon 24

[178] Acts 18:8; 1 Corinthians 1:14

[179] Colossians 4:14; 2 Timothy 4:10; Philemon 24

[180] Colossians 1:7, 4:12; Philemon 23

[181] Acts 19:22; Romans 16:23; 2 Timothy 4:20

[182] Acts 19:29, 20:4; Romans 16:23; 1 Corinthians 1:14; 3 John 1

[183] Acts 17:5-7, 17:9; Romans 16:21

[184] Acts 13:1; Romans 16:21

[185] Colossians 4:9; Philemon 10

[186] Mark 15:21; Romans 16:13

[187] Acts 18:17; 1 Corinthians 1:1

[188] Acts 20:4, 21:29; 2 Timothy 4:20

[189] Acts 20:4; Ephesians 6:21; Colossians 4:7; 2 Timothy 4:12; Titus 3:12

[190] For example: Achaicus (1 Corinthians 16:17), Ampliatus (Romans 16:8), Andronicus (Romans 16:7), Apelles (or Appella) (Romans 16:10), Apphia (Philemon 2), Aristobulus (Romans 16:10), Artemas (Titus 3:12), Asyncritus (Romans 16:14), Carpus (2 Timothy 4:10), Claudia (2 Timothy 4:21), Crescens (2 Timothy 4:10), Epaenetus (Romans 16:5), Epaphroditus

(Philippians 2:25, 4:18), Eubulus (2 Timothy 4:21), Euodia (Philippians 4:2), Fortunatus (1 Corinthians 16:17), Hermas (Romans 16:14), Hermes (Romans 16:14), Herodion (Romans 16:11), Julia (Romans 16:15), Junias (or Junia) (Romans 16:7), Lazarus (John 11:1-2, 11:5, 11:11, 11:14, 11:43, 12:1-2, 12:9-10, 12:17), Linus (2 Timothy 4:21), Narcissus (Romans 16:11), Nereus (Romans 16:15), Nicodemus (John 3:1, 3:4, 3:9, 7:50, 19:39), Nympha (or Nymphas) (Colossians 4:15), Olympas (Romans 16:15), Onesiphorus (2 Timothy 1:16, 4:19), Patrobas (Romans 16:14), Philemon (Philemon 1), Philologus (Romans 16:15), Phlegon (Romans 16:14), Pudens (2 Timothy 4:21), Quartus (Romans 16:23), Secundus (Acts 20:4), Simeon (a/k/a Niger) (Acts 13:1), Sopater (Acts 20;4), Sosipater (Romans 16:21), Stachys (Romans 16:9), Stephanas (1 Corinthians 1:16, 16:15, 16:17), Syntyche (Philippians 4:2), Tertius (Romans 16:22), Tryphaena (or Tryphena) (Romans 16:12), Tryphosa (Romans 16:12), Urbanus (Romans 16:9), and Zenas (Titus 3:13).

[191] Original quotation is from *St. Paul the Traveler and the Roman Citizen,* by Sir William Ramsay, as quoted in McDowell, *The New Evidence That Demands a Verdict*, p. 62.

[192] See Acts 18:2.

[193] Acts 19:27

[194] Acts 19:29, 31

[195] See Acts 17:6: "When they did not find them, they *began* dragging Jason and some brethren before the city authorities, shouting, 'These men who have upset the world have come here also. . . ."

[196] Acts 16:12 says: " . . . and from there to Philippi, which is a leading city of the district of Macedonia, a *Roman* colony; and we were staying in this city for some days."

[197] Gaius, who was hosting Paul when he wrote the letter to the Romans (Romans 16:23), was a member of the Corinthian church (see I Corinthians 1:14), implying that Paul was in Corinth at the time. In addition, in Romans 16:1-2, Paul commends Phoebe (who probably carried Paul's letter to the Romans), a member of the church at Cenchrea, which was located in close proximity to Corinth. (Corinth was located on the narrow isthmus—about four miles wide—which connects the Peloponne-

sus, or southern Greece, with the rest of Greece. Cenchrea was Corinth's eastern port.)

[198] While Paul did not see the risen Jesus in the flesh, he did have a vision of the risen Christ. See 1 Corinthians 15:8.

[199] Quoted from Suetonius' *Vita Neronis* (i.e., *Life of Nero*), xvi, as quoted in *Documents of the Christian Church*, p. 2).

[200] The ten official Roman persecutions were as follows:

First Roman persecution: ca. 64 A.D.
Second Roman persecution: ca. 81 A.D.
Third Roman persecution: ca. 108 A.D.
Fourth Roman persecution: about 177-180 A.D.
Fifth Roman persecution: 202-211 A.D.
Sixth Roman persecution: 235-238 A.D.
Seventh Roman persecution: 249-251 A.D.
Eighth Roman persecution: 257-261 A.D.
Ninth Roman persecution: 274-275 A.D.
Tenth Roman persecution: 303-311 A.D. (but continued in the eastern Roman Empire until 323 A.D.)

[201] See Acts 16:12 and 16:19-24

[202] See Acts 19:23-41.

[203] See footnote 35 and Acts 18:2.

[204] Acts 4:1-3, 5:17-18, 5:40

[205] Acts 12:3-11

[206] Acts 13:45-51 (Pisidian Antioch), 14:1-6 (Iconium), 14:19 (Lystra), 17:5-8 (Thessalonica), 17:13 (Berea), 18:12-13 (Corinth), 20:3 (unspecified city in Greece)

[207] See Acts 8:1, 9:1-2, 22:4-5, 26:9-11; 1 Corinthians 15:9; Galatians 1:13, 1:23

[208] Acts 14:19-20

[209] Acts 9:23-25 and 23:12-15

[210] See, for example, John 15:20-21; Romans 8:17-18; 1 Corinthians 4:8-12; 2 Corinthians1:4-9, 4:8-11, 4:16-17; Galatians 5:11, 6:12; Philippians 1:27-29; 1 Thessalonians 2:2, 2:14-16, 3:3-4; 2 Thessalonians 1:4-7; 2 Timothy

1:8, 1:12, 2:3, 2:9-10, 3:11-12; James 1:2-4; 1 Peter 2:19-20, 3:13-17, 4:1, 4:4, 4:12-16, 4:19; Revelation 2:9-10

211 See Acts 8:5-13 and 8:26-40. There is some uncertainty about whether this Philip is the apostle Philip or the Philip of Acts 6:1-5. The latter was a Greek Jew, one of the seven deacons of the early church (Acts 6:5), and was known as Philip the Evangelist. I believe the Philip of Acts 8:5-13 and 8:26-40 was Philip the Evangelist, primarily because Acts 8:14 says that "when the apostles in Jerusalem heard that Samaria had received the word of God" as a result of Philip's preaching, they sent Peter and John to Samaria, apparently to check on the situation there. Such supervision would seem unnecessary and even perhaps insulting for a fellow apostle, but quite appropriate for a deacon.

212 Peter traveled with John to Samaria, which was northern Palestine (Acts 8:14). He also went to the towns of Lydda (Acts 9:32), Joppa (Acts 9:38-39), and Caesarea (Acts 10:24-25).

213 See Acts 11:25-30, 12:25-21:14.

214 1 Peter 5:13 says: "She who is in Babylon, chosen together with you, sends you greetings, and *so does* my son, Mark."

215 This James should not be confused with either of the apostles named James, who are known as James the Greater and James the Lesser. James the Greater was the son of Zebedee and brother of the apostle John (Matthew 4:21, 10:2; Mark 1:19, 3:17, 10:35; Luke 5:10). James the Lesser was the son of Alphaeus (Matthew 10:3; Mark 3:18; Luke 6:15; Acts 1:13). Jesus' brother James—known as James the Just—became the leader of the Christians in Jerusalem. See Acts 12:17, 15:13, and 12:18; 1 Corinthians 15:7; Galatians 1:19, 2:9, 2:12; James 1:1; and Jude 1:1.

216 Acts 12:1-2

217 Acts 7:57-60

218 Matthias was a replacement for Judas Iscariot, who betrayed Jesus and subsequently killed himself. See Acts 1:23-26.

219 John 20:19

220 Acts 8:1, 8:3, 9:1-2, 9:21, 22:3-5, 26:9-11; 1 Corinthians 15:9; Galatians 1:13

221 Acts 9:3-9, 22:5-11, and 26:12-18

[222] Mark 3:21, 3:31-35. 6:1-4; John 7:3-5

[223] Acts 1:14, 15:13, 21:17-18; Galatians 1:19, 2:9, 2:12

[224] Letter of James and Letter of Jude, and in particular James 1:1 and Jude 1

[225] See Acts 12:17, 15:13, 21:18; Galatians 1:19, 2:9, 2:12; Letter of James (that this James "the Just" is not the son of Zebedee and the brother of John is evident from Acts 12:2, which records the death of John's brother, James)

[226] 1 Corinthians 15:7

[227] See also, Matthew 6:19-21, 19:21-24; Mark 4:18-19, 10:21-25; Luke 1:53, 6:24-25, 12:16-31, 12:33-34, 16:19-25, 18:22-25; Romans 1:29; Colossians 3:5; 1 Timothy 3:3, 3:8, 6:7-9, 6:17-19; 2 Timothy 3:2; Titus 1:7, 1:11; Hebrews 13:5; James 1:10-11, 2:2-6, 5:1-6; 2 Peter 2:14; Revelation 3:17-18

[228] See, for example, Matthew 5:38-46; Luke 6:27-36; Romans 12:14, 12:17-20; 1 Corinthians 13:4-7; 2 Corinthians 2:7, 6:1-3, 6:6; Galatians 5:22-23, 6:1; Ephesians 4:31-32; Colossians 3:12-13; Hebrews 13:2; James 3:17-18; 2 Peter 1:7;

[229] See Acts 3:14-17; Romans 13:1-7; 1 Corinthians 2:6-8; 1 Timothy 2:1-2; Titus 3:1; 1 Peter 2:13-14, 2:17; see also, Jude 1:8

[230] The author of Revelation—believed to be John the Apostle, the son of Zebedee—was temporarily exiled to the island of Patmos, a Roman penal colony, during the Second Roman Persecution, under the Emperor Domitian, in about 81 A.D. John was released in about 96 A.D. when Domitian died, and returned to Asia Minor where he died a few years later.

[231] See, for example, Romans 12:9; 1 Corinthians 5:8, 13:6; 2 Corinthians 1:12, 2:17, 6:7; Galatians 2:11-14; Ephesians 4:15, 4:25, 4:28, 5:8-9, 6:5, 6:13-14; Colossians 3:22; James 3:17; 1 Peter 2:1; 1 John 3:18

[232] Matthew 9:18-19, 9:24; Mark 5:35-40; Luke 8:49-53

[233] The quote is from a sermon by the late Dr. Gene Scott, former pastor of Faith Center in Glendale, California.

[234] Each of these books is cited in the Bibliography.

Chapter 3
WHY DO BAD THINGS HAPPEN (TO ME)?

Terrible things happen constantly: war, crime, natural disasters, disease, starvation, accidents. Life is often full of pain, suffering, and grief. Why does God permit these things to happen? Is He powerless to stop it? Does He not care enough to do anything about it? Or does He not exist at all? If we expect easy, sound-bite answers to these questions, we are fooling ourselves. But there are answers. We begin with God's self-restraint.

Free Will. I have a lot of fillings in my teeth, the result of too many cavities in my youth. Is God to blame for those, or is the real culprit my younger self's poor dental hygiene? I was once the victim of a theft. Is God responsible, or does the fault lie with the thief?

If we are honest with ourselves, we must admit that human beings are the primary cause of suffering in this life. Most of the evils you can name—violence, gossip, adultery, slander, drug abuse, theft, and even cavities—are caused by a human being hurting himself or others through words, deeds, or simple neglect. The human race's pain is largely self-inflicted. But doesn't God permit all of this? Of course He does. He has to.

Christianity teaches that God loves us more than we can possibly comprehend. However, His love is not a one-way street. He wants us to love Him back. He wants to have a loving relationship with us. The "greatest commandment" is to "love the Lord your God with all your heart, and with all your soul, and with all your mind." (Matthew 22:37-38) [1] However, love cannot be commanded, bought, sold, or required. It must be freely given.

What is this "love" that God wants from us? The Greek word is *agapaô*, which refers to "the kind of love shown even when the one loved has no merit for that love. It is love that must be chosen and willed"; [2] "giving love that seeks the highest good for the other"; [3] love that is deliberate and self-sacrificing. [4] It is "the antithesis of selfishness." [5] In other words, *agapaô* is neither a feeling nor an emotion, but a deliberate choice. When you read the English word "love" in the New Testament, most of the time the original Greek is *agapaô* or a form of it. [6]

If this is what God wants from us, then He must give us a real choice. Machines cannot love in this way, nor can animals. We can. But introducing choice into the world means that some of us will choose unwisely. We can follow Him and try to obey Him, or we can reject Him and do as we please. When we reject Him, we embrace, to a greater or lesser degree, the evils that He despises—what Paul refers to as the deeds of the flesh (Galatians 5:19-21). [7] As a result of our poor choices, people get physically and emotionally hurt. As sad as that situation is, He must live with it.

God could certainly eliminate evil by taking away our free will, but *agapaô* love would go with it. If we could no longer choose evil, we also could no longer choose Him. And so He does what He can to persuade us to make good choices: He commands, [8] He entreats, [9] He threatens, [10] He promises, [11] and He sent Jesus to demonstrate His love in the flesh. He gave mankind the following choice long ago, and continues to do so:

> "I call heaven and earth to witness against you today, that I have set before you life and death, the blessing and the curse. So choose life in order that you may live, you and your descendants, by loving the LORD your God, by obeying His voice, and by holding fast to Him. . . ."
>
> —Deuteronomy 30:19-20

If we insist on living our lives apart from God, He must live with the consequences. And so must we. That is the price of freedom.

Cause and Effect. But free will is not a complete answer to the question of why bad things happen. Maybe God feels compelled to let us choose, even if that means a lot of us will choose unwisely, but He could still prevent the resulting pain and suffering. For example, He certainly has the power to keep a drunk driver from hurting himself and others. So why doesn't He? Any parent, teacher, or judge can probably answer that one.

When I was a child, I saw a prickly pear cactus on my uncle's property. Carefully avoiding the long pointy needles, which were obviously sharp and threatening, I touched the apparently smooth skin of the cactus, and learned a painful lesson: the "smooth" skin has tiny needles that hurt like a splinter in your finger. Since then, I have always been cautious around cactus. Sometimes experience really is the best teacher. But my encounter with the cactus would have taught me nothing if not for the pain I felt.

Pain teaches us to avoid potential dangers. Similarly, unpleasant consequences teach us to avoid improper actions. When a child is disciplined for misbehavior, she learns not to misbehave. One reason we punish criminals is to convince them that crime is not worth the cost. Our suffering teaches us not to do foolish things. And sometimes we learn through the suffering of others. But we learn only because poor choices have consequences.

Substance abuse experts tell us that when friends and family members protect an alcoholic from the adverse effects of his drinking, he is unlikely to stop—because his drinking is not causing any adverse consequences *for him*. The best hope for that alcoholic is often to remove these shields and allow him to suffer the full effects of his drinking, even if that means the loss of job, money, family, etc.

Similarly, if God protected us from the adverse consequences of our bad choices, we would never learn to choose wisely. We would never learn to choose Him. And we would be the worse for it.

But I believe the problem goes even deeper. When we ask why our poor choices have unpleasant consequences, we are asking the wrong question. It is like asking, "why does a bad dog bite?" The dog doesn't bite because he's a "bad" dog—he is a bad dog because he bites. Similarly, decisions don't have harmful consequences because they are "bad" decisions; they are bad decisions because of their harmful consequences.

If I choose to rake the leaves in my yard, that is not ordinarily a poor decision. But if my yard is a minefield, the fact that I could blow myself up by raking leaves suddenly makes this a dreadful choice. The only thing that changed is the potential harmful consequences.

Moral choices are no different. God did not prohibit theft and murder because He wanted to deprive us of something fun, but because those acts hurt people. "Bad" choices are "bad" because of their adverse consequences—to the victim, of course, and also to the perpetrator. The purpose of the vast majority of God's commands in the Bible is to protect us from the consequences that inevitably flow from our poor choices, by teaching us how to make good moral decisions. In the Bible He has warned us to stay away from minefields, and He has even told us where the minefields are. If we go there anyway and get blown up, it's our own fault.

But perhaps you are now wondering why the consequences of our bad choices are sometimes so severe. Why does a teenager who drives foolishly have to end up dead, or permanently crippled? Couldn't God mitigate the consequences? Well, in many cases He does: physical pain and emotional distress generally subside; wounds heal; we adapt to disabilities; and we learn from our mistakes so that we don't repeat them. He gave us inventive minds which have come up with safety equipment to prevent or lessen injuries, as well as medicines to ease pain and speed healing. All of these factors help to mitigate the adverse consequences of our poor choices. In addition, He gave us the resiliency to bounce back and go on with life.

But why does He allow severe pain or disabilities at all? Why doesn't God moderate the consequences still further, perhaps by limiting our suffering to the pain I endure when I burn myself on a hot stove? We might as well ask why our courts don't impose a one-day jail sentence for murder. To teach us not to make horrible choices, sometimes God must allow the consequences of those choices to remain serious.

And if God did limit our pain and suffering to negligible levels, I would probably wish to eliminate even that much. Whatever level of pain and misery God permits, He could always allow less, and when we are in pain we quickly lose sight of its benefits. But some level of pain is *necessary*. People who cannot feel pain due to a genetic defect, [12] diabetes, leprosy, or another cause are constantly at risk for serious injuries and infections because they lack this early warning system.

On the other hand, God could have allowed much *greater* suffering than we now have. The consequences of our bad choices could include a lifetime of pain, but in His mercy He makes it temporary. Our poor decisions could routinely lead to disabilities, but because of His grace they do so only rarely. We regard some consequences as "severe" only because we haven't bothered to consider how much worse they could have been.

Yet some pain and suffering have nothing to do with our moral choices. Why does God allow people to suffer and die from disease and natural disasters? This question leads us to what I believe is the final part of the answer to why God allows bad things to happen: eternity.

The Eternal Perspective. We have seen that God allows suffering because that is the inevitable cost of allowing us to make our own moral choices, and that He gives us that freedom because He doesn't want machines, but people who can respond to Him in love and obedience. Yet that is still not a complete answer to the problem, because not all suffering is caused by our choices.

Victims of an earthquake, tornado, hurricane, or other natural disaster do not usually suffer because of any moral choice they have made, but because of circumstances beyond their control. Similarly, terrible and fatal diseases afflict people every day, often without regard to any moral choices they have made in life. And sometimes people—even infants and young children—die from such things. How can a loving and powerful God possibly permit this to happen?

The answer lies in the ephemeral nature of this life, which we too often overlook or simply refuse to see. Christ walked this earth two-thousand years ago, and none of us will live one-tenth that long. God, however, is eternal. [13] He has a different view of this life, because He realizes, as we often do not, that the life that begins after we die is the one that truly matters. Paul recognized this when he said: "For I consider that the sufferings of this present time are not worthy to be compared with the glory that is to be revealed to us." (Romans 8:18) [14] The primary focus of the New Testament is not on this temporary existence, but on God's promise of eternal life, [15] and on how to attain it.

So what does eternal life have to do with the bad things that happen in this life? Everything. If we could just see these "bad" events from God's eternal perspective, we would see that many of them—perhaps most of them—are not truly "bad" at all, but are instead blessings in disguise.

To be clear, I am not talking about God bringing good out of bad, as in Romans 8:28, although He can certainly do that. I mean that events that *appear* to be awful because they involve pain, suffering, or loss of life actually result in a much greater good that justifies the temporary anguish.

Nothing illustrates this point better than Jesus's crucifixion. His cruel and painful death appeared to be a tragedy for Him and a disaster for His followers. A few days later His resurrection changed everything.

The apostle Paul suffered many times and in many ways at the hands of the Jews and Romans, [16] yet his suffering vividly demonstrated the sincerity of his message, and as a result countless persons believed his testimony about Christ. If someone today were to ask Paul if his suffering was "bad," I am certain that he would answer in the negative. Indeed, he once said, "I rejoice in my sufferings," because he recognized the good it was producing. [17]

The seventy-year exile of the Jewish people in Babylon no doubt caused enormous hardships for them, but it also taught them to stop worshiping idols and trust God. [18]

In each case, suffering was necessary to achieve God's purposes and led to tremendous long-term benefits.

But what about the death of a child? Surely that qualifies as "bad," doesn't it? Maybe not. I believe we will one day see that a child who dies at a young age and goes to Heaven, [19] where crying, pain, and death do not exist, [20] and where "God will wipe every tear from their eyes" (Revelation 7:17), [21] is much more fortunate than the person who endures 90 years of pain, sorrow, trouble, and increasing debilitation in this life. Instead of dreading death, we should look forward to it, as Paul did: "For to me, to live is Christ and to die is gain." (Philippians 1:21) For those who belong to Christ, death is not an enemy to be feared, but a friend to be welcomed and embraced when the time comes.

Yet this is only half of the answer. God has another reason for not abolishing the diseases and natural disasters that are so frightening and destructive: He doesn't want us to grow attached to this life.

When things are going well for us, our natural inclination is to ignore God. We pretend we don't need Him. His Truth—and even His existence—become trivial matters, unworthy of our attention, because we believe we are doing just fine without Him. I was once such a person.

This attitude is often defeated by pain, suffering, or fear of death. Calamities force us to recognize how fragile and helpless each of us truly is. We are at the mercy of powerful forces all around us. And when we finally understand our own weakness, we are ready to turn back to God. [22]

This also explains why He does not prevent the deaths of young people. If He guaranteed each of us at least thirty years of life, far too many of us would delay making a decision about Him until we got close to our thirtieth birthday. Fear of death started me on the path that eventually led me to God.

The saying that "there are no atheists in foxholes" illustrates this principle: suffering and the fear of death can drive us back to God. If in the process I also receive eternal life, then the event that prompts my divine reconciliation is not ultimately "bad." From God's eternal perspective, the cancer that takes a man's life could be the best thing that ever happened to him if it leads him to Christ and eternal life.

Yes, but why are bad things happening to me? These explanations may make perfect sense unless *you* are the one suffering. Then the pain seems horribly unfair, as it did to poor Job. Through no fault of his own, Job lost everything—possessions, servants, children, and even his health. [23] Job felt mistreated, and accused God of cruelty and injustice. [24] God's response, in chapters 38 through 41 of the book of Job, can be summarized as: "I'm God and you're not, so just trust Me."

If our suffering seems unfair at times, then we must trust God and try to endure it, while always keeping in mind that this life is not the end. And we are not alone, for God is there in the midst of our suffering, comforting and strengthening us. [25]

Conclusion. The pain, suffering, and unhappiness that we experience in this life have many causes—a lot of them of mankind's own making—but these "bad things" also serve a purpose, much like guardrails on a highway. They can be damaging and painful if your car hits them, but they keep you on the road and protect you from greater dangers, such as oncoming cars or a sudden drop off a cliff. Similarly, the hurts of this life help to redirect us back to a loving relationship with our Creator, and are intended to protect us from something far worse: missing out on eternal life. As Jesus said, "For what does it profit a man to gain the whole world, and forfeit his soul?" (Mark 8:36) [26]

Endnotes for Chapter Three, "Why Do Bad Things Happen (to Me)?"

[1] See also Mark 12:28-30.

[2]*The Life Application Concise New Testament Commentary,* at Romans 12:14-21).

[3]*Ibid.* (at Ephesians 5:28)

[4]*Ibid.* (at 1 Peter 2:17)

[5]*New Unger's Bible Dictionary.*

[6] The following New Testament verses use the Greek term, *agapaô,* or a form of it, such as *agape*: Matthew 5:43-44, 5:46, 6:24, 19:19, 22:37, 22:39, 24:12; Mark 10:21, 12:30-31, 12:33; Luke 6:27, 6:32, 6:35, 7:5, 7:42, 7:47, 10:27, 11:42-43, 16:13; John 3:35, 5:42, 8:42, 10:17, 13:34-35, 14:15, 14:21, 14:23-24, 14:31, 15:9-10, 15:12-13, 15:17, 17:26, 21:15-16; Romans 5:5, 5:8, 8:28, 8:35, 8:39, 12:9, 13:8-10, 14:15, 15:30; 1 Corinthians 2:9, 4:21, 8:1, 8:3, 13:1-4, 13:8, 13:13, 14:1, 16:14, 16:24; 2 Corinthians 2:4, 2:8, 5:14, 6:6, 8:7-8, 8:24, 9:7, 11:11, 12:15, 13:11, 13:14; Galatians 5:6, 5:13-14, 5:22; Ephesians 1:4, 1:15, 2:4, 3:17, 3:19, 4:2, 4:15-16, 5:2, 5:25, 5:28, 5:33, 6:23, 6:35; Philippians 1:9, 1:16, 2:1-2; Colossians 1:4, 1:8, 2:2, 3:14, 3:19; 1 Thessalonians 1:3, 3:6, 3:12, 4:9, 5:8, 5:13; 2 Thessalonians 1:3, 2:10, 3:5; 1 Timothy 1:5, 1:14, 2:15, 4:12, 6:11; 2 Timothy 1:7, 1:13, 2:22, 3:10; Titus 2:2; Philemon 1:5, 1:7; Hebrews 6:10, 10:24, 12:6; James 1:12, 2:5, 2:8; 1 Peter 1:8, 1:22, 2:17, 3:10, 4:8, 5:14; 2 Peter 1:7; 1 John 2:5, 2:10, 2:15, 3:1, 3:10-11, 3:14, 3:16-18, 3:23, 4:7-12, 4:16-21, 5:1-3; 2 John 1:1, 1:3, 1:5-6; 3 John 1:6; Jude 1:2, 1:12, 1:21; Revelation 1:5, 2:4, 2:19, 12:11.

In contrast, the following New Testament verses use the term *phileô* (referring to brotherly love), or a form of it: Matthew 6:5, 10:37, 23:6; Luke 20:46; John 5:20, 11:3, 12:25, 15:19, 16:27, 21:15-17; Romans 12:10; 1 Corinthians 16:22; 1 Thessalonians 4:9; 1 Timothy 3:3, 6:10; Titus 2:4, 3:4, 3:15; Hebrews 13:1, 13:5; 1 Peter 1:22; 3 John 1:9; Revelation 3:19, 22:15. (There is some duplication in these lists, because a few verses contain both *agapaô* and *phileô*: John 21:15-16; 1 Thessalonians 4:9; 1 Peter 1:22.)

[7] Following Christ cultivates the fruit of the Spirit, per Galatians 5:22-23.

[8] For example, see Exodus 20:1-17 (the Ten Commandments). See also, Deuteronomy 6:5, 10:12, 11:1, 11:13, 11:22, 19:9, 30:16; and Joshua 22:5.

[9] For example, in Joshua 23:11 and Psalm 31:23, we are urged to love God.

[10] Such threats are found at Deuteronomy 7:10, 11:16-17, 30:15-20; Psalm 145:20; and 1 Corinthians 16:22.

[11] For examples of God's promises to those who love Him, see Deuteronomy 7:9, 11:13-15, 11:22-25, 30:15-20; Nehemiah 1:5; Psalms 18:1-3, 97:10, 145:20; James 1:12.

[12] This genetic condition is known as congenital insensitivity to pain (CIP), or congenital analgesia.

[13] See, for example: Deuteronomy 33:27; Isaiah 9:6; Romans 16:26; 1 Timothy 1:17

[14] See also 1 Corinthians 15:19.

[15] See, for example: Matthew 19:29, 25:46; Mark 10:30; Luke 18:30; John 3:15-16, 3:36, 4:14, 4:36, 5:24, 6:27, 6:40, 6:47, 6:54, 10:28, 12:25, 12:50, 17:2-3; Acts 13:46-48; Romans 2:7, 5:21, 6:22-23; Galatians 6:8; 1 Timothy 1:16, 6:12; Titus 1:2, 3:7; 1 John 2:25, 5:11-13; Jude 21.

[16] See Romans 11:23-27.

[17] Colossians 1:24

[18] For examples of the Jewish people's idolatry prior to the exile, see Jeremiah 1:16, 2:7-8, 2:11-13, 2:17, 2:20-23, 2:27-28, 2:32, 7:30-31, 13:10-11. Because of their idolatry and wickedness, Jeremiah prophesied that Jerusalem would be plundered and its people killed or carried into exile, and the land would be desolate. See Jeremiah 7:14-15, 7:32-34, 13:16-19, 13:24, 16:13-15, 20:4-6. The Babylonian exile was to last 70 years, per Jeremiah 25:11 and 29:10.

The Babylonian King Nebuchadnezzar conquered Jerusalem in about 605 B.C. and carried into exile a portion of its population, including the prophet Daniel. See II Kings 24:1-16, II Chronicles 36:6-7, and Daniel 1:1-6. In subsequent years the Babylonians destroyed the city and the Temple, and took most of the Jewish population into exile, in retaliation for repeated rebellions by their leaders. In about 539 B.C., the Babylonians were conquered by the Medo-Persians, led by King Cyrus. The following year,

Cyrus decreed that the Jewish people could return to their homeland. Two years later, in 536 B.C., more than 42,000 did. See Ezra 2:1-65. Others followed in subsequent years.

[19] I do not accept that God will condemn those who die as young children. I do not know exactly how God will deal with them, but I trust Him to deal with them fairly.

[20] Revelation 21:4

[21] See also Revelation 21:4.

[22] Perhaps nowhere is this principle better illustrated than in the Old Testament book of Judges. Time after time, the Israelites fall away from God and begin practicing evil, and each time they are brought to repentance through suffering. See Judges 3:5-9, 3:12-15, 4:1-3, 6:1-6, and 10:6-10. See also Exodus 2:23. And see Chapter 7, "Is Yahweh an Ogre?"

[23] Job 1:6-19 and 2:1-8

[24] See Job 30:20-21 and 31:35.

[25] See, for example, Philippians 4:13, 2 Corinthians 1:3-7, and 2 Thessalonians 2:16-17.

[26] See also Matthew 16:26.

Chapter 4
FOR GOD SO LOVED . . . WELL, WAIT A MINUTE

> [Jesus speaking] "For God so loved the world that He gave His only begotten Son, that whosoever believes in Him shall not perish, but have everlasting life."
>
> —John 3:16

When I was in college, in my days as an agnostic, many Christians tried to make a Christian out of me by quoting John 3:16 and telling me: "Just believe in Jesus Christ and you'll be saved." My response was always something like: "Then why doesn't Jesus come down here and show Himself to me? Then I *would* believe." For well over a year, none of those Christians gave me a satisfactory answer to that question. Now I see that my question completely misinterpreted the real meaning of John 3:16.

Salvation does not depend on "belief" in the sense of believing that Jesus Christ was a real person, or that He was a wise teacher who was cruelly and unjustly executed by the Roman Empire, or even that He is the Son of God and that He rose from the dead. Believing certain facts will not save you. If belief in this sense were all that was necessary, then Satan and his demons would all be saved, for they *know* that Jesus is the Son of God and that He rose from the dead. [1]

Other scriptures provide clues that my naïve, pre-Christian understanding of John 3:16 was simply wrong. In Romans 1:17, Paul said: "But the righteous man shall live by faith." If mere belief is sufficient, why does Paul emphasize faith? And Jesus said: " 'You will be hated by all because of My name, but it is the one who has endured to the end who will be saved.' " (Matthew 10:22) Then He further muddies the waters by asserting that the greatest commandment is to "love the Lord your God with all your heart, and with all your soul, and with all your mind, and with all your strength." (Mark 12:30) [2] If belief is all it takes, why does Jesus talk about endurance and love as though they were critical?

Our problem is that "believe" is an ambiguous word in English. I can say I *believe* the world is spherical, and I *believe* the football game begins at 3:30 p.m., and I *believe* aliens have visited the earth, and I *believe* the President is an honest man. In each of these statements, the word *believe* has a slightly different meaning, and none of them adequately conveys the true meaning of "believe" in John 3:16.

So to figure out what the New Testament is saying, we need to look at the original Greek. The English words "belief," "believe," and "faith" are all translated from the Greek word, *pistis*, or its verb form *pisteuô*, which means not only "belief" but "faith," "assurance," and "moral conviction," [3] as well as "trust" and "reliance on." [4] One commentary goes a bit further, saying that *pisteuô* involves "trust or personal commitment, to the extent of handing over one's self to another person." [5] This definition sounds a lot like what we mean by the word *surrender*.

Every time you read in the New Testament that we should "believe" in—or have "faith" in—God/Christ, the word is *pisteuô* or *pistis*. [6] In this context, the meaning of *pisteuô*—trusting God and making a strong personal commitment to Him—is similar to what Jesus said when He spoke of loving God with all of our heart, soul, mind, and strength. God wants far more than our mere belief that Christ is alive or that the Bible is true. He wants us to *live* as if we believe those things.

But wouldn't God get that by openly demonstrating His existence and power? In other words, if Jesus performed miracles on television or walked across the Atlantic Ocean, wouldn't everyone immediately commit themselves to Him? Sadly, no. Intimidation doesn't work. God has tried it.

In Exodus 19:16, He appeared to the people of Israel in the form of thunder, lightning, a thick cloud, and a sound like a loud trumpet. Their reaction was typical: they trembled with fear. In fact, they were so frightened that they begged Moses not to let God speak to them again. [7] However, they did *not* respond with love or trust—or even obedience. Within a short time, they built and worshiped a statue of a calf, [8] in flagrant disregard for God's commandment against worshiping idols. [9] In the Old Testament, God constantly reaches out to His people through miracles, prophets, and leaders, only to see them turn away from Him time after time.

When God confronts people in the Bible, their consistent reaction is not love or trust, but fear, or even terror. Adam felt this fear. [10] So did Moses, [11] Isaiah, [12] and Jesus's disciples. [13] Some of Jesus's miracles provoked fear, such as walking on water, [14] calming the sea, [15] and casting out demons. [16] The townspeople who heard about Jesus casting out the "Legion" of demons became so frightened that they asked Him to go away. [17]

Setting aside the Bible for a moment, almost everyone reacts with fear when they are confronted with a strong earthquake, hurricane, or some other natural disaster. How much greater is God's power than those! The awesome power of God created the Sun, which is the size of 1.3 million Earths and has an average surface temperature of 10,000 degrees Fahrenheit. The majestic power of God created the universe. God created life—and each of us. When we encounter such power, what can we do but shake with fear because of our own weakness and insignificance?

I am not talking about the "fear" mentioned in verses like Proverbs 9:10: "The fear of the LORD is the beginning of wisdom." [18] Such verses refer to the respect that leads us to listen and learn, just as we heed the counsel of a parent or mentor. Indeed, many commentaries and contemporary English translations prefer the terms "reverence" or "respect" in place of "fear" in these verses. The person who "fears" the Lord in this way will learn His ways and profit from them. [19]

By "fear" I mean the terror that makes us tremble and hide, like Adam and Eve did. [20] In the Bible, a direct confrontation with the power of God consistently provokes that kind of dread.

God could easily terrify us in this way if He wanted to. And if He merely wanted our belief—that is, our intellectual acknowledgement of His existence—I am convinced He would do exactly that. Fear and belief can co-exist quite nicely. I have no trouble believing in the tornado that is about to destroy my home and perhaps take my life, even though I may be petrified with fear.

However, my belief is useful to God only if it also causes me to trust Him and commit myself to Him, and leads me, eventually, to love Him as He loves me. As we have seen, the greatest commandment is to love God with our whole being. We were created by God to be in relationship with Him—to love Him and to be loved by Him. A majestic display of awesome power would frighten us, but it does not produce love. When we are afraid, we run, we hide, we withdraw. Fear elicits anxiety and worry, not love.

I will concede that we can sometimes love someone—or at least, *think* we love someone—of whom we are afraid. [21] A child may "love" a parent despite verbal or physical abuse. A wife may "love" an abusive husband. But I believe two truths are self-evident in such circumstances:

1. Love exists despite fear, not because of it. If a wife loves her abusive husband, it is probably because he sometimes is, or once was, caring and attentive to her needs. But her fear of his abuse does not enhance her feelings of love for him. Also,

2. Where love and fear do co-exist, love almost invariably develops first. A woman surely will not fall in love with a man who is abusive to her from the time they meet, for if she has any sense she will flee out of fear before love has a chance to develop.

In short, fear is an obstacle to the relationship God wants to have with each of us. If He frightens us, we may temporarily submit to Him, but we will not develop a loving relationship with Him.

So an open and obvious demonstration of His tremendous power simply undermines His own interests. For this reason, God must restrain His power, at least for the time being. He must be gentle with us. "For God so loved the world" that He came in a way that would not terrify us—as the man, Jesus.

God's goal is not to make us simply *believe* in His existence, but to demonstrate His great love for us, so that we will respond in love, and commit ourselves to Him. Love and trust, commitment and relationship—those are what John 3:16 is really all about.

Endnotes for Chapter Four, "For God So Loved . . . Well, Wait a Minute"

[1] For example, see James 2:19: "You believe that God is one. You do well; the demons also believe, and shudder." For other verses which demonstrate that demons recognized who and what Jesus was, see: Matthew 8:28-29; Mark 1:34, 5:2-9; Luke 4:41, 8:27-30.

[2] See also Matthew 22:37-38.

[3] Strong's Greek Lexicon search result for *pistis.*

[4] "What Is Faith?" TruthorTradition.com.

[5] Pfeiffer and Harrison, eds., *The Wycliffe Bible Commentary*, p. 1185.

[6] The perceptive reader may be wondering about the word translated "believe" in James 2:19, quoted above. Yes, it is also *pisteuô*. Yet, in context, "believe" seems an appropriate translation, since James says the demons "*pisteuô*" (believe) a fact—that "God is one." Faith in Christ is more than merely believing facts.

[7] See Exodus 20:18-19.

[8] See Exodus 32:1-8.

[9] See Exodus 20:3-5.

[10] See Genesis 3:9-10: "Then the LORD God called to the man, and said to him, 'Where are you?' He said, 'I heard the sound of You in the garden, and I was afraid because I was naked; so I hid myself.' "

[11] See Exodus 3:5-6.

[12] See Isaiah 6:5.

[13] See Matthew 17:5-6.

[14] See Matthew 14:26-27.

[15] See Mark 4:39-41.

[16] See Mark 5:15.

[17] Mark 5:15-17, Luke 8:35-37

[18] See also, for example: Job 28:28; Psalms 25:12, 25:14, 111:10; Proverbs 1:7, 1:29, 2:5, 8:13, 10:27, 14:27, 15:33, 16:6, 19:23

[19] See, for example: Psalm 25:12-15; Proverbs 1:1-5, 2:6-8, 8:10-11, 9:9, 9:11, 10:24-30, 14:26-27, 15:29-32, 16:6-7, 19:20-23.

[20] Genesis 3:8-10

[21] However, I will not concede that trust can co-exist with fear. How can we trust someone to have our best interests at heart if we are afraid that person may hurt us, either physically or emotionally?

Chapter 5
WHAT HELL IS REALLY LIKE

I date my conversion to Christianity from January 3, 1976, but I actually toyed with the idea about five years earlier when a well-meaning friend introduced me to Christ. My infant faith soared for about a week, until my agnostic father shot it down by assailing me with questions for which I had no answers. One of those questions was, "Why would a loving God inflict pain and torture on some of His creatures for all eternity?" I had to admit that it did not make any sense. What I did not know at the time was that this view of Hell finds scant support in the Bible. [1]

The image of Hell which too many Christians uncritically accept envisions a place where unbelievers and the wicked are tortured endlessly. I will refer to this vision as the "traditional" view of Hell. For Christians, this picture of Hell—and what it says about God—should be deeply troubling.

After all, the New Testament tells us that God is a loving Father. According to the first letter of John, "God is love." (1 John 4:8 and 4:16) Jesus told us to " 'love one another, just as I have loved you.' " (John 15:12) Could a just God—much less the loving and compassionate God we see in the New Testament—impose everlasting pain and torment on *anyone*? Only the most compelling Scriptural evidence would convince me to say "yes."

This is not to say that God must, or will, let everyone into Heaven. If Heaven is to be a place without crying or pain, [2] then God may have to exclude those who selfishly insist on hurting others, or Heaven would cease to be Heaven.

But what purpose does God advance by inflicting pain and torment upon those He has excluded? Torturing the damned will not make Heaven a better place. To the contrary, He would cause unnecessary grief for those in Heaven who care about some of the condemned. Could you be happy in Heaven if you knew that someone you love was being tortured in Hell?

However, before I go further, let me frankly state that I am not a clergyman. I am a lawyer. As such, I bring a slightly different perspective to this discussion. The law follows a rule which I believe is useful in interpreting Scripture—the doctrine of *pari materia* (which is Latin for "on the same subject"). Simply stated, it says that we should interpret laws so that they are consistent with each other, so long as they address the same general subject, or have the same general purpose. [3]

This principle recognizes that lawmakers do not deliberately enact laws that conflict with each other, so every effort should be made to avoid such conflicts when interpreting the law. I believe a similar rule makes sense in Biblical interpretation: we should interpret verses, whenever possible, so that they are in harmony with one another. A corollary is like it: if two verses appear to be in conflict, then we are interpreting at least one of them incorrectly.

With this in mind, let's take a detailed look at the verses that talk about Hell, either explicitly or by implication.

1) First, a large number of verses speak of "judgment," "wrath," and "condemnation," but give us no specifics. [4] I also include in this category verses which mention "Hell" or "Hades," but without elaboration. [5] Frankly, these verses do not help us, because they are vague about the nature of Hell and can easily be interpreted to support any of several possibilities. Eternal torture would certainly be consistent with God's judgment, wrath, and condemnation, but so would other types of punishment, such as death or exile. I mention the verses in this category only for the sake of completeness, but I will not spend any further time discussing them.

2) Another group of verses associates the fate of the damned with "fire," as in John's Gospel where Jesus says: " 'If anyone does not abide in Me, he is thrown away as a branch; and dries up; and they gather them, and cast them into the fire and they are burned.' " (John 15:6) [6]

3) A third group of New Testament verses speaks of "death" and/or "destruction." In Matthew 10:28, Jesus warns His followers: " 'Do not fear those who kill the body but are unable to kill the soul; but rather fear Him who is able to destroy both soul and body in hell.' " [7]

4) Jesus also spoke of Hell as a place where there is "weeping and gnashing of teeth," [8] and as an "abyss" or a place of darkness. [9]

5) Finally, some verses speak of "punishment" or "torment." [10] Certainly, the most graphic of these is Jesus's parable of Lazarus and the rich man, in Luke 16:22-31:

> "Now the poor man died and was carried away by the angels to Abraham's bosom; and the rich man also died and was buried. In Hades he lifted up his eyes, being in torment, and saw Abraham far away and Lazarus in his bosom. And he cried out and said, 'Father Abraham, have mercy on me, and send Lazarus so that he may dip the tip of his finger in water and cool off my tongue, for I am in agony in this flame.' But Abraham said, 'Child, remember that during your life you received your good things, and likewise Lazarus bad things; but now he is being comforted here, and you are in agony. And besides all this, between us and you there is a great chasm fixed, so that those who wish to come over from here to you will not be able, and *that* none may cross over from there to us.' And he said, 'Then I beg you, father, that you send him to my father's house—for I have five brothers—in order that he may warn them, so that they will not also come to this place of torment.' But Abraham said, 'They have Moses and the Prophets; let them hear them.' But he said, 'No, father Abraham, but if

someone goes to them from the dead, they will repent!' But he said to him, 'If they do not listen to Moses and the Prophets, they will not be persuaded even if someone rises from the dead.' "

Punishment and Torment. We begin with this last group of Scriptures, which appear to most strongly support the traditional view of Hell. This group consists of a mere nine Scriptures. Of these, four appear in the Gospels (Matthew 18:34-35, Matthew 25:41-46, Luke 12:46-48, and Luke 16:22-31), three in the epistles (Romans 2:5-9, 2 Peter 2:9, and Jude 6-7), and two in the Book of Revelation (Revelation 14:9-11, and Revelation 20:10).

Three of the four Gospel Scriptures are drawn from parables:

(1) Luke 16:22-31 is of course the parable of Lazarus and the rich man, which is quoted above.

(2) Matthew 18:34-35 is from the parable of the unforgiving slave, who refused to forgive a small debt after he was forgiven a large debt. Verse 34 says that this unforgiving slave was handed over to "the torturers until he should repay all that was owed him," and verse 35 adds: "My heavenly Father will also do the same to you, if each of you does not forgive his brother from your heart."

(3) The third of the parables, Luke 12:46-48, discusses the fate of the disobedient slave who is caught by his master's unexpected return. Jesus tells us that the slave will receive "many lashes," will be cut to pieces, and will be assigned "a place with the unbelievers."

Can we conclude from these parables that the fate of the unbelievers will include burning, torture, and lashes? If so, then shouldn't we also conclude that Jesus advocated robbery when He compared Himself to a robber who overpowers Satan? [11] Shall we strive to be dishonest, like the unrighteous steward whom his master praised? [12] Are the stories of the Prodigal Son, [13] the Good

Samaritan, [14] and the angry dinner host [15] to be accepted as literal fact rather than simply stories? Are men trees, bearing both good and bad "fruit"? [16]

Jesus's parables are stories which teach a lesson. We must therefore be careful not to read too much into them. Nowhere is this truer than in the parable of Lazarus and the rich man.

In that parable, Jesus deliberately exaggerates the ferocity of Hell. The rich man (who, by the way, should be screaming in agony, not carrying on a calm conversation with Abraham) requests an absurdly trivial favor: that Lazarus be allowed to dip the mere tip of his finger in water and cool off nothing but the rich man's tongue. I would have asked for at least a bucket of ice water. Perhaps Jesus used such hyperbole to emphasize the complete separation of the saved from the unsaved. But He also used it to prophetically illustrate that some people simply refuse to accept God's salvation; neither threats of consequences nor Jesus's own resurrection from the dead are sufficient to convince them ("they will not be persuaded even if someone rises from the dead," Luke 16:31).

We also find horrific images of Hell in the Book of Revelation. Revelation 14:9-11 says that those who worship the "beast" and receive his mark "will be tormented with fire and brimstone in the presence of the holy angels and in the presence of the Lamb," and "the smoke of their torment goes up forever and ever. . . ." And Revelation 20:10 says the "beast" and the "false prophet" will be thrown into the lake of fire, where "they will be tormented day and night forever and ever." However, any person knowledgeable about the Book of Revelation will concede that it contains a great deal of symbolism.

In Revelation 20:15, those whose names are not found in the "book of life" are thrown into the "lake of fire." But just before this, in Revelation 20:14, we read: "Then death and Hades were thrown into the lake of fire. This is the second death, the lake of fire." [17] In 20:14, the image of "death and Hades" being cast into a lake of fire must be symbolic, since death and Hades are not real beings, but mere symbols. The "lake of fire" also seems to be symbolic, since it is said to be "the second death." Thus, as with Jesus's parables, Revelation's images regarding Hell are not meant to be taken literally.

We have now discussed five of the nine Scriptures in this group. What about the other four? Paul, in Romans 2:8-9, says there will be "tribulation and distress" for evil-doers, while 2 Peter 2:9 talks of "punishment" for the unrighteous in the day of judgment. Yet Peter and Paul do not tell us specifically what this tribulation, distress, and punishment will be.

Jude 6-7 talks of "the punishment of eternal fire" that will be imposed on wicked angels. Does Jude mean that they will be tortured by that fire? Or simply that fire will be the means by which their "punishment," whatever that may be, will be carried out? Thus, these three Scriptures are quite ambiguous, and will therefore tolerate a variety of interpretations, including those which are relatively benign.

Finally, in the last of our nine Scriptures, Matthew 25:31-46, Jesus presents an image of the final judgment, in which people are divided into sheep (those who are saved) and goats (the unsaved). The latter are told, " 'Depart from Me, accursed ones, into the eternal fire which has been prepared for the devil and his angels. . . .' " (Matthew 25:41) Their fate is described as follows: " 'These will go away into eternal punishment, but the righteous into eternal life.' " (Matthew 25:46) This language, while similar to that of Jude, is also stronger, since the punishment suffered by the damned is now "eternal." I believe these verses in Matthew provide the strongest New Testament support for the traditional view of Hell. And yet, "eternal punishment" is still vague enough that it could be consistent with something other than eternal pain and torture.

If the New Testament were otherwise silent, these nine Scriptures would make a reasonably strong case for the view of

Hell as eternal pain and torture. But remember that these verses must be interpreted in the light of other Scriptures. And there we will find strong reasons to doubt that traditional view.

But next we will address the second group of Scriptures—those that associate the fate of the damned with "fire"—as we consider the question, when is "fire" not really fire?

Fire. The traditional view of Hell includes fire as a central element. And we have already mentioned several New Testament verses which associate fire with the afterlife and the fate of unbelievers. Another instance is found in Matthew 18:8-9:

> "If your hand or your foot causes you to stumble, cut it off and throw it from you; it is better for you to enter life crippled or lame, than to have two hands or two feet and be cast into the eternal fire. If your eye causes you to stumble, pluck it out and throw it from you. It is better for you to enter life with one eye, than to have two eyes and be cast into the fiery hell." [18]

But does "fire" mean literal scorching, burning, pain-inducing fire? Frequently in the Bible, the concept of "fire" carries a symbolic meaning. In Romans 12:20, Paul, quoting Proverbs 25:21-22, uses "burning coals" to symbolize guilt and remorse:

> But if your enemy is hungry, feed him, and if he is thirsty, give him a drink; for in so doing you will heap burning coals on his head.

James uses fire as a symbol of wickedness in James 3:5-6:

> So also the tongue is a small part of the body, and *yet* it boasts of great things. See how great a forest is set aflame by such a small fire! And the tongue is a fire, the *very* world of iniquity; the tongue is set among our members as that which defiles the entire body, and sets on fire the course of *our* life, and is set on fire by hell. [19]

Fire also symbolizes God's wrath or judgment, as in Nahum 1:6:

> Who can stand before His indignation?
> Who can endure the burning of His anger?
> His wrath is poured out like fire,
> And the rocks are broken up by Him. [20]

Fire can be a symbol of God's presence, His Spirit, and His word:

> "For I," declares the Lord, "will be a wall of fire around her [Jerusalem], and I will be the glory in her midst."
>
> —Zechariah 2:5

> And there appeared to them tongues as of fire distributing themselves, and they rested on each one of them.
>
> —Acts 2:3 [21]

God even uses "fire" to modify or correct His people's behavior, as in Malachi:

> But who can endure the day of His coming? And who can stand when He appears? For He is like a refiner's fire and like fullers' soap. He will sit as a smelter and purifier of silver, and He will purify the sons of Levi and refine them like gold and silver, so that they may present to the Lord offerings in righteousness.
>
> —Malachi 3:2-3 [22]

These verses, and others cited in the endnotes, illustrate the plausibility of a symbolic interpretation of such verses as Matthew 5:22 and 18:8-9, which talk of the "fiery hell," and Mark 9:43, which talks of the "unquenchable fire" of hell. But how do we decide whether the literal or the symbolic interpretation is correct? The answer will be found in other verses, which are difficult or impossible to reconcile with anything but a symbolic interpretation. As a starting point, we turn to one of the letters of

Peter, which provides another clue that the "fire" of Hell is not literal.

Death and Destruction. 2 Peter 3:7 warns us that: "by His word the present heavens and earth are being reserved for fire, kept for the day of judgment and destruction of ungodly men." In this verse, "fire" does not torture and inflict pain, but instead destroys. This is but one of many New Testament Scriptures that talk about the fate of unbelievers in terms of "death" or "destruction." Here are some examples:

> Do you not know that when you present yourselves to someone *as* slaves for obedience, you are slaves of the one whom you obey, either of sin resulting in death, or of obedience resulting in righteousness?
>
> —Romans 6:16 [23]

> "Do not fear those who kill the body but are unable to kill the soul; but rather fear Him who is able to destroy both soul and body in hell."
>
> —Matthew 10:28

> These will pay the penalty of eternal destruction, away from the presence of the Lord and from the glory of His power. . . .
>
> —2 Thessalonians 1:9

> "But for the cowardly and unbelieving and abominable and murderers and immoral persons and sorcerers and idolaters and all liars, their part *will be* in the lake that burns with fire and brimstone, which is the second death."
>
> —Revelation 21:8

These verses, and others, [24] which speak of "death," destruction of the soul, "eternal destruction," and the "second death," are not merely talking about the physical death of the body, which all of us—saved and unsaved alike—must one day suffer. Instead, these verses refer to a spiritual death, which suggests one of two interpretations: (1) the literal death of the soul—truly a "second death" as stated in Revelation 21:8; or (2) spiritual death through separation from God—as Paul says, "away from the presence of the Lord." (2 Thessalonians 1:9)

The death of the soul—the "second death"—is probably the more merciful of the two, because the alternative, separation from God, would be a horrid existence, even without any physical pain or torture. Unsaved souls who are separated from God would be estranged from the source of everything good and kind and loving—a life without everything that makes life worthwhile, including hope.

The literal death of the soul also avoids two questions inherent in the idea of mere separation from God. First, while souls separated from God would be spiritually "dead," how are they "destroyed" as some verses assert? And, more critically, where could these souls possibly go to escape the omnipresence of God? [25]

If wicked souls are punished through a "second death"—the death of the soul—then the traditional view of Hell as eternal torture becomes untenable, for no souls would remain upon whom to inflict pain and torture in Hell. Thus, the "furnace of fire" and the "lake that burns with fire and brimstone" could simply be the means of destruction. Or perhaps "fire" symbolizes the guilt these souls feel as they are judged by God.

On the other hand, those who believe that a loving God would be unable to bring Himself to kill *any* of His human creatures, no matter how wicked, may prefer to interpret "death" and "destruction" in these verses as a spiritual death through separation from God. If we adopt this second interpretation, then we must ask whether separation from God is inconsistent with the traditional view of Hell. Couldn't God banish the wicked to a place of eternal torture? Of course He could. But scriptures in the final category suggest otherwise.

"Weeping and Gnashing of Teeth" and "Darkness." In Matthew 13:41-42, Jesus says:

> "The Son of Man will send forth His angels, and they will gather out of His kingdom all stumbling blocks, and those who commit lawlessness, and will throw them into the furnace of fire; in that place there will be weeping and gnashing of teeth."

In Matthew 8:12, Jesus speaks of the fate of some Jews, saying that they

> "will be cast out into the outer darkness; in that place there will be weeping and gnashing of teeth."

Of course, the "furnace of fire" and the "outer darkness" cannot both be literal, since a fiery furnace would hardly be a place of darkness. But aside from that, the reference to "gnashing of teeth" in these and other verses [26] does *not* signify pain. In the Bible, gnashing of teeth always refers to anger or rage, as in Job:

> His anger has torn me and hunted me down.
> He has gnashed at me with His teeth;
> My adversary glares at me.
>
> —Job 16:9

Job is not saying that God is in pain, but that God is angry with him. Similarly, other Old Testament verses use "gnashing of teeth" to refer to anger or rage, not pain. [27]

The phrase is also used in the New Testament, describing the anger of Stephen's enemies before they put him to death: "Now when they heard this, they were cut to the quick, and they *began* gnashing their teeth at him." (Acts 7:54)

Hell is a place of "weeping and gnashing of teeth" because the residents will either blame themselves for their fate, and weep, or they will blame God, and rage. Pain does not enter the picture.

Jesus always chose His words carefully. If He meant pain or torture, He certainly would have said so. His repeated use of the phrase, "weeping and gnashing of teeth," is therefore significant, especially when juxtaposed with the "furnace of fire," as in Matthew 13:42 and Matthew 13:50.

Hell is also referred to as "the outer darkness," [28] the "abyss," [29] "pits of darkness," [30] "black darkness," [31] or simply "darkness." [32] In this context, "darkness" probably symbolizes evil, as in John 3:19: "men loved the darkness rather than the Light; for their deeds were evil." Darkness may also imply sadness or loneliness, but the term does not connote physical pain or torture.

Thus, to the extent that the unbelievers continue to live after they have been judged, these verses demonstrate that their lives include regret and/or burning rage—but not pain. If there is any pain or torment in Hell, I am certain that the residents, not God, will inflict it.

Conclusion. God cannot share Heaven with evil. But the kind, loving, and merciful Father of whom Jesus spoke would not—could not—inflict everlasting and unnecessary torture upon even the most evil of mankind. Such cruelty would be against His nature. That, combined with the paucity of evidence in the New Testament to support the traditional view of Hell, and the abundant verses that conflict with such a view, leads to the inescapable conclusion that the traditional view of Hell as an eternal torture chamber is inaccurate. So what is Hell really like?

Only two interpretations are consistent with all of the many New Testament verses which discuss the ultimate fate of the damned: (1) God will end their existence, once and for all; or (2) God will quarantine their evil in "Hell." [33]

If the first interpretation is correct, then the Scriptures regarding "death" and "destruction" must be accepted as literal fact, and the Scriptures which talk of "weeping and gnashing of teeth" merely describe a temporary condition. On the other hand, if the wicked are separated from God, rather than destroyed, then they will "die" only in the spiritual sense of being separated from the Source of all life, and "weeping and gnashing of teeth" describes their permanent existence. Both possibilities are sad to contemplate. But unlike the traditional view of Hell, neither is inconsistent with God's nature.

Endnotes for Chapter Five, "What Hell Is Really Like"

[1] In this essay I only discuss what the New Testament says about Hell. The Old Testament talks of Sheol, rather than Hell, and says little about the nature of Sheol except that it is a place for departed souls. See Genesis 37:35, 42:38, 44:29, 44:31; Numbers 16:30, 16:33; Deuteronomy 32:22; 1 Samuel 2:6; 2 Samuel 22:6; 1 Kings 2:6, 2:9; Job 7:9, 11:8, 14:13, 17:13, 17:16, 21:13, 24:19, 26:6, 33:18; Psalm 6:5, 9:17, 16:10, 18:5, 30:3, 31:17, 49:14-15, 55:15, 86:13, 88:3, 89:48, 116:3, 139:8, 141:7; Proverbs 1:12, 5:5, 7:27, 9:18, 15:11, 15:24, 23:14, 27:20, 30:16; Ecclesiastes 9:10; Song of Solomon 8:6; Isaiah 5:14, 7:11, 14:9, 14:11, 14:15, 28:15, 28:18, 38:10, 38:18, 57:9; Ezekiel 31:15-17, 32:21, 32:27; Hosea 13:14; Amos 9:2; Jonah 2:2; Habakkuk 2:5.

[2] See Revelation 21:4.

[3] See 53 Texas Jurisprudence 2nd, "Statutes," Section 186, page 280, as quoted in *Cheney v. State,* 755 S.W.2d at 126. See also Black, *Black's Law Dictionary,* "pari materia," at p. 1004.

[4] See Matthew 3:7, 10:15, 11:22, 11:24; Mark 12:40, 16:16; Luke 12:58-59, 20:47; John 3:18-19, 3:36, 5:29; Romans 2:5-6, 2:8-9, 11:22; 1 Corinthians 11:32; Ephesians 2:3, 5:5-6; Colossians 3:5-6, 3:25; 1 Thessalonians 5:9; 2 Thessalonians 2:11-12; Hebrews 2:2-3; 1 Peter 4:5-6; 2 Peter 2:4, 2:9, 3:7; Jude 6; Revelation 20:12-13.

[5] See Matthew 5:22, 5:29-30, 10:28, 11:23, 16:18, 18:9; Mark 9:43, 9:45, 9:47; Luke 10:15, 12:5, 16:23; Acts 2:27, 2:31; Ephesians 4:9; James 3:6; 2 Peter 2:4; Revelation 1:18, 20:13-14.

[6] See also, Matthew 3:10, 3:12, 5:22, 7:19, 13:30, 13:40, 13:42, 13:50, 18:8-9, 25:41; Mark 9:43, 9:49; Luke 3:9, 3:17, 16:24; 1 Corinthians 3:13, 3:15; 2 Thessalonians 1:7; James 3:6, 5:3; 2 Peter 3:7; Jude 7, 23; Revelation 19:20, 20:10, 20:14-15, 21:8.

[7] See also Matthew 7:13, 10:39; Mark 8:35-36; Luke 13:3, 13:5, 13:9, 19:27; Acts 3:23, 13:46; Romans 6:16, 6:23, 7:5, 7:9-11, 7:24, 8:6, 8:10, 8:13; 1 Corinthians 3:17; 2 Corinthians 2:15-16, 4:3, 7:10; Ephesians 2:5; Philippians 1:28; 1 Thessalonians 5:3; 2 Thessalonians 1:9, 2:10; James 5:20; 2 Peter 2:3, 2:12, 3:7, 3:16; Jude 10; Revelation 2:11, 11:18, 20:6, 20:14, 21:8.

[8] See Matthew 8:12, 13:42, 13:50, 22:13, 24:51, 25:30; Luke 13:28.

[9] See Matthew 8:12, 22:13, 25:30; Luke 8:31; John 3:19; 2 Peter 2:4; Jude 6, 13; Revelation 20:1, 20:3.

[10] Matthew 18:34-35, Matthew 25:41-46, Luke 12:46-48, Luke 16:22-31, Romans 2:5-9, 2 Peter 2:9, Jude 6-7, Revelation 14:9-11, and Revelation 20:10

[11] See Luke 11:21-22, Mark 3:27, and Matthew 12:29.

[12] Luke 16:1-8

[13] Luke 15:11-32

[14] Luke 10:25-37

[15] Luke 14:16-24

[16] Luke 6:43-45; Matthew 7:16-20

[17] A similar image is presented in Revelation 21:8.

[18] Similarly, see Mark 9:43-50.

[19] Similarly, see Isaiah 9:18-19 and Psalm 39:3.

[20] For other references to fire as a symbol of God's wrath or judgment, see: Isaiah 65:3-5 and 66:15-16; Jeremiah 4:4, 5:14, 21:12, and 48:45; Lamentations 2:3-4; Ezekiel 21:31, 22:20-22, 24:1-13, 28:18, 36:5, and 38:19; Amos 5:6-7. Fire is also used to *carry out* God's judgment, as in Genesis 19:24; Leviticus 10:1-2; Numbers 11:1; and 2 Kings 1:10 and 1:12.

[21] Other verses which use fire as symbolic of God's presence or His word include: Exodus 3:2-4 and 13:21; Judges 6:21; 1 Kings 18:36-39; 1 Chronicles 21:26; Isaiah 31:9; Jeremiah 20:9 and 23:28-29; Daniel 7:9-10; Matthew 3:11; and 2 Thessalonians 1:6-9.

[22] For additional verses which use "fire" in this way, see Zechariah 13:9; Matthew 3:11; Mark 9:49; and 1 Peter 1:7. See also 1 Corinthians 3:12-15.

[23] See also Romans 6:23 and 2 Corinthians 7:10.

[24] See Matthew 7:13, 10:39; Mark 8:35-36; Luke 13:3, 13:5, 13:9, 19:27; Acts 3:23, 13:46; Romans 7:5, 7:9-11, 7:24, 8:6, 8:10, 8:13; 1 Corinthians 3:17; 2 Corinthians 2:15-16, 4:3; Ephesians 2:5; Philippians 1:28; 1 Thessalonians 5:3; 2 Thessalonians 2:10; James 5:20; 2 Peter 2:3, 2:12, 3:7, 3:16; Jude 10; Revelation 2:11, 11:18, 20:6, 20:14.

[25] See Psalm 139:7-8 and Jeremiah 23:24.

[26] See Matthew 13:50, 22:13, 24:51, 25:30; Luke 13:28.

[27] See Psalm 35:15-16, Psalm 37:12, Psalm 112:10, and Lamentations 2:16.

[28] Matthew 8:12, 22:13, 25:30

[29] Luke 8:31 and Revelation 20:1-3

[30] 2 Peter 2:4

[31] Jude 13

[32] Jude 6

[33] And perhaps there is a third option—that God will allow each person to choose whether to live apart from Him or to not live at all.

Chapter 6
THREE LIES PEOPLE TELL ABOUT GOD

People lie to us all the time. Advertisers tell you their product will make you happy, popular, successful, or attractive to the opposite sex. [1] Politicians announce the wonderful things they have no intention of doing if they are elected. Many people tell little white lies to make you feel better. A few lie to try to take advantage of you. We even lie to ourselves, especially about the inevitability of growing old and dying. But the most destructive lies people tell are about God, because they have eternal implications. Let's look at three of them.

Lie #1: God wants to make you wealthy. Preachers who just want your money will assure you that if you give to God, He will make you wealthy—or at least comfortably well off. They often quote what Jesus says in Matthew 19:29 to show that God has promised to bestow riches on those who make sacrifices for His church:

> "And everyone who has left houses or brothers or sisters or father or mother or children or farms for My name's sake, will receive many times as much, and will inherit eternal life." [2]

These prosperity preachers may even tell you that you will receive good health and an easy life in the bargain. But they are wrong.

First of all, history refutes their claim. Jesus and His followers did not live lives of wealth and ease. Instead, they lived simple lives and traveled extensively to spread the Gospel. The Christians in Jerusalem—where the Christian church was born—were so poor that the apostle Paul raised money in Asia Minor and Greece to help them. [3]

Nor did the early Christians have an easy life. Jesus was crucified, and many of His followers were also martyred because of their preaching about Jesus. For three centuries after Christ's death, many Christians lost their property, their freedom, and even their lives for the crime of being a Christian.

Nowhere is this suffering better illustrated than in the life of the apostle Paul. He traveled throughout the eastern Roman Empire: Palestine (i.e., Israel), Syria, Cyprus, Asia Minor (now Turkey), Macedonia (northern Greece), and Achaia (southern Greece). He probably also traveled to Crete and Spain.

I previously mentioned the many hardships he had to bear, per II Corinthians 11:23-27 (see page 48), which included whippings, beatings, a stoning, three shipwrecks, hunger, thirst, sleepless nights, and many dangers. Paul tells us that he learned to be content even when he was in humble surroundings and had little food. [4] And he also had to endure what he called a "thorn in the flesh" (2 Corinthians 12:7), which was probably some type of chronic health problem. Ultimately, Paul was beheaded in Rome because of his Christian faith.

If faith in Christ is supposed to bring health, wealth, and an easy life, the early followers of Jesus somehow missed out.

This notion that God wants Christians to be wealthy is also inconsistent with the attitude of Jesus and the New Testament writers toward money. For example, the writer of the letter to the Hebrews gives this advice: "*Make sure that* your character is free from the love of money, being content with what you have. . . ." (Hebrews 13:5) And Paul warns us that

> the love of money is a root of all sorts of evil, and some by longing for it have wandered away from the faith and pierced themselves with many griefs.
>
> —1 Timothy 6:10 [5]

Jesus told the rich young ruler to give away all of his possessions to the poor, so that he would have treasure in heaven. [6] Jesus gave similar advice to His own followers, telling them not to horde earthly possessions, [7] but instead to give them away:

> "Sell your possessions and give to charity; make yourselves money belts which do not wear out, an unfailing treasure in heaven, where no thief comes near nor moth destroys. For where your treasure is, there your heart will be also."
>
> —Luke 12:33-34 [8]

Jesus told us to not even be concerned about the necessities of life, like food and clothing, [9] but instead to " 'seek His kingdom, and these things will be added to you.' " (Luke 12:31) [10] Indeed, Jesus seems to say that Christianity is opposed to wealth—or perhaps more accurately, the lust for wealth:

> "No servant can serve two masters; for either he will hate the one and love the other, or else he will be devoted to one and despise the other. You cannot serve God and wealth."
>
> —Luke 16:13 [11]

> And Jesus said to His disciples, "Truly I say to you, it is hard for a rich man to enter the kingdom of heaven. Again I say to you, it is easier for a camel to go through the eye of a needle, than for a rich man to enter the kingdom of God."
>
> —Matthew 19:23-24 [12]

Jesus knew that the wealthy would be tempted to seek their happiness and security through money rather than God. In this way, wealth impedes the development of the relationship God longs to have with each of us, for He insists that we make Him the most important thing in our lives. [13] That cannot happen so long as money occupies that top spot.

In addition, a focus on money leads us down the wrong path by emphasizing this earthly life. Christianity is more concerned with eternal life. That is why Jesus's followers were willing to sacrifice *everything,* including their own lives, to win eternity.

As Paul said: "If we have hoped in Christ in this life only, we are of all men most to be pitied." (1 Corinthians 15:19) [14]

Thus, making us wealthy often runs counter to God's interests. Wealth encourages us to focus on the pleasures and worries of this earthly life, rather than on God and eternal life. In light of this, why would God want to inflict riches on anyone?

However, this does not mean that Matthew 19:29 is a lie, for " 'God is not a man, that He should lie. . . .' " (Numbers 23:19) [15] Anyone who leaves home or family for God *will* receive many times as much, because she will become part of the much larger family of God and will be welcomed by God's many true followers. And that is a reward greater than any promised by the prosperity preachers.

Lie #2: God punishes us in this life. Another lie that too many Christians (and non-Christians, also) accept—either explicitly or implicitly—is that God punishes us in this life for the evils we do and the mistakes we make. When something terrible happens in their lives, they immediately wonder what they did to cause God to bring such a calamity upon them.

Jesus's contemporaries thought that way, but Jesus refused to buy into the idea. When His disciples asked whether a man had been born blind because of his parents' sin or because of his own sin, Jesus responded: " '*It was* neither *that* this man sinned, nor his parents; but *it was* so that the works of God might be displayed in him.' " (John 9:3) Similarly, Jesus refuted the idea that the victims of two misfortunes of His day had been punished by God for their sins:

> Now on the same occasion there were some present who reported to Him about the Galileans whose blood Pilate had mixed with their sacrifices. And Jesus said to them, "Do you suppose that these Galileans were *greater* sinners than all *other* Galileans because they suffered this *fate?* I tell you, no, but

> unless you repent, you will all likewise perish. Or do you suppose that those eighteen on whom the tower in Siloam fell and killed them were *worse* culprits than all the men who live in Jerusalem? I tell you, no, but unless you repent, you will all likewise perish."
>
> —Luke 13:1-5

While the Old Testament often speaks of God punishing individuals and nations in this life because of their bad behavior, the New Testament is curiously silent on that subject. Instead, the New Testament focuses on God's judgment *in the next life*—life after death. [16]

Of course, people who break man's laws are punished in this life, but such punishment comes from God only in the indirect sense that the authorities who enforce those laws owe their positions to God. [17] As a general rule, the New Testament writers do not suggest that God inflicts earthly punishment for bad behavior, and the exceptions to this are both limited and specific.

One such exception is Paul's reference to Christians who suffer because they have failed to respect the sacred nature of the Lord's Supper: [18]

> Therefore whoever eats the bread or drinks the cup of the Lord in an unworthy manner, shall be guilty of the body and the blood of the Lord. But a man must examine himself, and in so doing he is to eat of the bread and drink of the cup. For he who eats and drinks, eats and drinks judgment to himself if he does not judge the body rightly. For this reason many among you are weak and sick, and a number sleep [i.e., have died]. But if we judged ourselves rightly, we would not be judged. But when we are

> judged, we are disciplined by the Lord so that we will not be condemned along with the world.
>
> —1 Corinthians 11:27-32

Two other exceptions are found in Revelation, where John threatens the false prophetess Jezebel and her followers in the Christian church at Thyatira with sickness and tribulation, [19] and then warns the Christians of Laodicea that the Lord will "reprove and discipline" them to shake them out of their arrogance and complacency. [20]

Each of these exceptions is quite narrow. Revelation threatens punishment (or discipline) against two specific groups, while Paul's warning addresses those who profane the Communion meal. As such, these exceptions apply to Christians only in certain circumstances, and not at all to non-Christians. [21]

Now to be sure, the New Testament does speak of Jesus and His followers suffering, and especially suffering persecution. [22] But this suffering cannot be equated with punishment from God. Instead, most of this suffering is unwarranted and unjust, and yet also a cause for rejoicing:

> "Blessed are you when *people* insult you and persecute you, and falsely say all kinds of evil against you because of Me. Rejoice and be glad, for your reward in heaven is great; for in the same way they persecuted the prophets who were before you."
>
> —Matthew 5:11-12 [23]

Suffering can result from a variety of causes, including our own actions, but the reason for our suffering is rarely, if ever, punishment from God.

Lie #3: God will let you into Heaven if your good works outweigh your bad deeds. I remember my mother telling me that she was raised to believe that God kept a record of everything she did—good and bad—and that her eternal destiny would be determined by whether she had more marks on the "Good" side of the ledger than on the "Bad" side.

What a tragedy that many people seem to accept this view of God. Those who believe this lie will waste their whole lives in a vain effort to balance out their failings with good deeds. Or they will simply give up in despair, realizing at some point that we can never do enough to earn God's love or approval.

The good news of Christianity is that we don't have to. God is not a divine scale, weighing our good works against our bad behavior. He is instead a loving Father, who stands ready and eager to forgive us for all of our wrongdoing, and to welcome us back with open arms. There is only one catch: we must return to Him of our own free will, for He will not compel us. God wants our love, but love must be freely given.

Many New Testament verses teach this truth, but let's begin with one of the most famous, John 3:16: "For God so loved the world, that He gave His only begotten Son, that whoever believes in Him shall not perish, but have eternal life." We saw in Chapter Four that the word translated "believes" is the Greek word, *pisteuô,* the meaning of which is really closer to our English words "trust" or "commitment." It connotes giving our lives to God wholeheartedly.

A related concept is that of repentance, which translates the Greek word, *metanoeô,* meaning to turn back or change direction. When we repent, we turn back to God and change the direction of our lives. The New Testament often speaks of the need for repentance, [24] just as it speaks of the need to trust God and commit our lives to Him. These concepts are all interrelated—we cannot truly do one without the others.

When we turn back and commit ourselves to God, we are immediately forgiven for the wrongs we have done and given the free gift of eternal life. This forgiveness and salvation are not anything we deserve. We don't receive eternal life because we go to church every Sunday or because we do a lot of good deeds. We receive salvation because God loves us and wants to give it to us. This is grace, which means *unmerited favor*. Because of His love for us, God gives us what we need, not what we deserve.

We see this truth expressed throughout the New Testament. In his letter to the Romans, Paul says: "For the wages of sin is death, but the free gift of God is eternal life in Christ Jesus our Lord." (Romans 6:23) Or again, from Paul's letter to the Ephesians:

> For by grace you have been saved through faith; and that not of yourselves, *it is* the gift of God; not as a result of works, so that no one may boast.
>
> —Ephesians 2:8-9 [25]

God's eagerness to save us, without regard to our own merit, is the point of Jesus's parable of the prodigal son. [26] The younger son went away and wasted his money on profligate living, but ultimately decided to return home. His father (who is of course God) did not come after the boy when he left, but as soon as he got close to home the father was eager to forgive him—running to meet his son as he approached. The son did not have to do any good deeds to earn his father's forgiveness; the boy merely returned to his father, and received an enthusiastic welcome.

The same is true for us. When we repent and turn back to God, we are immediately accepted by Him, and Heaven rejoices: " 'I tell you that in the same way, there will be *more* joy in heaven over one sinner who repents than over ninety-nine righteous persons who need no repentance.' " (Luke 15:7) [27]

This idea of God's grace is unique to Christianity. In many religions, God (or the gods) is a powerful and terrifying Judge and Avenger, who must be placated. Those religions have rules for what you must do, or how you must act, in order to avoid God's wrath and win His favor. Of course, Christianity has "rules" as well, such as to act with love and kindness toward everyone (even enemies). But unlike adherents of other religions, Christians do this as a *response* to God's love, not in an effort to earn it.

One final point—if God is so loving and wants to forgive us, why is repentance even necessary? Why doesn't God simply let everyone into Heaven? Well, it's kind of like that old joke: "I wouldn't want to join any club that would accept me as a member."

Heaven is a special place not only because of Who is there, but also because of who is not. Heaven would not be Heaven if God accepted people who are selfish, mean, or hateful *and wish to remain so*. How could a bigot share Heaven with the object of his bigotry? How could a woman share Heaven with the ex-husband she despises? For Heaven to be Heaven, all of its inhabitants must embrace God's way of love and forgiveness. I believe we must enter Heaven God's way, or not at all.

Conclusion. We must stop lying to ourselves about who God is and what He wants from us. He is not a vending machine, dispensing wealth when we put in a few coins. Nor is He a school teacher who slaps our hands each time we step out of line. And most important of all, He is not a scorekeeper who decides our eternal fate based on a ledger of our good and bad deeds.

He is instead a loving parent, who wants to forgive us, embrace us, and give us eternal life. Maybe that is what Jesus meant when He said:

> "If you continue in My word, *then* you are truly disciples of Mine; and you will know the truth, and the truth will make you free."
>
> —John 8:31-32

Endnotes for Chapter Six, "Three Lies People Tell About God"

[1] My favorite "lies" that advertisers tell:

1. "Free" – Actually, it's almost always just included in the price.
2. "You deserve. . . ." – If I truly *deserve* it, why do I have to pay for it? Of course, we deserve very little of what we get.
3. "Everybody knows. . . ." – If *everyone* knows, then you don't need to tell us.
4. "Everybody is talking about. . . ." - Similarly, if *everyone* is talking about it, there is no need to tell us.
5. "No one is better" – Doesn't that just mean that you are about the same as your competitors?
6. "Today only" – Yet it always seems to be available tomorrow, too.
7. "Just pay shipping and handling" – Of course, that more than covers the product's cost, too.
8. "Free shipping" – Like "free," it's simply included in the price.
9. "Save" – How do I save money by spending it?
10. "Wholesale prices" – Wholesalers don't sell to the public. If you do, you are not a wholesaler.
11. "We treat you like family" – That is, like family members with money to spend.
12. "You need. . . ." – Although we may *want* what they are selling, we probably don't really *need* it.

[2] See also Mark 10:29-30 and Luke 18:29-30.

[3] See 1 Corinthians 16:1-4; 2 Corinthians 8:1-15; and Romans 15:25-26. See also Acts 19:21.

[4] See Philippians 4:11-12.

[5] Similarly, one of the qualifications for an elder is that he be "free from the love of money." See 1 Timothy 3:3.

[6] Matthew 19:21; Mark 10:21; Luke 18:22

[7] See Matthew 6:19: " 'Do not store up for yourselves treasures on earth, where moth and rust destroy, and where thieves break in and steal.' "

[8] See also Matthew 6:20-21.

[9] Luke 12:22-30 and Matthew 6:25-32

[10] Similarly, see Matthew 6:33.

[11] Similarly, see Matthew 6:24.

[12] Similarly, see Mark 10:23-25 and Luke 18:24-25. Of course, Jesus also assures us that the rich ***can*** be saved, for " 'with God all things are possible.' " (Matthew 19:26; Mark 10:27; Luke 18:27)

[13] The most important of God's commandments is to love God with all of our heart, soul, mind, and strength. See Mark 12:28-30, Matthew 22:36-38, and Luke 10:25-27.

[14] See also Ecclesiastes 2:1-11, which points out that wealth and possessions cannot bring happiness or fulfillment.

[15] Similarly, Paul tells us in Titus 1:2 that God "cannot lie."

[16] See, for example, Matthew 25:31-46, where Jesus speaks of God's eternal judgment. 2 Thessalonians 1:6-10 speaks of God punishing those who are persecuting the Thessalonian Christians, but the punishment is "eternal destruction, away from the presence of the Lord" (2 Thessalonians 1:9), which obviously refers to the afterlife. In addition, the time of this punishment is not the present, but "when the Lord Jesus will be revealed from heaven with His mighty angels" (2 Thessalonians 1:7), a reference to His Second Coming. Romans 2:2-10 speaks of God's judgment upon the unrighteous, but in the context of eternal life. (See Romans 2:7.) Many other examples could be cited from the New Testament.

[17] See Romans 13:1-3. And see 1 Peter 2:13-15.

[18] The Lord's Supper, also known as the Communion, commemorates Jesus' last night before his crucifixion, when he used bread and wine to symbolize his body and blood, and asked His disciples to eat and drink "in remembrance of Me." See Luke 22:19-20 and 1 Corinthians 11:23-26; see also Matthew 26:26-28 and Mark 14:22-24.

[19] Revelation 2:20-23

[20] Revelation 3:19

[21] Another example is that of Ananias and Sapphira in Acts 5:1-10. Note that this example too has no application to non-Christians.

[22] See, for example, Matthew 5:11, 5:44, 10:23, 13:21, 16:21, 17:12, 23:34, 24:9; Mark 4:17, 8:31, 9:12; Luke 9:22, 11:49, 17:25, 21:12, 22:15, 24:26, 24:46; John 15:20, 16:33; Acts 3:18, 5:40-41, 8:1, 9:15-16, 11:19, 13:50, 17:3, 26:23; Romans 5:3, 8:17, 8:35, 12:12, 12:14; 2 Corinthians 1:4-9; Galatians 1:1; Philippians 1:29; 1 Thessalonians 2:2, 3:3-4; 2 Timothy 1:12, 2:3, 2:9; Hebrews 10:32-39; 1 Peter 2:19-21, 3:14, 3:17, 4:12-16, 4:19, 5:9-10; Revelation 1:9, 2:9-10.

[23] See also Romans 5:3-4.

[24] See, for example, Matthew 3:2, 4:17; Mark 1:15, 6:12; Luke 13:3, 13:5; Acts 2:38, 3:19, 8:22, 17:30, 26:20.

[25] The Greek word which is translated as "faith" is *pistis*—the noun form of *pisteuô*—so again the meaning is trust or commitment. For more on this, see Chapter 4, "For God So Loved . . . Well, Wait a Minute."

[26] See Luke 15:11-24.

[27] See also Luke 15:10.

Chapter 7
IS YAHWEH AN OGRE? [1]

He utterly destroyed Sodom and Gomorrah, killing all of the inhabitants of both cities (except Lot and his family). [2] He ordered Moses to slay the leaders of the Israelites when they worshiped the Moabites' false gods. [3] He prescribed the death penalty for sorcery, [4] idolatry, [5] and false prophecy, [6] as well as for adultery, [7] murder, [8] rape, [9] and many other offenses. [10] Early Christian heretics—such as the Marcionites, [11] the Paulicians, [12] and Gnostic Christians [13]—believed that He was evil, and that this world, as His creation, was also evil.

In the Old Testament, God at first seems much different than He is portrayed in the New Testament. Certainly, the Old Testament can be difficult to understand. When I first tried to read it after becoming a Christian, I struggled through the early books before finally abandoning the effort somewhere around Deuteronomy. Yet as I have grown in my faith, I have come to understand that the Old Testament's Yahweh is the same loving, compassionate, and merciful God we see in the New Testament. God did not change—we did.

He's the Same God. What Jesus called the Greatest Commandment [14] actually comes from the book of Deuteronomy in the Old Testament: " 'You shall love the LORD your God with all your heart and with all your soul and with all your might.' " (Deuteronomy 6:5) [15] The Second Greatest Commandment [16] also comes from the Old Testament, Leviticus 19:18: "you shall love your neighbor as yourself." Kindness to enemies—an idea which Jesus and Paul certainly promoted [17]—has its roots in the Old Testament:

> If your enemy is hungry, give him food to eat;
> And if he is thirsty, give him water to drink. . . .
>
> —Proverbs 25:21 [18]

> "If you meet your enemy's ox or his donkey wandering away, you shall surely return it to him."
>
> —Exodus 23:4 [19]

The New Testament encourages Christians to be kind and generous to the poor, [20] but so does the Old Testament:

> "If there is a poor man with you, one of your brothers, in any of your towns in your land which the LORD your God is giving you, you shall not harden your heart, nor close your hand from your poor brother; but you shall freely open your hand to him, and shall generously lend him sufficient for his need *in* whatever he lacks. . . . You shall generously give to him, and your heart shall not be grieved when you give to him. . . ."
>
> —Deuteronomy 15:7-8 and 15:10 [21]

The compassion we associate with Jesus is evident in the Old Testament's insistence upon proper treatment of widows, orphans, and strangers:

> "You shall not wrong a stranger or oppress him, for you were strangers in the land of Egypt. You shall not afflict any widow or orphan."
>
> —Exodus 22:21-22

Many other parallels exist between the Old and New Testament portrayals of God. Isaiah calls Him "Father" and "Redeemer" (Isaiah 63:16), names reminiscent of the New Testament, and adds that God "longs to be gracious to you, and therefore He waits on high to have compassion on you" (Isaiah 30:18). The Psalmist testifies that God often restrained His anger and forgave His people, even when they were unfaithful to Him. [22]

Just as Jesus and John the Baptist called upon people to repent, so does Ezekiel. [23] And when the people of the Assyrian city of Nineveh did repent, God forgave them. [24] People thought Jesus's prohibition of divorce [25] was new, but Malachi spoke of God's hatred for divorce centuries before Christ. [26]

Many of the New Testament teachings are trees grown from the seeds of the Old Testament. So why does God *seem* so different in the Old Testament? Let's start with what people were like back then—and what God was trying to teach them.

It's All About Trust. A wise parent does not discipline a two-year-old the same way he disciplines a teenager. A teenager needs firm guidance combined with the freedom to make many of her own decisions—and mistakes. But a two-year-old would be lost if given such freedom. He needs strict rules which are strictly enforced, and a great deal of supervision. In terms of spiritual maturity, Jesus was teaching teenagers, while Yahweh was working with two-year-olds.

In early Old Testament days, God's people had little knowledge or experience of God. The Psalms had not yet been written, and none of the Prophets had appeared on the scene. The coming of Jesus and the Holy Spirit was not even on the horizon. God still had a lot to teach His people, beginning with the most important lesson: Trust Me and do what I tell you to do.

We see this as early as the story of Adam and Eve. [27] God made it simple for the first man and woman. He gave them only one rule: don't eat the fruit of the tree of the knowledge of good and evil. [28] People with ill motives toward God have criticized Him for trying to keep Adam and Eve from acquiring knowledge—knowledge they were not ready for, by the way. But this criticism misses the point. The story of Adam and Eve is all about trust. The serpent convinced Eve that God had lied to her, and so she trusts the serpent rather than God. [29] Adam in turn trusts Eve rather than God, and disobeys God, too. [30] Adam and Eve received a failing grade for their lesson in trust, and were banished from Eden because of it. [31]

God continued this lesson in trust with the Israelites, the descendants of Abraham, Isaac, and Jacob. [32] And as a first step,

God gave them rules: the Ten Commandments and the Law, as detailed in the first five books of the Bible (the Pentateuch). [33] Like any parent, He promised rewards for obedience and punishments for disobedience. [34] Unfortunately, the Israelites repeatedly fell into idolatry and wickedness, so they were often punished. [35] The punishments God inflicted may seem harsh in our eyes, but perhaps they would seem otherwise if we truly understood whom God was dealing with. Let's look at the world of the Israelites.

The Way They Were: The Canaanites. If God dealt harshly with the Israelites, He was much harder on the peoples nearby. Before the Israelites entered the land of Canaan (modern Israel), which they were to occupy, God gave them this command:

> "I will fix your boundary from the Red Sea to the sea of the Philistines, and from the wilderness to the River *Euphrates;* for I will deliver the inhabitants of the land into your hand, and you will drive them out before you. You shall make no covenant with them or with their gods. They shall not live in your land, because they will make you sin against Me; for *if* you serve their gods, it will surely be a snare to you."
>
> —Exodus 23:31-33

God ordered the Israelites to drive out the Canaanites—or to kill them if they refused to leave—and not to allow any of them to live in the land. [36] All evidence of their religion was to be obliterated. [37] Sometimes God even commanded the Israelites to leave no survivors, as in the city of Ai, [38] or in the conquest of southern Canaan. [39] This may seem cruel, but only because we have forgotten who the Canaanites were.

Simply put, the Canaanites were barbaric. Their religious worship included human sacrifice—*and even child sacrifice*—and the Israelites (contrary to God's instructions) adopted that same monstrous practice. [40] The Canaanites may have even practiced a form of cannibalism, by eating the human flesh which had been sacrificed. [41]

Following the Canaanite customs, the Israelites began to worship idols (i.e., false gods), and this idolatry became a chronic problem for them until after their return from exile in Babylon. [42] The Israelites also learned witchcraft, sorcery, [43] and temple prostitution [44] from the Canaanites. Eventually, the Israelites' wickedness *exceeded* that of the Canaanites. [45] The Psalmist sums up the problem:

> They did not destroy the peoples,
> As the LORD commanded them,
> But they mingled with the nations
> And learned their practices,
> And served their idols,
> Which became a snare to them.
>
> —Psalm 106:34-36 [46]

By ordering the Israelites to drive out or kill the Canaanites, God was trying to save His people from savagery and immorality, which were far more dangerous than any hot stove for a two-year-old. God saw that the Israelites would quickly descend into a moral abyss if they were exposed to the Canaanites for long. And, unfortunately, that is exactly what happened. The Israelites failed to drive out the Canaanites, and soon began to adopt all of their depraved practices.

Viewed in its proper context, God's order to kill or drive out the Canaanites was an act of mercy toward the Israelites. If they had obeyed, they would have been much better off. As for the Canaanites, shall we have much sympathy for people who killed children as part of their religious worship?

Of course, what about the Canaanite children? Was it truly necessary to kill even children and infants? We may well ask what alternative did the Israelites have? With the parents dead, the younger children would have faced a painful death from starvation or dehydration, while the older children would have represented a serious threat once they grew up and sought vengeance for the killing of their people. However, let's look at another, more complete answer that we must always keep in mind when trying to understand the Old Testament, or the Bible as a whole.

The Eternal Perspective. Yahweh seems ogre-like to us primarily because so many people die in the Old Testament. When the Israelites worshipped the Golden Calf, Moses brought them back into line by ordering the Levites to kill—and 3,000 men died. [47] To punish the Amalekites, who had attacked the Israelites as they fled from Egypt, [48] God ordered Saul to destroy them—every man, woman, child, and animal. [49] Jehu murdered the descendants of the wicked King Ahab and the worshippers of the false god Baal, and God praised him for it. [50]

We see all of this death, much of it done in Yahweh's name or at His command, and our first thought is that He must be terribly evil to inflict so much death, even if many of the deceased probably deserved it. But our initial reaction is wrong, because it is based on a false assumption.

We too often view death as the ultimate evil, because we assume that death is the end of life. If this assumption were true, then the Old Testament would be reprehensible, and Yahweh would be morally indefensible. But death is not the end. Death is merely a door to eternal life. Yahweh knew this, as did Jesus. When we view the Old Testament from God's eternal perspective, everything changes.

We must not assume that those who died in the past are gone forever, or that they can never make it to Heaven, for the New Testament says otherwise. In John 5:25-29, Jesus proclaims that the dead will live again, and that some of them will receive eternal life. 1 Peter 3:18-20 says that after Jesus died, "He went and made proclamation to the spirits *now* in prison, who once were disobedient" (1 Peter 3:19-20)—that is, to those who had died. 1 Peter 4:6 is more explicit:

> For the gospel has for this purpose been preached even to those who are dead, that though they are judged in the flesh as men, they may live in the spirit according to *the will of* God.

This preaching was not mere idle chatter for the amusement of the dead, but an opportunity for them to embrace God's mercy, forgiveness, and salvation. The implication is that many who died in Old Testament times will make it to Heaven with us.

Judging Yahweh is a perilous undertaking, for our understanding of this life and this world are necessarily limited. From God's perspective, the deaths of people in the Old Testament were unfortunate, but necessary to preserve His message: "Trust Me." That message was more important than any individual life, because He was trying to lead people toward faith, righteousness, and, eventually, eternal salvation. Those who opposed that message were obstructions which had to be removed for the greater good of all.

Both the Canaanites and the rebellious Israelites suffered exile or death for their opposition to God. Shall we now judge Yahweh in how He chose to deal with them, or in how He will deal with all who are now dead? I prefer to embrace the lesson of the Old Testament and trust Yahweh to judge them with justice, mercy, and compassion.

Endnotes for Chapter Seven, "Is Yahweh an Ogre?"

[1] Yahweh (also rendered as Jehovah) is one of the Hebrew names for God in the Old Testament. Some other names for God in the Old Testament include Elohim (the Creator-God of Genesis), Adonai (Lord), and El Shaddai (the all-sufficient God, or God Almighty). In this chapter, I will use "Yahweh" to refer to God as He is presented in the Old Testament.

[2] Genesis 19:24-25

[3] Numbers 25:1-4

[4] Exodus 22:18; see also Leviticus 20:27

[5] Exodus 22:20, Deuteronomy 13:1-10, 17:2-7

[6] Deuteronomy 18:20

[7] Leviticus 20:10, Deuteronomy 22:22-24

[8] Exodus 21:12-14; Leviticus 24:17, 24:21; Numbers 35:16-21, 35:30-31; Deuteronomy 19:11-13

[9] Deuteronomy 22:25-27 (note that only the rapist is punished—the rape victim is considered innocent of any sin, and therefore she is not to be punished)

[10] For example, death is ordered for the following offenses, among others:

> violating various rules regarding the priests and the Tabernacle (Exodus 28:35, 28:43, 30:20-21; Leviticus 8:31-35, 10:6-9, 16:2, 16:13, 22:9; Numbers 1:51, 3:5-10, 3:38, 4:15, 4:19-20, 18:2-3, 18:7, 18:22, 18:25-32);
>
> cursing, striking, or persistently disobeying a parent (Exodus 21:15, 21:17; Deuteronomy 21:18-21);
>
> kidnapping (Exodus 21:16; Deuteronomy 24:7);
>
> bestiality (Exodus 22:19; Leviticus 20:15-16);
>
> homosexuality (Leviticus 20:13);
>
> certain types of incest (Leviticus 20:11-12);
>
> premarital sex when betrothed to another (Deuteronomy 22:20-21);
>
> child sacrifice (Leviticus 20:2);

profaning the Sabbath (Exodus 31:14-15, 35:2; Numbers 15:32-36);

allowing a dangerous animal to kill someone (Exodus 21:29);

cursing or blaspheming God (Leviticus 24:15-16);

refusing to abide by the decision of a priest or judge (Deuteronomy 17:12)

[11] Marcionism, an early Christian heresy, taught that Jesus had only the appearance of an earthly body, and thus denied His humanity. The Marcionites forbid both marriage and sex, and required married couples to live apart and practice celibacy.

[12] Paulicians first made their appearance in the 7th century A.D., south of Armenia. Believing that flesh is evil and that spirit is good, they denied Jesus' humanity, and thus claimed that his life and death were illusory.

[13] Gnostics believed in a "Gnosis," or Truth, revealed in all religions. Gnosticism was really a separate religion, rather than part of Christianity, but many early Christians attempted to blend elements of Gnosticism with Christianity. These Gnostic Christians taught that the flesh, with its desires and lusts, was evil, and that salvation required freeing the spirit from these fleshly desires. Since flesh was regarded as evil, most Gnostic Christians denied that Jesus had existed in the flesh, and thus denied or minimized his earthly life, death, and resurrection.

[14] Matthew 22:36-38; Mark 12:28-30; Luke 10:27

[15] Other verses which remind the Israelites to love God above all else include: Deuteronomy 10:12, 11:1, 11:13, 11:22, 13:3, 19:9, 30:6, 30:16; Joshua 22:5, 23:11; 1 Samuel 12:20.

[16] Matthew 22:39; Mark 28:31; Luke 10:27

[17] Matthew 5:44; Luke 6:27-28, 6:35; see also Romans 12:20, which expresses a similar sentiment.

[18] Paul quotes this verse in Romans 12:20.

[19] In this verse, the Lord is speaking to Moses, giving him laws for the Israelites to follow.

[20] Matthew 19:21; Mark 10:21; Luke 14:13, 18:22, 19:8; Romans 15:26; Galatians 2:10; James 2:2-6, 2:15-16

[21] Similarly, see Ezekiel 18:7, and Isaiah 58:6-7 and 58:10.

[22] Psalm 78:36-39

[23] Ezekiel 14:6

[24] Jonah 4:11 (even if you view the book of Jonah as allegory, as many do, the lesson it teaches about forgiveness and mercy is unchanged)

[25] See Matthew 5:31-32, 19:3-9; Mark 10:2-12.

[26] See Malachi 2:13-16.

[27] For purposes of this discussion, I do not care whether you consider the story of Adam and Eve to be history, allegory, or parable. The lesson is the same.

[28] Genesis 2:16-17

[29] Genesis 3:1-6

[30] Genesis 3:6

[31] Genesis 3:23-24

[32] Abraham was the father of Isaac and the grandfather of Jacob, who was also known as Israel. See Genesis 21:2-3, 25:21-26, and 32:28. Israel in turn became the father of twelve sons. See Genesis 29:31-30:24, 35:16-18. The descendants of Israel became known as the Israelites.

[33] The Pentateuch refers to the first five books of the Old Testament: Genesis, Exodus, Leviticus, Numbers, and Deuteronomy

[34] For example, Deuteronomy 28:1-14 describes the blessing God will grant the Israelites if they obey Him, including many children, abundant rain, plentiful crops, fruitful flocks and herds of animals, and victory over enemies. But Deuteronomy 28:15-68 describes the consequences of disobedience, which include diseases, drought, defeat in war, oppression by enemies, exile to a foreign land, insects eating their crops, captivity, hunger, thirst, deprivation, exile, fear, and slavery. Similarly, compare Leviticus 26:1-13 (blessings of obedience) and Leviticus 26:14-39 (consequences of disobedience). See also Deuteronomy 4:25-27 and Deuteronomy 29:19-21 (consequences of idolatry).

[35] See, for example: Numbers 21:4-6 (God sends poisonous snakes to punish the Israelites for grumbling against God and Moses); Judges 2:11-23 (the Israelites returned to idolatry each time God delivered them from oppression); 1 Kings 11:9-13 (Solomon's unfaithfulness results in the di-

vision of his kingdom after his death); 1 Kings 12:25-13:5, 1 Kings 14:1-18, 1 Kings 15:28-30, and 2 Kings 23:20 (the idolatry of King Jeroboam and its consequences); 2 Chronicles 5:1-8 (Egypt conquers Judah because of the people's unfaithfulness to God); 2 Chronicles 21:12-19 (King Jehoram's idolatry and wickedness and its consequences); 2 Chronicles 25:14-28 (the idolatry of King Amaziah and its consequences); 1 Kings 16:31-34, 1 Kings 21:20-24, and 2 Kings 9:14-10:11 (the idolatry of King Ahab and its consequences); 2 Kings 17:5-18 (because of the idolatry and wickedness of Israel, they are conquered and scattered by the Assyrians); 2 Kings 22:14-17 and 2 Kings 24:1-20 (the Babylonians conquer Judah and carry its people into exile because of their idolatry and wickedness).

[36] Most of the Old Testament verses say that the Israelites were to drive out the Canaanites (i.e., the inhabitants of Canaan), not necessarily kill them. See, for example, Exodus 23:28-30, Exodus 33:2, Exodus 34:11, 34:24, Leviticus 20:23, Numbers 33:51-52, Deuteronomy 11:23, Deuteronomy 18:12, Joshua 13:6, Joshua 17:18, Joshua 23:5, Joshua 24:12, 24:18, Judges 11;23, Psalm 44:2, Psalm 78:55, Psalm 80:8. However, some verses do speak of "destroying" the Canaanites: Exodus 23:23-24; Deuteronomy 7:1-2, 9:3, 20:16-18. Of course, any Canaanites who refused to be "driven out" would have to be killed.

[37] Deuteronomy 12:2-3; see also, Exodus 23:24

[38] In Joshua 8:2, God instructs Joshua to "do to Ai and its king just as you did to Jericho and its king." The Israelites killed all of the inhabitants of Jericho except Rahab and her family, although the Old Testament does not clearly state that this was done at God's command. See Joshua 6:17-21. Similarly, Joshua left no survivors from his battle with the kings of northern Canaan, and the implication is that this was in accordance with God's instructions to Moses. See Joshua 11:6-15.

[39] See Joshua 10:40.

[40] Many Old Testament verses refer to this practice of human sacrifice, including the following: Deuteronomy 12:29-31, 18:9-10; 2 Kings 16:3-4, 17:17, 17:31, 21:6, 23:10; 2 Chronicles 28:3, 33:6; Psalm 106:37-38; Isaiah 57:5; Jeremiah 7:31, 19:4-5, 32:35; Ezekiel 16:20-21, 16:36, 20:26, 20:31, 23:36-39. To "pass through fire," as in Deuteronomy 18:10, 2 Kings 16:3, Ezekiel 16:21, and Ezekiel 23:37 is a euphemism for human sacrifice.

(Compare 2 Kings 16:3 with 2 Chronicles 28:3; similarly, compare Ezekiel 16:20 with Ezekiel 16:21, and Ezekiel 23:37 with Ezekiel 23:39.) God's law expressly prohibited any type of human sacrifice, on pain of death. See Leviticus 18:21, 20:2-5; Deuteronomy 12:29-31, 18:9-10.

[41] See Ezekiel 23:37 (emphasis supplied): " 'For they have committed adultery, and blood is on their hands. Thus they have committed adultery with their idols and even caused their sons, whom they bore to Me, **to pass through *the fire* to them as food**.' "

[42] Judges 8:24-27; 1 Kings 11:4-8, 12:26-32, 15:11-14, 16:30-33, 21:25-26, 22:51-53; 2 Kings 17:7-12, 21:2-5; 2 Chronicles 21:11, 28:22-25, 33:2-5, 33:22; Jeremiah 2:5-28, 3:6-10, 7:9-10, 11:17, 32:33-34; Ezekiel 16:15-19, 16:26-29, 20:30-32; Hosea 1:1-5:14, 9:1-17

[43] See 2 Kings 21:6 and 2 Chronicles 33:6. Witchcraft, sorcery, and similar types of magic were forbidden by Deuteronomy 18:9-12, which also makes clear that the inhabitants of Palestine practiced these things; see also Exodus 22:18 and Leviticus 20:27, which prescribe the punishment of death for those who practice such things.

[44] 1 Kings 14:24, 1 Kings 15:12; Hosea 4:14; prostitution, including religious prostitution, is forbidden by Leviticus 19:29 and Deuteronomy 23:17

[45] 2 Kings 21:9 and 2 Chronicles 33:9

[46] Other verses agree that the Israelites fell into idolatry and evil because they followed the practices of the previous inhabitants of Palestine. See, for example, Judges 3:1-8; 1 Kings 14:22-24; 2 Kings 17:7-12, 21:2-5; 2 Chronicles 28:2-3.

[47] Exodus 32:25-28

[48] See Exodus 17:8-16.

[49] 1 Samuel 15:1-3

[50] 2 Kings 10:1-30

Chapter 8
ISLAM'S CREDIBILITY PROBLEM

Of the four religions with the most adherents—Christianity, Islam, Buddhism, and Hinduism—only Christianity claims to have a monopoly on Truth.

I freely admit that this is an audacious claim. If I wanted to be politically correct and avoid offending anyone, I would say that all religions are equally valid. However, the claim is not mine, but Christ's: "I am the way, and the truth, and the life; no one comes to the Father but through Me." (John 14:6) [1]

Is His claim valid? Does Christianity have any right to consider itself the One True Religion? To answer that question we must know a lot about both Christianity and the other religions so that we can compare them. In the next chapter we will discuss Buddhism, and indirectly, Hinduism. But we begin with Islam.

We waste words if we merely look at individuals or history, for mankind has often misused religion for wicked purposes. (People have misused patriotism this way, too.) So we must not judge Islam by its wars of conquest in the seventh and eighth centuries, its discrimination against non-Muslims, or the violence of modern-day Muslim terrorists, any more than we should judge Christianity by the Inquisition, Europe's religious wars of the sixteenth and seventeenth centuries, or the Salem witch trials. We must instead judge Islam by what it says about itself. We must delve into its holy book, the Qur'ân (or Koran).

Like the Old and New Testaments, the Qur'ân preaches one God [2] and holds Abraham in high esteem. [3] It speaks of the mercy and forgiveness of God [4] and promises eternal life to those who follow its teachings, [5] while warning of God's ultimate judgment upon the wicked. [6] So is there any difference between Christianity and Islam, between the Bible and the Qur'ân? There is all the difference in the world.

The Qur'ân immodestly calls itself a perfect book, a revelation of God's truth, "without any crookedness"; [7] thus, "no falsehood could enter it." [8] The great proof that Islam is true, according to Muslims and the Qur'ân itself, is that its founder, Muhammad, a man who was said to be illiterate, could produce a book of such poetry, eloquence, quality, and substance. [9] But for me, the Qur'ân itself proves that Islam cannot be from God. For the Qur'ân has a credibility problem.

The Qur'ân and the Old Testament

The Qur'ân explicitly acknowledges that parts of the Bible are from God, and declares that the Qur'ân corroborates these previous Scriptures:

> He has revealed to thee the Book with truth, verifying that which is before it, and He revealed the Torah and the Gospel aforetime, a guidance for the people. . . . [10]

The Qur'ân contains many references to people in the Old Testament, including Noah, Moses, Abraham, Ishmael, and Joseph. The author has a superficial familiarity with stories from Genesis and Exodus, for he retells many of them. But he makes mistakes in the retelling—some minor, some not. What the Muslim holy book says is often inconsistent with—and sometimes flatly contradicts—the Old Testament. Did the Qur'ân's author misremember these stories, or were they already garbled when he heard them? Either way, the Qur'ân—this "perfect" book—often gets it wrong. To see what I mean, let's quickly review what Genesis says about Joseph.

The Story of Joseph in Genesis. When Joseph was about seventeen he dreamed that his brothers would bow down to him, [11] a dream that would later come true in Egypt. [12] They were already jealous of him because he was their father's favorite, so the recounting of the dream only inflamed their anger. [13] Jacob, their father, later sent Joseph to check on them and the flocks they were shepherding, [14] and the brothers saw their chance. They sold him to some

Midianite traders, who took him to Egypt. [15] The brothers then fooled their father by smearing animal blood on Joseph's coat. [16] Jacob believed his favorite son had been killed by a wild beast. [17] Meanwhile, the Midianites sold the boy to Potiphar, Pharaoh's captain of the guard. [18]

Joseph prospered in his new position until Potiphar's wife tried to seduce him. [19] When the young man refused her advances, she accused him of trying to rape her, and her husband immediately cast him into prison. [20]

Sometime later, Pharaoh became angry with his baker and cupbearer and put both into prison—the same prison where Joseph was confined. [21] The baker and the cupbearer each had a dream, which Joseph interpreted for them, informing them that in three days the cupbearer would be restored to his position, but the baker would be executed. [22] Three days later Pharaoh reconciled with his cupbearer, but the unfortunate baker suffered the predicted tragic end. [23]

The cupbearer kept silent about poor Joseph until two years later when Pharaoh had a dream that needed interpreting. [24] The cupbearer belatedly told Pharaoh about Joseph's talent for interpreting dreams, so Pharaoh summoned the young man. [25] Again, with God's help, Joseph had the answer: Egypt was about to enjoy seven years of tremendous abundance, followed by seven years of severe famine. [26] Joseph suggested that twenty percent of the harvests during the first seven years be set aside to feed the people during the seven years of famine, and that Pharaoh appoint a wise person to supervise the operation. Pharaoh appointed Joseph. [27]

The famine extended beyond Egypt, affecting Jacob and his family. [28] Desperate for food, the old patriarch twice sent his sons to Egypt to buy grain, [29] and since they did not recognize Joseph, [30] he was able to exact a measure of revenge by playing a trick on them. On their second journey, Joseph framed Benjamin, the youngest brother, on a charge of theft and had him arrested. [31] Joseph's deception of his brothers collapsed when he became emotional and confessed his true identity. [32] The family subsequently reunited and prospered in Egypt for many years. [33]

The Story of Joseph in the Qur'ân. The differences in the Qur'ân's retelling of Joseph's story begin with Jacob, [34] who now seems almost prophetically gifted. Twice he foresees his sons' future plot against Joseph, yet does nothing to prevent it.

The first time occurs when Joseph tells his dream to Jacob—rather than to his brothers—and his father warns him not to repeat it to them "or they will scheme against you." [35] The second time happens when the sons ask to take Joseph with them—rather than Jacob sending him to them—and their father is reluctant: "It saddens me that you should take him, and I fear that the wolf would eat him if you would be absent of him." [36] Nor does Jacob's insight end there. When his sons return with Joseph's bloody coat, he is not so easily fooled as in Genesis, but instead remarks: "You have invented this tale yourselves." [37]

As significant as these discrepancies are, the most glaring is found in the story of Joseph and Potiphar's wife, for the Qur'ân says that her accusation is investigated and actually discovered to be false:

> . . . and a witness from her family gave testimony: "If his shirt was torn from the front, then she is truthful, and he is the liar. And if his shirt is torn from behind, then she is lying, and he is truthful." So when he saw that his shirt was torn from behind, he said: "This is from your female scheming, your female scheming is indeed great! Joseph, turn away from this. And you woman, seek forgiveness for your sin; you were of the wrongdoers." [38]

Thus, in Muhammad's retelling of the story Joseph is *exonerated*. Yet the rest of the story requires that Joseph be imprisoned, so the Qur'ân simply adds: "But it appealed to them, even after they had seen the signs, to imprison him until a time." [39] Thus, according to Islam's holy book, Joseph's Egyptian master—who thought highly of Joseph, by the way [40]—cleared him of all guilt and then had him thrown into prison anyway, for no apparent reason. This exemplifies the Qur'ân's credibility problem, since confining Joseph under these circumstances borders on the nonsensical.

Once Joseph is imprisoned, the Qur'ân's retelling of the story closely parallels that of Genesis, with only a few minor differences. Instead of Joseph being brought to Pharaoh to interpret his dream, the cupbearer goes to Joseph in prison to obtain the interpretation. [41] And Joseph does not merely accept the position as second-in-command in Egypt, as in Genesis, but affirmatively requests it: "He [Joseph] said: 'Make me keeper over the granaries of the land, for I know how to keep records and I am knowledgeable.' " [42] Finally, the trick Joseph plays on his brothers by having Benjamin framed and arrested seems quite improbable of success in the Qur'ân, which says Joseph disclosed his identity to Benjamin at their initial meeting, prior to the arrest. [43]

The Story of Moses in Exodus. Exodus tells us that long after the time of Jacob and Joseph, the Pharaoh grew fearful of the explosive population growth of the Israelites. [44] So he ordered that all male Israelite babies be killed. [45] In the face of this decree, Moses' mother hid him for three months after he was born and then placed him in a basket in the Nile River, where he was found by Pharaoh's daughter. [46] Moses' sister, who was spying nearby, approached the princess and offered to find an Israelite woman to nurse the child—which of course turned out to be Moses' mother. [47] Thereafter, Moses was raised by Pharaoh's daughter as her own son. [48]

When Moses was grown, he killed an Egyptian who was beating an Israelite and then hid the body. [49] The next day, as Moses was trying to break up a fight between two Israelites, he learned from one of them that his murder of the Egyptian had become known, so he fled to Midian to escape Pharaoh's wrath. [50]

In Midian, Moses got married and built a new life, until one day God—"the God of Abraham, the God of Isaac, and the God of Jacob" (Exodus 3:6) [51]— spoke to him from a burning bush and told him to return to Egypt to lead the Israelites to freedom. [52]

Moses and his brother Aaron confronted Pharaoh, who refused to let the Israelites leave. [53] So God performed ten miracles: (1) Aaron's staff turned into a serpent; (2) the Nile River turned to blood; (3) frogs; (4) gnats; (5) insects; (6) disease killed Egyptian livestock; (7) boils and sores erupted on people and animals; (8) hail; (9) locusts; and (10) the death of every first-born Egyptian and animal. [54]

After the fourth miracle, Pharaoh's magicians realized these were no ordinary tricks and advised him to agree to Moses' demands, but Pharaoh refused. [55] Only after the tenth miracle did Pharaoh let the Israelites go. [56] And when he had a change of heart and pursued them, God drowned the Egyptian army in the sea. [57]

The Israelites reached Mount Sinai, where Moses received the Ten Commandments and various other laws, as well as detailed instructions for constructing the tabernacle and its accoutrements. [58] But when Moses did not come down from Mount Sinai for some time, the people became restless and asked Aaron to make them a god to worship. He did: the infamous golden calf, which caused Moses to shatter the tablets on which the commandments were written. [59]

Moses and the Qur'ân. As with Joseph, the story of Moses in the Qur'ân parallels the Old Testament, but with a few significant changes.

The story of baby Moses in the Qur'ân has only two minor differences from Exodus: in Muhammad's retelling Moses is raised by Pharaoh's wife [60] instead of Pharaoh's daughter, and his mother is chosen to nurse him only after he refuses to nurse from other women. [61]

But the story of Moses' murder of the Egyptian varies in two critical details. First, the Israelite is no longer the victim of a beating but merely a participant in a fight. Second, the Qur'ân appears to blame him rather than the Egyptian, since Moses discovers the Hebrew fighting again the next day and realizes that he is simply "a trouble maker." [62]

This blame-shifting from the Egyptian to the Israelite seems to reflect a bias by the Qur'ân against the Jewish people. We see another example of this apparent bias in the conspicuous absence from the Qur'ân of the phrase, "the God of Abraham, the God of Isaac, and the God of Jacob," which is so prominent in Exodus. Instead, when God speaks to Moses from the burning bush He refers to Himself as "your Lord," [63] "God, the Lord of the worlds," [64] and "God, the Noble, the Wise." [65]

While thus de-emphasizing the importance of Isaac and Jacob, ancestors of the Jewish people, the Qur'ân elevates Abraham's other son, Ishmael, the ancestor of the Arabs, to the status of a prophet: "And recall in the Scripture Ishmael; he was truthful to his promise, and he was a messenger prophet." [66]

In keeping with this apparent bias against the Jewish people, the Qur'ân rejects the validity of God's covenant with them, which Genesis 17:7 says would be "everlasting." [67] In Leviticus 26:14-39, God warns that He would punish the Israelites if they broke their part of the covenant, but Leviticus 26:44-45 emphasizes that God would *never* reject His people or break His covenant with them:

> "Yet in spite of this, when they are in the land of their enemies, I will not reject them, nor will I so abhor them as to destroy them, breaking My covenant with them; for I am the LORD their God. But I will remember for them the covenant with their ancestors, whom I brought out of the land of Egypt in the sight of the nations, that I might be their God. I am the LORD." [68]

The Qur'ân easily dismisses this everlasting, unbreakable covenant:

> And Abraham was tested by commands from His Lord, which he completed. He said: "I will make you a leader for the people."
>
> He said: "And also from my progeny?"
>
> He said: "My pledge will not encompass the wicked." [69]

When Moses reaches Egypt to confront Pharaoh, the Qur'ân again diverges from Exodus. In the Qur'ân, the Egyptian magicians become convinced of Moses' divine authority after the first miracle, in which Aaron's staff [70] becomes a serpent and swallows the magicians' staffs, rather than remaining skeptical until after the fourth miracle (gnats). [71]

Of course, Pharaoh's heart is hardened and he refuses to allow the Israelites to leave. However, Exodus and the Qur'ân differ about how this hardening occurred. In Exodus, Pharaoh hardens his own heart at first, and later God hardens it further. [72] But in the Qur'ân, this hardening results from a prayer of Moses which is granted by God:

> And Moses said: "Our Lord, you have given Pharaoh and his commanders adornments and wealth in this worldly life so that they will misguide from Your path. Our Lord, wipe out their wealth and bring grief to their hearts; for they will not believe until they see the painful retribution."
>
> He said: "I have answered your prayer, so keep straight and do not follow the path of those who do not know." [73]

The Qur'ân repeats Pharaoh's order to kill the Israelite children, but now it comes as a response to Moses' efforts rather than at the time of Moses' birth: [74]

> And We had sent Moses with Our signs, and a clear authority. To Pharaoh, Haamaan, and Qaa-roon. But they said: "A lying magician!"

> Then, when the truth came to them from Us, they said: "*Kill the children of those who believed with him*, and rape their women." But the scheming of the rejecters [that is, unbelievers—those who reject God or Islam] is always in error. [75]

Finally, in the famous story of the golden calf, Moses' brother, Aaron, is largely relieved of culpability in the Qur'ân, which says the golden calf was built by the "Samarian" (or "Samiri") rather than by Aaron. [76]

The Story of Noah in Genesis. Noah lived in a time of great wickedness, so much so that God decided to wipe out mankind from the earth. [77] But Noah was righteous, so God saved him and his family by instructing him to build an ark that would preserve them when He unleashed flood waters on the world. [78] When the time came, Noah, his wife, his three sons (Shem, Ham, and Japeth) and their wives, seven of each "clean" animal, [79] and two of every other kind of animal entered the ark. [80] Then the flood waters arose and all of humanity drowned—except those in the ark. [81]

Noah in the Qur'ân. In the Qur'ân, one of Noah's sons (we are not told which one) refuses to board the ark and is drowned in the flood, [82] but his loss is balanced by the rescue of a few believers [83] who respond to a warning from Noah. [84] As for the unbelievers who reject Noah's warning, Noah prays that God would destroy them:

> And Noah said: "My Lord, do not leave on the Earth any of the rejecters at all. If you are to leave them, then they will misguide Your servants and they will only give birth to a wicked rejecter." [85]

The Qur'ân acknowledges that the details it supplies are not part of the original story of Noah, but asserts that this is new information that was previously secret. [86]

Secret or not, the Qur'ân's story of Noah seems deliberately crafted to parallel many of the early experiences of Muhammad and his followers. Like Muhammad, Noah is accused of inventing his story [87] and appears to be a man of no special gifts or importance, while his followers are poor and humble. [88] Perhaps most striking, in the Qur'ân Noah and Muhammad utter virtually identical language about themselves:

> [Noah] *"Nor do I say to you that I have the treasures of God, nor do I know the future, nor do I say that I am an Angel,* nor do I say to those whom your eyes look down upon that God will not grant them any good. God is more aware of what is in their souls; in such case I would be among the wicked." [89]

> [Muhammad] "Say: *'I do not say to you that I possess God's treasures, nor do I know the future, nor do I say to you that I am an Angel.* I merely follow what is inspired to me.' Say: 'Are the blind and the seer the same? do you not think?' " [90]

Since the Qur'ân accepts the Torah [91]—which includes Genesis and Exodus—as Scriptural, the contradictions and inconsistencies between the Bible and the Muslim holy book make it difficult to accept the latter as anything more than stories told by a man with an imperfect knowledge of the Jewish Scriptures. When we turn to the New Testament, we find the same difficulties.

The Qur'ân and the New Testament

The Qur'ân talks about several people mentioned in the Gospels, including Jesus, Mary, John the Baptist, and Zacharias (John's father), and the two holy books do agree on some facts. The Muslim scriptures attest that Mary was a virgin when Jesus was conceived. [92] It attributes miracles to Jesus, such as healing the blind and lepers, bringing the dead back to life, and making a live bird from clay. [93] The Qur'ân regards Jesus as a prophet, [94] states that He was guided by God, [95] and even refers to Him as the Messiah. [96] But the differences dwarf these similarities.

We saw in Chapter One that Jesus claimed to be God, or at least God-like. The Qur'ân emphatically rejects such claims, as well as the Christian doctrine of the Trinity—i.e., that God consists of three persons in one: Father, Son, and Holy Spirit. [97] In fact, the Qur'ân asserts that Jesus Himself would reject any claim to divine status:

> And God will say: "O Jesus son of Mary, did you tell the people to take you and your mother as gods instead of God?"
>
> He said: "Be you glorified, I cannot say what I have no right of. If I had said it then You know it, You know what is in my soul while I do not know what is in Your soul. You are the Knower of the unseen." [98]

The Qur'ân also denies the reality of Jesus's crucifixion, maintaining that God lifted Jesus up to heaven and left the illusion of the crucifixion for the Jews to see:

> And their saying: "We have killed the Messiah Jesus the son of Mary, the messenger of God!" They did not kill him, nor did they crucify him, but it appeared to them as if they had. [99] Those who dispute are in doubt of him, they have no knowledge except to follow conjecture; they did not kill him for a certainty. For God raised him to Himself; and God is Noble, Wise. And from the people of the Scripture are few who would have believed in him before his death, and on the Day of Resurrection he will be witness against them. [100]

Thus, Islam's sacred scripture takes the bizarre—and apparently contradictory—position of recognizing the authority of the Gospels, and of Jesus's status as a prophet, while rejecting the core teachings of Jesus Himself and His disciples: the divinity, crucifixion, and resurrection of Christ. [101] The Qur'ân denounces Christianity for proclaiming the "gross blasphemy" that Jesus is

God's Son, [102] but nevertheless capitalizes on His reputation by attributing to Him a prophecy about the coming of Muhammad:

> And when Jesus, son of Mary, said: "O children of Israel, I am God's messenger to you, authenticating what is present with me of the Torah and bringing good news of a messenger to come after me whose name will be acclaimed." [103]

This duplicity concerning Christianity can also be seen in various verses which address the fate of Christians. On the one hand, the Qur'ân seems to promise that at least some Christians (and Jews) will be saved:

> Surely those who believe, and those who are Jewish, and the Nazarenes [i.e., Christians], and the Sabiens; any one of them who believes in God and the Last Day, and does good work, they will have their reward with their Lord, with no fear over them, nor will they grieve.[104]

Yet the Qur'ân also contains many verses which promise God's condemnation upon Christians and Jews:

> Rejecters indeed are those who have said: "God is the Messiah son of Mary!" And the Messiah said: "O Children of Israel, serve God, my Lord and your Lord. Whoever sets up partners with God, then He will forbid Paradise for him, and his destiny will be the Fire; and the wicked will have no supporters."
>
> Rejecters indeed are those who have said: "God is a trinity!" There is no god but One god. If they do not cease from what they are saying, then those who reject from among them will be afflicted with a painful retribution. [105]

> And they [Jews and Christians] said: "Our hearts are sealed!" No, it is God who has cursed them for their rejection, for very little do they believe.
>
> And when a Scripture came to them from God, authenticating what is with them; while before that they were mocking those who rejected; so when what they knew came to them, they rejected it! God's curse be upon the rejecters. [106]
>
> Those who rejected from the people of the Scripture and those who set up partners are in the fires of Hell abiding therein, those are the worst of creation.[107]

Perhaps these verses in the Qur'ân regarding the fate of Jews and Christians can be reconciled, although I do not see how. But this much is undeniable: Islam and Christianity cannot be reconciled with each other. Either the Muslim scriptures are from God, and Christianity is a false religion, or Christianity is true and the Qur'ân is, at best, inaccurate, misguided, and man-made.

If the Qur'ân is man-made, rather than from God, then we would expect to find within its pages some of the human foibles of its author (or authors). And we do. For nowhere are those foibles more on display than in what Islam's holy book says about the fate of its enemies.

Hell

As mentioned at the outset, the Qur'ân speaks often of the mercy and forgiveness of God. Yet its view of Hell is neither merciful nor forgiving. It is a fire which burns and torments the damned, [108] "a gathering place for the rejecters." [109] The condemned drink "boiling water that cuts up their intestines," [110] and eat "pollutants," [111] "food that chokes," [112] and the foul fruit of the "tree of bitterness." [113] Surrounded by "fierce hot winds," "boiling water," and "a shade that is unpleasant," [114] they are bound in long chains and shackles, and cry out for death. [115] But they cannot die, for they are condemned to dwell in Hell forever. [116]

The Qur'ân often uses vivid, horrific images to describe Hell:

> For Hell is in wait. For the transgressors it is a dwelling place. They will abide in it for eons. They will not taste anything cold in it nor drink. Except for boiling water and filthy discharge. An exact recompense. They did not expect the reckoning. And they denied Our revelations greatly. And everything We have counted in a record. So taste it, for no increase will come to you from Us except in retribution. [117]

> O you who believe, many of the Priests and Monks consume people's money in falsehood, and they turn away from the path of God. And those who hoard gold and silver, and do not spend it in the cause of God, give them news of a painful retribution. On the Day when they will be seared in the fires of Hell, and their foreheads and sides and backs will be branded with it: "This is what you have hoarded for yourselves, so taste what you have hoarded!" [118]

> . . . as for those who rejected, outer garments made from fire are cut out for them, and boiling water is poured from above their heads. It melts the inside of their stomachs and their skin. And they will have hooked rods of iron. Every time they want to escape the anguish, they are returned to it. Taste the retribution of the burning! [119]

The Qur'ân's descriptions of Hell seem to portray God as a sadist who tortures and torments the damned for all eternity—and for no apparent purpose other than His own vengeful amusement. [120] For He could simply destroy them and be done with it, but chooses instead to inflict endless pain and misery. Yet isn't this exactly what we should expect from the mind of a mere mortal? He seems to be a man who, like most men, prays that his enemies would receive what he believes they deserve instead of the mercy he desires for himself.

Notice also how worldly the imagery is. It depicts Hell as little more than the sufferings of earthly life taken to extremes: the dead eat and drink; they are enchained and imprisoned, beaten and burned. In the Qur'ân immortality closely parallels mortal existence. Because this life is all he knows, the author fails to consider the more likely possibility that the life of an eternal soul will bear little or no resemblance to our current reality. This failure is even more pronounced in the Qur'ân's descriptions of Heaven.

Heaven

Islam's holy book often compares Heaven to gardens [121] with abundant water, [122] describing it as "gardens with rivers flowing beneath." [123] Heaven contains many fine homes and palaces, [124] and the believers are dressed in silks and adorned with gold. [125] They rest on comfortable furnishings, couches, and carpets. [126] Food, especially fruit, will abound. [127] There will be rivers of water, milk, wine, and honey for the believers to drink. [128] They will be surrounded by lovely virgins, [129] and will marry spouses who are always faithful ("pure" spouses). [130] Heaven is a place of peace [131] and eternal bliss, [132] where the believers "will have what they wish." [133]

As appealing as this portrait of Heaven may be, it seems curiously man-made. The Qur'ân emphasizes sensual pleasures: eating and drinking, fine clothes and comfortable furniture—even, it appears, sexual relations. When viewed as a man-made construct, this makes perfect sense. Rich gardens and abundant food and water would indeed be Heaven to a person who lived in the desert climate of Arabia, as did Muhammad and his early followers.

But when viewed as a divine revelation, the Qur'ân's imagery seems strangely incongruent with the eternal nature of the afterlife, for why would an eternal soul need food, drink, or sexual reproduction? [134] Are there no heavenly joys that can surpass these earthly delights?

Then again, what is perhaps even more striking is the failure to discuss the relationship and interaction of the saved with the Almighty. The Qur'ân says that men in Heaven will question one another, [135] but does not say that they will even converse with Allah. He seemingly rewards the faithful with everything they could want, and then disappears from the scene, like the Genie in the magic lamp.

Is Islam a Religion of Peace or Violence?

For me, one of the great proofs of Christianity is that so many of Jesus's teachings don't sound like something a mere man would invent, because they run counter to the way people think. His followers must have been astonished when Jesus told them to love their enemies and be kind to them, [136] to not strike back, [137] to be humble and serve others, [138] and to forgive others without limit. [139] He even forgave the men who were crucifying Him. [140]

You will find few, if any, such counter-intuitive notions in Islam's holy book. It reads like men think: love your friends (Muslims) and hate your enemies (everyone else). And as its depictions of Heaven and Hell illustrate, Allah seems to think the same way.

Indeed, a debate is raging within the Muslim community as to whether Islam should be a religion of peace or violence. Those Muslims who oppose the use of violence (such as terrorism) point to this famous verse from the Qur'ân to support their claim that Islam opposes violence, especially against the innocent:

> It is because of this that We have decreed for the Children of Israel: "Anyone who kills a person who has not committed murder, or who has not committed corruption in the land; then it is as if he has killed all the people! And whoever spares a life, then it is as if he has given life to all the people." [141]

Similarly, another famous verse from the Qur'ân seems to prohibit war, except in self-defense: "And fight in the cause of God against those who fight you, but do not transgress, God does not like the aggressors." [142]

Yet this is not a one-sided argument, [143] for the Muslims on the other side can quote many verses from the Qur'ân in support of violence and hatred against non-Muslims. [144] Here is a sampling:

> So when the sacred months have passed, slay the idolaters, wherever you find them, and take them captive and besiege them and lie in wait for them in every ambush.[145]
>
> O you who believe, fight those of the disbelievers who are near to you and let them find firmness in you. And know that Allah is with those who keep their duty. [146]
>
> There has been a good example set for you by Abraham and those with him, when they said to their people: "We are innocent from you and what you serve besides God. We have rejected you, and it appears that there shall be animosity and hatred between us and you until you believe in God alone." [147]

Indeed, the Muslim scripture mandates that able-bodied male Muslims participate in war. [148] Those who fulfill this obligation—especially those who die in battle—receive God's favor, mercy, and eternal rewards, [149] while those who shirk it risk being cast into Hell with the unbelievers. [150]

The Prophet's Special Privileges

I have repeatedly asserted that the Qur'ân reads like a book written by a man rather than God. Nowhere is this more apparent than in the special privileges it decrees for its founder and prophet, Muhammad. For example, it prohibits Muslims from marrying more than four wives, and warns about the dangers of marrying more than one, [151] yet grants an exclusive exemption from this rule for Muhammad, [152] who had thirteen wives after his first wife died. [153] God absolved the Prophet from his promise to avoid a certain slave-girl, [154] and also gave him permission to marry the divorced wife of his adopted son, Zayd. [155] The Qur'ân contains detailed instructions to Muhammad's followers to protect the privacy of the Prophet, [156] as well as the chastity of his wives, [157] and even forbids his wives to remarry (presumably after divorce or Muhammad's death). [158]

These special rules, which are suspiciously convenient for him personally, raise doubts about the Prophet's good faith concerning at least some of his claimed revelations.

Conclusion

I have no use for any religion which is not true. And while I recognize that everyone must decide for themselves whether a particular religion is true or false, I believe Islam stands or falls on the basis of its holy book, the Qur'ân. [159] That book appears to be the product of a devout, monotheistic man (or men) who made a lot of mistakes in writing or dictating it.

How else are we to explain the many contradictions between the Qur'ân and the Old Testament? Does the Muslim explanation—that the Jews got it wrong—hold water? The story of Joseph alone is enough to embarrass this explanation, when viewed with common sense rather than zeal. The story of Joseph in the Old Testament reads like real life, with elements of jealousy, lust, lies, and injustice. The story as presented in the Qur'ân does not even make sense. Similarly, the Qur'ân's credibility is seriously undermined by its flawed renderings of the stories of Noah and Moses, and its apparent bias against the Jewish people.

What are we to think of a book that accepts the virgin birth of Christ, acknowledges His miracles, recognizes Him as a prophet of God, and endorses the divine authority of the Gospels—and then denies the most important things those Scriptures say about Him?

The descriptions of Heaven and Hell also convince me that the Qur'ân is the product of a human mind. Their focus is almost entirely on sensual pleasures and pain—as if Heaven and Hell are no more than extensions of our earthly existence. I believe the Qur'ân's portrait of a cruel, sadistic Allah who tortures people in Hell for eternity must have come from the mind of man—probably the same man who endorsed hatred and war against the "enemies" of Islam.

There is much in Islam to commend it. I admire its emphasis on devotion to God, prayer, and charity. There is no doubt that Islam furthered the cause of monotheism in the parts of the Middle East untouched by Judaism or Christianity. And as hard as this may be to believe today, Islam actually improved the condition of women and children in Muhammad's Arabia. The unity and brotherhood of the majority of Muslims around the world has much to teach ecumenical Christianity.

Yet I could never choose a religion based on its social desirability—it also has to be true. And any attempt to prove Islam to be true inevitably runs up against one insurmountable obstacle: the Qur'ân. Its lack of credibility is a big problem for Islam.

APPENDIX: A BRIEF HISTORY OF EARLY ISLAM

The founder of Islam was Muhammad, who was born in Mecca, in what is now Saudi Arabia, in about 569 A.D. Orphaned by the age of six, he was primarily raised by his uncle, Abu Talib. Muhammad often traveled with passing caravans, and by the age of twenty-five became a caravan leader for a middle-aged widow, Khadija, who would soon thereafter become his wife. The caravans exposed Muhammad to the monotheism of Judaism, Christianity, and monotheistic Arabs.

In the year 610, at about the age of 40, Muhammad went to a mountain near Mecca to devote himself to prayer. While there, he claimed to have had a vision of the angel Gabriel, who told him that he was to be the messenger of Allah. With the support of his family, Muhammad began to proclaim the message that there is only one God—Allah. But his wife and uncle died in 619, and he met stiff resistance to his preaching in Mecca.

So in 622 Muhammad moved his family and followers to the city of Yathrib, where he found a population much more receptive to his message. He became known there as "The Prophet," and the city was renamed Medinat al-Nabi, "City of the Prophet"—which was soon shortened to Medina. Muhammad became the city's religious leader, but he also ruled the city as its political leader. In a succession of wars with Mecca from 624 to 630, Muhammad not only successfully defended his new religious stronghold, but triumphed by capturing Mecca itself. Before long he unified the entire Arabian peninsula under his rule.

Muhammad claimed to have visions and revelations from God throughout the remainder of his life. These were memorized by some of his followers, and were later written down and organized after his death, resulting in the Qur'ân. Many of these revelations helped instill morality, defeat idolatry, and end harmful superstitions.

Muhammad never tried to hide the fact that he was a mere man. He readily admitted his mistakes and ignorance. He made no claims of deity for himself, and did not attempt to perform miracles or foretell the future. He remained humble despite his rise in power, living simply and accumulating no wealth. He extended mercy and kindness to all but his most determined enemies. He gave generously of his time and money to those in need, and he judged both wisely and with incorruptible justice. He appointed honest judges and efficient, trustworthy administrators. Perhaps the greatest tribute that can be paid to the man was the single-minded devotion shown by all who knew him.

At the age of fifty-nine, Muhammad began to experience fevers, which gradually grew more frequent and more debilitating. At age sixty-three he experienced a fever which lasted two weeks and confined him to bed. A few days later, on June seventh or eighth, 632, he died.

Muhammad named no political successor, which led to an immediate dispute about who should rule after his death. The struggle was primarily between Ali, a son-in-law of Muhammad, and Abu Bekr, a father-in-law of the Prophet. The hostility between the two camps led to the division in Islam between the Shi'ites (followers of Ali) and the Sunnis (followers of Abu Bekr). Abu Bekr emerged triumphant, as the first of the four "rightly-guided caliphs." [160]

Although his rule lasted only two years (632-634), Abu Bekr was an able leader. He avoided any hint of corruption in his administration. He required his military leaders to wage war humanely, by protecting non-combatants and avoiding unnecessary killing and destruction. Perhaps most importantly, he insisted on the equality of all Muslims—which proved to be tremendously helpful in converting people to the new religion. Thanks to Abu Bekr's enlightened rule—and the brilliance of his leading general, Khalid ibn al-Walid—the Arabs defeated both the Persians and the Byzantines, and carried Islam into Syria.

Before Abu Bekr died, he named as his successor another father-in-law of the Prophet, Umar Abu Hafsa ibn al-Khattab (Omar or Umar, for short). Omar continued many of the practices of his predecessor which had proved so beneficial. He also enjoyed tremendous military successes. His armies conquered Syria, Palestine, Egypt, Iran (then known as Persia), and Iraq. Omar granted Jews and Christians religious toleration and the same legal protections enjoyed by Muslims, but he also required that all non-Muslims leave the Arabian peninsula. Omar was murdered in 644, and a six-man committee chose his successor, Othman ibn Affan, a son-in-law of Muhammad and a member of the Meccan aristocracy (the Umayyads).

Othman ruled for about 12 years. His caliphate was marked by widespread corruption, but also by further expansion of the growing Arab Empire into Afghanistan, Asia Minor, and the southern Caucasus.

In 656, Othman, like Omar, was assassinated. His successor was the one man Muslim leaders believed could unify Sunni and Shi'ite Muslims: Ali. But it was not to be. Ali's attempts to reverse the corruption of Othman's government, as well as his failure to capture and punish the assassins of Othman, angered many, and he found himself facing multiple rebellions before finally being assassinated in 661.

Power was now seized by the amir of Syria, Mu'awiya, the first of the Umayyad Caliphate, which would rule the Arab Empire until 750. Mu'awiya was an exceptional administrator, who used many Jews and Christians in his government. He also turned the caliphate into a hereditary monarchy so that his son, Yezid, could succeed him—which he did in 680.

Under the Umayyads, the Empire expanded into northern Afghanistan, central Asia, Pakistan, North Africa, and Spain. Only Charles Martel's victory at the Battle of Tours (732 A.D.) stopped this Muslim expansion from taking over all of France, and possibly all of Europe. Islam has since been carried into other parts of Asia,

Africa, Europe, and even the Americas—sometimes by conquest, but also through Muslim merchants, immigrants, and missionaries.

Since the Qur'ân requires that conversion to Islam be voluntary, [161] forced conversion to Islam has been exceptionally rare in Muslim history—and also unnecessary. The relatively enlightened rule of the Arabs and their successors, as well as the Muslim ideal of equality and brotherhood among believers, attracted many to the new religion. So did the routine imposition of disabilities upon non-Muslims, such as higher taxes and exclusion from government service. In addition, economic incentives were sometimes offered to encourage conversion to Islam, [162] and a few were convinced by the occasional persecution of non-Muslims.

For these and other reasons, people in areas which came under Muslim control usually converted to Islam within a few generations. That is why Christians are now a minority in such former strongholds as Turkey (Asia Minor), Palestine, and Egypt.

Endnotes for Chapter Eight, "Islam's Credibility Problem"

[1] Contrary to what some say, this does not necessarily mean that only Christians will be saved; salvation is ultimately up to God. But it does mean that if God saves some non-Christians (and I believe He will), He will do so through Jesus Christ, and because of what He did for all of us on the cross.

[2] For example, see the following verses in the Qur'ân: 2:255, 3:6, 3:18, 3:62, 5:73, 6:19, 6:102, 6:106, 9:31, 29:46, 37:4, 37:35, 38:65, 39:6, 40:3, 40:65, 41:6, 44:8, 47:19, 59:22, 59:23, 73:9, 112:1. (The Qur'ân has 114 chapters, each of which is named. For example, Chapter 2 is "The Cow." For convenience, only chapter numbers, not chapter names, are used in citations herein.)

[3] Qur'ân,2:130, 2:135, 3:67-68, 3:95, 4:125, 6:161, 16:120-123.

[4] Qur'ân,1:3, 2:37, 2:54, 2:160, 2:173, 2:182, 2:218, 2:235, 3:30-31, 3:74, 3:89, 3:155, 4:25, 4:29, 4:43, 4:64, 4:96, 4:99-100, 4:106, 4:110, 4:152, 5:3, 5:34, 5:39, 5:74, 5:98, 6:54, 8:69-70, 9:27, 9:102, 16:18, 16:47, 17:25, 24:22, 25:6, 25:70, 26:9, 33:5, 33:24, 33:43, 33:50, 33:59, 33:73, 34:2, etc.

[5] Qur'ân, 11:108, 18:30-31, 25:15-16, 39:73-75, 43:69-73, 82:13, 83:22-24.

[6] Qur'ân,4:168-169, 5:10, 18:49, 21:47, 23:102-103, 33:63-68, 33:73, 34:3-5, 39:68-72, 56:1-9, 69:13-18, 77:1-37, 81:1-14, 82:1-5, 82:9-19.

[7] For example, Qur'ân, 39:27-28 says:

> And We have cited for the people in this Quran from every example, that they may take heed. A Quran in Arabic, without any crookedness, that they may be righteous.

See also Qur'ân, 2:176, 4:82, 6:66, 17:105, 18:1, 41:41-42, 69:40-43, 98:1-3.

Except as otherwise indicated, all quotes from the Qur'ân are from "Quran," an English translation by the Progressive Muslims Organization.

For those who would prefer an easier read, I recommend *The Koran*, translated with notes by N. J. Dawood (Penguin Books 1999). For example, Dawood translates 39:28, in relevant part, as: "a Koran in the Arabic tongue, free from any flaw. . . .")

[8] Qur'ân 41:42

[9] Qur'ân, 10:38, 11:12-14, 16:103, 28:48-49, 52:33-34

[10] Qur'ân, 3:3 (quoted from "The Holy Qur'ân," translated by Maulana Muhammad Ali); see also, 2:89, 2:91, 2:101, 5:46, 5:48, 5:68, 10:37, 46:12, 46:29-30.

[11] Genesis 37:2-11

[12] Genesis 42:6, 43:26, 43:28, 44:14

[13] Genesis 37:3-4, 8

[14] Genesis 37:12-17

[15] Genesis 37:25-28

[16] Genesis 37:31-32

[17] Genesis 37:32-35

[18] Genesis 37:36 and 39:1

[19] Genesis 39:2-7

[20] Genesis 39:8-20

[21] Genesis 40:1-4

[22] Genesis 40:5-19

[23] Genesis 40:20-22

[24] Genesis 40:23-41:13

[25] Genesis 41:14

[26] Genesis 41:15-32

[27] Genesis 41:33-44

[28] Genesis 41:53-57

[29] Genesis 42:1-7 and 43:1-15

[30] Genesis 42:7-8

[31] Genesis 44:1-17

[32] Genesis 44:18-45:4

[33] Genesis 45:16-50:26; see also Exodus 1:8-10

[34] The Qur'ân refers to Jacob as "Israel," a name by which he is also known in Genesis. See Genesis 32:28.

[35] Qur'ân, 12:4-5

[36] See the Qur'ân, 12:11-13. The Qur'ân does not explain why Israel (Jacob) let Joseph go despite these concerns. (The Qur'ân may be conflating the stories of Joseph and Benjamin. Jacob *was* reluctant to send Benjamin to Egypt with his brothers, saying, " 'I am afraid that harm may befall him.' " (Genesis 42:4) However, this occurred long after Joseph's brothers had sold him into slavery in Egypt.)

[37] Qur'ân, 12:18

[38] Qur'ân, 12:26-29. Indeed, the wife eventually confesses that she lied. Qur'ân, 12:50-53.

[39] Qur'ân, 12:35

[40] See Genesis 39:1-6.

[41] Qur'ân, 12:43-50

[42] Qur'ân, 12:55

[43] Compare Genesis 43:16-44:3 with the Qur'ân, 12:68-70, and especially 12:69.

[44] Exodus 1:8-10; and see Exodus 12:40-41

[45] Exodus 1:15-22

[46] Exodus 2:1-6

[47] Exodus 2:4-9

[48] Exodus 2:10

[49] Exodus 2:11-12

[50] Exodus 2:13-15

[51] See also, for example, Exodus 3:15-16 and 4:5.

[52] Exodus 2:16-4:17

[53] Exodus 4:14, 4:27-21

[54] Exodus 7:8-12:30

[55] Exodus 7:8-8:19

[56] Exodus 12:31-32

[57] Exodus 14:1-30

[58] Exodus 19:1-31:18

[59] Exodus 32:1-6, 15-19

[60] Qur'ân, 28:7-13, and especially 28:9

[61] Compare the Qur'ân, 28:11-13 with Exodus 2:7-9.

[62] Compare the Qur'ân, 28:15-18 with Exodus 2:11-14.

[63] Qur'ân 20:12, 28:32

[64] Qur'ân 26:16, 27:8, 28:30

[65] Qur'ân 27:9.

[66] Qur'ân, 19:54; see also Qur'ân, 2:136, 2:140, 3:84, 4:163, 6:84-86.

[67] See also: Genesis 17:10, 17:13, 17:19, 17:21; Exodus 2:24, 6:3-5, 34:27; Leviticus 26:9; Deuteronomy 4:23, 4:31, 7:12, 8:18; Judges 2:1

[68] See also Judges 2:1.

[69] Qur'ân, 2:124

[70] In the Qur'ân, Moses, not Aaron, possesses the staff and casts it down. See 26:45, as well as 7:117 and 20:69.

[71] Compare Exodus 7:8-8:19 with the Qur'ân, 7:117-126, 20:65-73, 26:41-51.

[72] Exodus 8:15, 8:19, 8:32, 9:7, 9:12, 9:34-35, 10:1, 10:20, 10:27, 11:10, 14:8

[73] Qur'ân, 10:88-89

[74] See Exodus 1:22-2:2:10.

[75] Qur'ân, 40:23-25 (emphasis added); similarly, see Qur'ân, 7:127. (N. J. Dawood, in *The Koran*, translates Pharoah's order as, "Put to death the sons of those who share his faith, and spare only their daughters.") Several other verses in the Qur'ân mention the exodus from Egypt as a deliverance from this edict, implying that the two were contemporaneous events. See, for example, Qur'ân, 2:49, 7:141, 14:6.

[76] Qur'ân, 20:85-97; compare Exodus 32:1-24

[77] Genesis 6:5-7, 11-13

[78] Genesis 6:8, 13-18

[79] The "clean" animals were those that God allowed the Israelites to eat, so the extra five animals probably provided food and sacrifices during and after the flood.

[80] Genesis 6:10, 6:19 - 7:16

[81] Genesis 7:17-23

[82] Qur'ân, 11:42-43

[83] Qur'ân, 11:40

[84] Qur'ân, 71:1-10; Noah's warning is also discussed in 10:71-73 and 11:25-49. In Genesis, the people receive no warning from either God or Noah. See Genesis 6:5 – 7:24.

[85] See the Qur'ân, 71:26-27.

[86] Qur'ân, 11:49

[87] See the Qur'ân, 11:35. The Qur'ân acknowledges that the same was said of Muhammad; see 10:38, 25:4-5, 34:8.

[88] Qur'ân, 11:27; compare to 43:31, where Muhammad's opponents criticize him for appearing to be a man of no importance. And see 17:89-93, where they criticize him for the lack of miracles associated with his message.

[89] Qur'ân, 11:31 (emphasis added)

[90] Qur'ân, 6:50 (emphasis added)

[91] The Torah usually refers to the Pentateuch—i.e., the first five books of the Old Testament: Genesis, Exodus, Leviticus, Numbers, and Deuteronomy. These five books contain the Jewish Law.

[92] See the Qur'ân, 3:47, 19:19-22, 21:91, and 66:12; compare with Matthew 1:18-25 and Luke 1:26-35.

[93] Qur'ân, 3:49, 5:110; see also, 2:253 (however, making a live bird from clay is not a miracle mentioned in the Gospels)

[94] Qur'ân, 2:136, 4:163, 33:7

[95] Qur'ân, 2:87, 3:48, 5:46, 57:27

[96] Qur'ân, 3:45, 4:157, 5:17, 5:72, 5:75, 9:31

[97] Qur'ân, 4:171, 5:72-73, 5:75, 6:100-102, 9:30-31, 10:68, 17:111, 18:4-5, 19:34-35, 19:88-92, 23:91, 25:2, 39:3-4, 43:81, 72:3

[98] Qur'ân, 5:116

[99] This would be literally translated: "he was made to resemble another for them." See Dawood, *The Koran*, at p. 76, fn. 1.

[100] Qur'ân, 4:157-159

[101] Jesus Himself claimed divine status in a variety of ways, as discussed in Chapter 1, "Christianity Is Different." Similarly, Christ's crucifixion and resurrection are featured prominently in the Gospels, in the rest of

the New Testament, in the writings of early Christians, and even in some ancient secular sources. See Chapter 2, "Is Jesus' Resurrection Fact or Fairy Tale?"

[102] Qur'ân, 19:88-92; see also: 4:171, 5:72-73, 9:30-31, 10:68-69, 17:111, 18:4-5, 19:34-35, 23:91, 25:2, 39:3-4, 72:3

[103] Qur'ân, 61:6.

[104] Qur'ân, 2:62; see also: 3:113-3:115, 3:199, 5:69, 28:52-55, 57:27

[105] Qur'ân, 5:72-73. The reference to setting up "partners with God" in 5:72 may refer to giving Christ divine status co-equal with God. Maulana Muhammad Ali translates this passage as: "Surely who ever associates (others) with Allah, Allah has forbidden to him the Garden and his abode is the Fire." See Ali, "The Holy Qur'an."

[106] Qur'ân, 2:88-89

[107] Qur'ân, 98:6 (the "people of the Scripture" are Jews and Christians). For other examples of verses that speak of the condemnation of Jews and Christians, see: 2:75, 2:83, 2:84-85, 2:88-89, 2:91-96, 2:105, 3:19, 3:21-23, 3:64, 3:79, 3:110-112, 3:187, 4:44, 4:46, 4:51-52, 4:54-56, 4:150-151, 4:153-155, 4:160-161, 4:171, 5:13-14, 5:17, 5:43, 5:59, 5:61-64, 5:72-73, 5:77-82, 9:30-31, 10:68-70, 17:111, 18:4-5, 39:2-4, 57:16, 57:26-27, 59:11, 62:5-7.

[108] Qur'ân, 2:81, 2:167, 3:16, 3:181, 3:191-192, 4:14, 4:55-56, 5:72, 6:27, 9:63, 9:68, 11:98, 11:105-106, 11:113, 13:35, 14:30, 18:53, 22:9, 25:11, 31:21, 32:20, 33:64, 34:42, 39:8, 39:16, 39:19, 40:72, 41:19, 41:24, 41:28, 52:13-14, 55:35, 56:94, 57:15, 58:17, 59:3, 64:10, 66:6, 67:5, 67:10-11, 69:31, 70:15, 73:12, 74:29-31, 76:4, 77:31-32, 82:14, 98:6

[109] Qur'ân, 17:8

[110] Qur'ân, 47:15, 56:54, 56:93

[111] Qur'ân, 69:36

[112] Qur'ân, 73:13

[113] Qur'ân, 37:62-66, 44:43-44, 56:52-53; this "tree of bitterness" is described in 37:63-68:

> We have made it a punishment for the transgressors. It is a tree that grows in the midst of Hell. Its shoots are like the devils' heads. They will eat from it, so that their bellies are filled up.

Then they will have with it a drink of boiling liquid. Then they will be returned to Hell.

[114] Qur'ân, 56:41-43

[115] Qur'ân, 25:13-14, 34:33, 40:71, 43:77, 69:30-32, 73:12, 76:4

[116] Qur'ân, 2:161-162, 2:167, 4:168-169, 9:68, 14:17, 16:85, 18:53, 20:74, 33:65, 35:36-37, 41:28, 43:74-75, 43:77, 82:14-16, 98:6. See also: 2:81, 3:192, 4:14, 4:93, 5:80, 9:63, 16:29, 32:14, 39:72, 40:76, 41:24, 58:17, 64:10. On the other hand, Qur'ân 6:128 implies that the damned may have some hope that God could change His mind: "He said: 'The Fire is your dwelling, in it you shall abide eternally, except as your Lord wishes.' " Similarly, see 11:107.

[117] Qur'ân, 78:21-30

[118] Qur'ân, 9:34-35

[119] Qur'ân, 22:19-22; another translation of this passage is as follows: "So those who disbelieve, for them are cut out garments of fire. Boiling water will be poured out over their heads. With it will be melted what is in their bellies and (their) skins as well. And for them are whips of iron. Whenever they desire to go forth from it, from grief, they are turned back into it, and (it is said) Taste the chastisement of burning." Ali, "The Holy Qur'an."

[120] Of course, the New Testament has also been said to portray God and Hell in similar terms, but I believe mistakenly so. See Chapter 5, "What Hell Is Really Like."

[121] The Arabic word for Heaven is "Jannah," which literally means "garden."

[122] Qur'ân, 5:65, 15:45, 16:31, 18:31, 22:56, 31:8, 37:43, 37:45-46. 39:20, 44:51-52, 55:46, 55:50, 55:62, 55:66, 56:12, 56:31, 56:89, 76:17-18, 77:41, 78:31-32

[123] Qur'ân, 3:15, 3:195, 3:198, 4:13, 4:57, 4:122, 5:85, 9:72, 9:100, 13:35, 16:31, 20:76, 22:14, 22:23, 25:10, 57:12, 58:22, 64:9, 65:11, 66:8, 98:8

[124] Qur'ân, 9:72, 25:10, 39:20, 61:12

[125] Qur'ân, 18:31, 22:23, 44:53, 76:12, 76:21

[126] Qur'ân, 18:31, 36:56, 55:54, 55:76, 76:13

[127] Qur'ân, 13:35, 36:57, 37:42, 38:51, 44:55, 47:15, 55:52, 55:54, 55:68, 56:20-21, 56:32, 69:23, 76:14, 77:42-43

[128] Qur'ân, 47:15; see also, 76:17, 76:21

[129] Qur'ân, 37:48-49, 38:52, 55:56, 55:70-74, 56:22, 56:36-38

[130] Qur'ân, 3:15, 4:57, 44:54; another verse may indicate that those who were married in their earthly life will be reunited with their spouses: "Both them and their spouses, they will be shaded, reclining on high furnishings." (36:56) However, this verse could also refer to spouses obtained in heaven.

[131] Qur'ân, 39:73, 44:51, 56:25-26, 56:91

[132] Qur'ân, 11:108, 39:73-74, 43:71, 82:13, 83:22-24

[133] Qur'ân, 16:31, 25:16, 36:57, 41:31, 43:71

[134] Compare Matthew 22:30, where Jesus says: "For in the resurrection they neither marry nor are given in marriage, but are like angels in heaven." Similar: Mark 12:25 and Luke 20:34-35.

[135] Qur'ân, 37:50

[136] Luke 6:31-36; see also See Matthew 5:44 and Luke 6:27

[137] Luke 6:29; see also Matthew 5:39

[138] Matthew 23:11-12; see also: Matthew 18:4, Luke 14:11, 18:14

[139] Matt 18:21-22; see also Luke 17:3-4

[140] Luke 23:33-34

[141] Qur'ân, 5:32

[142] Qur'ân, 2:190

[143] Of course, Christianity has had its share of violence and hatred in its history, including the Crusades, the excesses of the Inquisition, and the 16th and 17th century religious wars between Catholics and Protestants. Yet such incidents are thankfully rare nowadays, due in large part, I believe, to the printing press and high literacy rates, which enabled Christians to read the clear and consistent message of the New Testament in opposition to violence, revenge, and hatred. Unlike Christianity, I do not believe Muslim violence can be attributed to ignorance, because the Qur'ân presents a decidedly mixed message on this subject. Indeed, many of today's Muslim terrorist leaders are well educated, knowledge-

able, and sophisticated, and they can find ample support for their views within the pages of the Qur'ân.

[144] The Qur'ân explicitly prohibits Muslims from fighting each other, except in the case of open aggression by one Muslim nation or group against another. See, for example, 49:10: "The believers are brothers; so reconcile between your brothers, and be aware of God, that you may receive mercy." See also, 49:9.

[145] Qur'ân, 9:5 (quoted from Ali, "The Holy Qur'an")

[146] Qur'ân, 9:123 (quoted from Ali, "The Holy Qur'an"). Other verses in the Qur'ân which counsel Muslims to fight or make war upon unbelievers include: 2:191, 2:193, 4:76, 4:104, 9:29, 9:73, 47:34-35, 48:29, 66:9. Three of these verses—9:73, 48:29, and 66:9—are specifically addressed to Muhammad, and many Muslims argue that all such verses should be limited to that time period, when Muslims were being persecuted and attacked. However, most of these verses are not explicitly so limited. In addition, many verses forbid friendship between Muslims and non-Muslims, including Jews and Christians: 3:28, 3:118, 4:138-139, 4:144, 5:51, 5:57, 5:80-81, 6:159, 9:23, 58:14-15, 58:22, 60:13.

[147] Qur'ân, 60:4

[148] Qur'ân, 2:216, 3:167-168, 4:77, 4:84, 9:12-14, 9:111, 47:20-21

[149] Qur'ân, 2:218, 3:146, 3:157-158, 3:169-174, 3:195, 4:74, 4:95-96, 4:100, 8:74-75, 9:19-22, 9:41, 16:110-111, 47:4-6, 57:10, 61:4

[150] Qur'ân, 8:15-16, 9:38-39, 9:44-45, 9:49-56, 9:81-87, 9:93-95, 33:18-19, 48:11-12, 48:16-17, 49:15

[151] See the Qur'ân, 4:3:

> And if you fear that you cannot be just to the orphans, then marry those whom you see fit from their mothers, two, and three, and four. But if you fear you will not be fair, then only one, or whom you are already betrothed to. This is best that you do not face financial hardship.

[152] See the Qur'ân, 33:50:

> O prophet, We have made lawful for you the wives to whom you have already given their dowry, and the one who is committed to you by oath, as granted to you by God, and the

> daughters of your father's brothers, and the daughters of your father's sisters, and the daughters of your mother's brothers, and the daughters of your mother's sisters, of whom they have emigrated with you. Also, the believing woman who had decreed herself to the prophet, the prophet may marry her if he wishes, *as a privilege given only to you and not to the believers.* We have already decreed their rights in regard to their spouses and those who are still dependant. This is to spare you any hardship. God is Forgiver, Merciful.

(Emphasis supplied.)

[153] In fairness, some of Muhammad's marriages were acts of diplomacy, in an effort to build alliances through matrimony, while others were acts of kindness to widows of slain Muslims. Nevertheless, the Qur'ân recognizes no such exception for any other Muslim, regardless of the circumstances.

[154] See the Qur'ân, 66:1-5:

> O you prophet, why do you prohibit what God has made lawful for you, seeking to please your wives? God is Forgiver, Merciful. God has already given the law, regarding the cancellation of oaths. And God is your Lord, and He is the Knowledgeable, the Wise. And when the prophet disclosed a matter in confidence to some of his wives, then one of them spread it, and God revealed it to him, he recognized part of it and denied part. So when he informed her, she said: "Who informed you of this?" He said: "I was informed by the Knowledgeable, the Expert. If the two of you repent to God, then your hearts have listened. But if you band together against him, then God is his ally, and so are Gabriel and the righteous believers. Also, the Angels are his helpers. It may be that he would divorce you, then his Lord will substitute other wives in your place who are better than you; surrendering, believing, obedient, repentant, worshipping, pious, previously married, and first born."

Regarding these verses, N. J. Dawood, in *The Koran*, at p. 398, footnote 1, adds: "Muhammad, we are told, was once found by his wife Hafsah with a Coptic slave from whom he had promised her to separate. Of this Hafsah secretly informed Aishah, another wife of his. To free Muhammad from his promise to Hafsah was the object of this chapter. Some of the references are obscure."

[155] Qur'ân, 33:37-38

[156] Qur'ân, 33:53

[157] Qur'ân, 33:32-33; see also 33:53

[158] Qur'ân, 33:53

[159] Many Muslims also accept the "Hadith" as authoritative. The Hadith is a collection of traditions about Muhammad and his early followers, which were collected during the Abbasid Caliphate (750-1058), more than 100 years after Muhammad's death. These traditions are often cited by moderate Muslims in an effort to soften the interpretation of some verses in the Qur'ân. For example, 4:34 tells Muslim husbands to deal with disobedient wives by first admonishing them, then terminating sexual relations with them, and finally by beating them. A tradition in the Hadith says that when a Muslim asked Muhammad what the husband should use to beat his wife, Muhammad showed him a tooth brush. Emerick, *Idiot's Guide to Understanding Islam*, p. 260. Nevertheless, most Muslims do not regard the Hadith as authoritative on a level with the Qur'ân.

[160] The term, "caliph," is derived from the title Abu Bekr took for himself, *Khalifat al-Rasul al-Allah,* meaning "Representative of the Messenger of God." The four rightly-guided caliphs were Abu Bekr, Omar, Othman, and Ali.

[161] See the Qur'ân, 2:256: "There is no compulsion in religion." (quoted from Ali, "The Holy Qur'an") And see Qur'ân, 50:45.

[162] For example, in 744 A.D., Christians in Egypt were offered a temporary tax exemption if they would convert to Islam. 24,000 accepted.

Chapter 9
BUDDHISM
(AND NOW FOR SOMETHING COMPLETELY DIFFERENT)

In the previous chapter, I pointed out many ways in which I believe Islam fails the test of credibility. Hinduism and Buddhism are not so easily appraised. Hinduism, like Judaism, is an ancient religion, and Buddhism is considerably older than Christianity. Both Hinduism and Buddhism have their own sacred scriptures, and do not accept any portion of the Bible as scriptural. Their worldview differs so radically from Christianity, Judaism, and Islam that evaluating Buddhism from a strictly Judeo-Christian perspective is like arguing about the nature of God with an atheist.

Although Buddhism and Hinduism share many fundamental beliefs, I will primarily focus on Buddhism. Our goal is not to attack or disprove Buddhism, but to understand it. However, I believe one thing will become abundantly clear in this discussion: Buddhism (and Hinduism) and Christianity cannot both be true.

The Four Fundamental Beliefs That Distinguish Buddhism From Christianity. In many ways, Buddhism and Christianity are strikingly similar. Both grew out of an ancient religion that still exists today: Christianity of course developed from Judaism, while Buddhism had its roots in Hinduism. Like Christianity, Buddhism had a single founder, Siddhartha Gautama (known as the Buddha), who embraced society's outcasts. Like the teachings of Jesus, Paul, and the apostles, Buddhism condemns such evils as killing, lying, stealing, and sexual misconduct (for example, adultery, rape, and promiscuity), while embracing values like compassion, generosity, humility, self-control, forgiveness, and nonviolence.

Paralleling Jesus's Sermon on the Mount [1] (which came more than 500 years later), the Buddha urged people to be moral and kind in their actions, speech, and thoughts. Thus, Buddhism disapproves of gossip, slander, insults and other hurtful speech, as well as hatred, anger, greed, covetousness, and self-centeredness. [2] Indeed, Buddhism arguably imposes a higher moral standard on its adherents than does Christianity, for Buddhists are forbidden to harm any living creature, whether human, animal, or insect. (For this reason, strict Buddhists are vegetarians.) Christianity and Buddhism also agree that lust for wealth is undesirable, and Buddhism says the same thing about a yearning for power, fame, sex, food, intoxicants, and other pleasures.

And yet as similar as Buddhism and Christianity are in many ways, four fundamental Buddhist beliefs are so radically different from anything in Christianity that they dwarf these similarities. Those four beliefs are: [3]

1. There is no personal God.
2. The universe is subject to the law of karma.
3. People have no eternal souls.
4. People constantly live in *samsara*, or "cyclic existence" (what we generally refer to as reincarnation).

No Personal God. Siddhartha Gautama was born in the city of Kapilavastu, in northeastern India, near present-day Nepal, in about 566 B.C. [4] He was the son of a wealthy rajah (a feudal lord), Suddhona, of the Shakya clan.

Early Buddhist scriptures tell us that Suddhona consulted a soothsayer at the time of the boy's birth, and was told that he would be either a great ruler or an even greater religious leader. In an effort to steer his son toward the former, Suddhona carefully insulated the boy from any persons who were sick, old, dying, or religious—that is, anyone who might cause disillusionment with this earthly life.

Siddhartha lived in luxury, took a bride (Yasodhara), and had a son (Rahula). Yet Siddhartha frustrated his father's plans by venturing into a nearby town and witnessing exactly what his father had tried to isolate him from: sickness, old age, death, and a Hindu monk. Siddhartha immediately fell into despair when he realized the transitory nature of life. Not long after, at the age of 29, he snuck out of his father's palace and took up the religious life. Buddhists call this the Great Renunciation.

For six years Siddhartha studied with Hindu masters and practiced extreme asceticism with five disciples, but by the end of that time he was much closer to death than he was to finding peace and happiness. So he abandoned the way of extreme asceticism. After eating a meal, he settled under a fig tree [5] to meditate, vowing not to move until he found enlightenment. And by the next morning, we are told, he found it. In his remaining 45 years, Siddhartha gained many followers through his wisdom and compassion. He died at age 80 from accidental food poisoning.

An example of the Buddha's compassion is his rejection of the Hindu caste system. Traditionally, Hinduism has had four castes. The highest ranking caste was that of the priests, followed by, in order: rulers and warriors, merchants, and manual laborers. Below the manual laborers was a group referred to as "Untouchables," who performed work no one else wanted to do, such as handling garbage and dead bodies. Hindus did not associate with members of other castes, and everyone shunned the Untouchables. [6] Siddhartha was in the second caste, that of rulers and warriors. However, he treated everyone as his equals, regardless of caste, including even the "Untouchables."

Siddhartha professed to have found the way to peace and happiness, but he never claimed to be anything more than a man who could show others the way. When people asked him if he was a god or a supernatural being, he denied both. So they asked, "Then what are you?," and he replied: "I am awake." Thus he became known as the Buddha, an "awakened one" or "enlightened one."

Despite achieving enlightenment, Siddhartha still lived in a Hindu culture. Hindus believe in a pantheistic God, Brahman, which is ultimate reality—infinite, immutable, and indescribable. Brahman is not a personal God like Yahweh or Christ. Brahman does not interact with people or intervene in human affairs. Brahman is not the Creator of everything, nor is He merely in everything—He *is* everything. If all living things are like drops of water in the ocean, Brahman is the ocean. If all living things are like a single cell in the body, Brahman is the body.

The Buddha refused to endorse the Hindu concept of Brahman, [7] as well as the countless lesser Hindu gods and goddesses [8] whom Hindus believe are both willing and able to intervene in human affairs. Strictly speaking, the Buddha was more agnostic than atheist. He declined to state whether or not the gods existed; he simply believed they were irrelevant, and certainly not helpful. He did not accept the existence of a God or gods which intervene in human affairs, or to whom people could turn for help. Instead, he emphasized that each person must rely on his or her own efforts to achieve enlightenment. The Buddha's last words just before he died are typical of this emphasis on individual self-reliance: "Work out your own salvation with diligence."

Although the Buddha had no desire to be called a god, Buddhists in the ensuing centuries idealized him, deified him, and ascribed miracles to him. This was particularly true in the Mahayana tradition, which began to develop within 100 years after the Buddha's death. The deification of the Buddha was probably well established by the third century B.C., about 200 years after his death.

Mahayana Buddhism grew to become the more popular form of the religion—as indicated by the name Mahayana, which means "the large raft." [9] This form of Buddhism eventually split from its more traditional cousin, Theravada Buddhism (Theravada means "teachings of the elders"). [10] In theory, if not always in practice, Theravada Buddhism remained true to the Buddha's original teachings, which denied his divinity.

Neither Mahayana nor Theravada Buddhism accepts the Judeo-Christian concept of a monotheistic Creator God who listens to human prayers and takes an interest in human affairs. In Mahayana Buddhism—which predominates in China, Taiwan, Tibet, Mongolia, Korea, and Japan—such divine help is sought from a variety of Buddhas (for they believe there have been many besides Siddhartha Gautama himself), as well as divine beings known as Bodhisattvas.

Theravada Buddhism, which is dominant in Sri Lanka and the nations of southeast Asia, [11] tends to adhere more closely to the Buddha's original insistence on self-reliance, although elements of Mahayana's polytheism are sometimes found.

While some Buddhists believe in divine beings that provide assistance on the path to enlightenment, while others deny their existence, no Buddhist believes that they determine his future. Only karma and the Four Noble Truths can do that.

Karma. After the Buddha achieved enlightenment, he sought his five former disciples in the Deer Park at Sarnath, and taught them The Four Noble Truths. [12] The first of these Noble Truths is that *life is full of suffering.*

The word in the original Pali language of the Buddhist scriptures is *dukkha,* which literally means that life is dislocated or out-of-joint. The word connotes suffering in all its many forms, from dissatisfaction to anguish. To the non-Buddhist, this seems like a very pessimistic view of life. The Buddhist would counter that it is instead a very *realistic* view of life.

Of course, we suffer when we are in physical pain or discomfort. But *dukkha* means far more. It also includes hurt feelings; confronting unpleasant circumstances; frustration from unfulfilled desires; disappointment due to unmet expectations; overindulgence in pleasure; and the pain of loss. Since each of these forms of *dukkha* is relatively common, Buddhism says that suffering is our natural condition.

The ultimate example of this is life itself. Each of us daily grows closer to death, and we can do nothing to change that. And so we suffer because we know that death is inevitable.

The Second Noble Truth is that *we suffer because we crave the impermanent things of this world*. This Noble Truth recognizes that the things we desire are necessarily impermanent: a friend, spouse, or family member will grow old and die; reality displaces romance; possessions wear out; health deteriorates. Nothing stays the same. In addition, we often exaggerate the merits of what we want, because ultimately they will prove to be unsatisfying. For these reasons, the Buddha said that everything in the world is *maya*—an illusion.

The things we crave are as difficult to grasp as smoke. Yet in our ignorance we yearn for them like a thirsty man longs for a drink of water. And when we make our happiness dependent upon obtaining them, our happiness is at best temporary, even if we obtain them. To add to the problem, *dukkha* generates unfavorable emotions, such as anger and hatred, as well as wicked thoughts and actions; those emotions, thoughts, and actions lead to further adverse consequences due to the law of karma—the second fundamental difference between Christianity and Buddhism.

Karma is a basic Hindu belief which the Buddha adopted. Karma is essentially cause and effect, but for Hindus and Buddhists it is not only a physical law but a moral law as well. Good karma comes from virtuous and altruistic thoughts, emotions, intentions, speech, behavior, and results, while bad karma arises from the opposite of these things.

The strength of the karma depends upon the intensity and combination of these factors. Thus, an evil thought combined with wicked behavior and a harmful result generates more bad karma than an evil thought alone. Similarly, murder causes more bad karma than a mere insult, since the resulting harm is much worse. [13]

If something terrible happens to me, a Buddhist would say that it is not due to bad luck or punishment from above, but the result of bad karma. In this way, suffering can become a vicious circle by arousing negative thoughts, emotions, and actions that produce more bad karma—which results in more suffering in the future. To a Hindu or a Buddhist, the moral law of karma is as inevitable and unavoidable as the law of gravity. Therefore, Hindus and Buddhists believe breaking this cycle of suffering is imperative. And that is the subject of the Buddha's Third Noble Truth.

No eternal soul. The Buddha's solution to the problem of suffering is the Third Noble Truth: *The way to eliminate suffering is to eliminate craving*. If I do not hunger after my possessions, I will not suffer when they are gone. Similarly, if I do not yearn to be with a spouse, family members, or friends, I will not suffer when they leave or die.

These principles are also true for life itself. The Buddhist would say that I fear death because I am afraid of losing my attachment to this life and the things of this life. If I free myself from that attachment, I will no longer fear death. At the heart of this Third Noble Truth we find the third fundamental difference between Buddhism and Christianity: the lack of belief in an eternal soul.

To a Buddhist, *nothing* about this life has any permanence, including each of us. The Buddha taught that every person is made up of a mind and a body—nothing else—and that both of these are impermanent in the sense that they are constantly changing and will eventually cease to function.

I may think I have a continuing self, but most Buddhists would say that this is *maya*, an illusion, for I am a different person now from whom I was as a child, or as an adolescent, or as a young adult. Whatever I am today will be different tomorrow, and whatever I become will not survive the death of my mind and body. Buddhism says that I must lose my attachment to this impermanent "self."

If by an "eternal soul" we mean a consciousness and personality that survive death, then most Buddhists would deny the existence of an eternal soul, [14] the fate of which is one of Christianity's chief concerns. For the Buddhist, death is simply part of *samsara,* the fourth and final fundamental difference between the Christian and Buddhist belief systems.

Samsara. The Buddha adopted the Hindu belief in *samsara,* or cyclic existence. This means that death begins a new life in a different form. According to Buddhist doctrine, this new life may be in the form of a human being, an animal, or one of several other life forms. [15] When I die, my energy passes into the next life, but my consciousness and personality do not, because both are impermanent. To explain this, the Buddha used the analogy of the flame of a dying candle being passed to a new candle. The energy passes from old to new, but everything else is different.

Karma determines what my future life will be. Good karma will result in an advantageous future life—hopefully as a human being with favorable circumstances, such as plenty to eat, good health, and long life. Bad karma results in a more adverse future life, perhaps as an animal, an insect, or worse.

Karma can express itself over a single lifetime, present or future, or over multiple lifetimes, usually depending on the strength of the karma. A Buddhist would say that everything I am, and everything that happens to me, has a cause somewhere in this life or in one of my past lives. Thus, my good karma from a previous life has caused me to be reborn as a human being—which is the most beneficial life form, by the way, since only humans can become enlightened.

However, neither Hinduism nor Buddhism seeks merely to accumulate good karma in order to achieve a better future life. The goal in both religions is to escape this cyclic existence, and thereby leave behind the suffering that it entails, for the law of karma applies only to those who are trapped in *samsara*.

In Hinduism the possibility of escape from *samsara* is limited to the Brahmin caste—the priestly caste—which necessarily also limits this possibility to males. For women and members of the lower castes, the only hope is to rise to a higher caste in a future life by living virtuously and performing the duties of your caste.

The Buddha disagreed with Hinduism on this point, teaching that escape from *samsara* is available to any person who achieves enlightenment, regardless of sex or caste, and that anyone who lives a virtuous life can achieve enlightenment. According to Buddhism, our attachment to life—that is, our strong will to exist—is what produces *samsara*. We are bound to this life because we crave it. That craving results from our ignorance regarding the true, impermanent nature of the self. To escape *samsara*, we must obtain wisdom to counter our ignorance and end our craving for this life. We must become "enlightened." And that leads us to the Fourth Noble Truth.

The Noble Eightfold Path to Nirvana. Achieving enlightenment is not easy, for it requires a person to eliminate his attachments to the impermanent things of this life. The Buddha's fourth Noble Truth tells us how to do this: *The way to eliminate these attachments is through the Noble Eightfold Path*. That Path includes: (1) right understanding, (2) right thought or intention, (3) right speech, (4) right action, (5) right livelihood, [16] (6) right effort, (7) right mindfulness, and (8) right concentration.

In simple terms, the Noble Eightfold Path is a way of life. As in Christianity, faith is necessary, but instead of faith in a person, Christ, Buddhism requires faith in a methodology: the Four Noble Truths. Understanding and accepting these "truths" is essentially what is meant by "right understanding" and "right thought." The goal of the Noble Eightfold Path is to engender wisdom, virtue, and altruism, by disciplining the mind, body, and tongue through deep meditation and concentrated focus—that is, through "right mindfulness" (#7) and "right concentration" (#8). Many Buddhists consider meditation and focus to be the keys to reaching enlightenment.

Through the Noble Eightfold Path, the Buddhist learns to accept, and be happy with, life as it comes. Instead of trying to change the world around him, he tries to change himself and the way he reacts to the world. When life is pleasant, the enlightened Buddhist can simply enjoy it without worrying about when it may end, and when life is difficult he can accept it in the knowledge that it is not a permanent condition. Perhaps the Buddha said it best when he remarked that the secret to happiness is wanting what you have and not wanting what you don't have. This philosophy seems similar to what Paul said in Philippians 4:11: " . . . I have learned to be content in whatever circumstances I am."

Buddhism teaches that following the Eightfold Path eventually leads to *Nirvana,* which literally means "blown out" or "extinguished"—as in a candle flame being snuffed. All Buddhists agree that *Nirvana* is the cessation of suffering, craving, and negative emotions, and freedom from *samsara.* And of course, all agree that *Nirvana* is the ultimate goal. Beyond these basics, Buddhists disagree about exactly what *Nirvana* is. [17]

Most Buddhists say an enlightened person reaches *Nirvana* after death, but some say enlightenment and *Nirvana* are the same thing, and therefore both can be achieved in this lifetime. Some think of *Nirvana* as a place, while others think of it as a mental state or attitude. Buddhists even hold opposing views on whether a person's consciousness and personality survive in *Nirvana.* Many Buddhists say that *Nirvana* cannot be explained through words, but must be experienced to be understood. The Buddha himself, when questioned about the nature of *Nirvana,* said only that it is "bliss."

Conclusion. One thing seems clear—Buddhism and Christianity cannot both be true. We have seen in Chapters 1 and 2 that

Christ's claims of divinity and the evidence for His resurrection provide sound historical reasons for faith in Christ. I find nothing of the sort in Buddhism. Buddha himself never claimed to be anything but a man, and his followers did not contend otherwise until long after his death.

Aside from this, Buddhism also doesn't *help* me. Before I became a Christian, I was tortured by the idea that my life would be short and meaningless. I wanted to be immortal. Buddhism says I want the wrong thing, and that instead of wanting to be immortal I should simply learn to accept that my life will be short and meaningless (to be followed by additional short and meaningless lives after I die). To me, this is like an oncologist telling her patient to simply accept that he is going to die soon. That may be fine advice if there is no cure, but I'd prefer the cure.

Christianity is the cure. It says I can have what I want, which of course is eternal life, through a faithful and loving relationship with God. So although Christianity and Buddhism may share many morals and values, I won't be seeking "enlightenment" in this lifetime. I am confident I've already found it.

Endnotes for Chapter Nine, "Buddhism"

[1] See Matthew chapters 5, 6, and 7.

[2] Most Buddhist monks and nuns have special rules they must follow, which can vary from place to place. For example, such rules may require abstention from some or all of the following: sexual relations, intoxicants, singing, dancing, music, perfumes, adornments, various luxuries, and the handling of money.

[3] Not all of these beliefs are universally held by all Buddhists, for Buddhism today encompasses a wide range of beliefs.

[4] Buddhism is not without its myths, many of which address the Buddha's birth. These myths claim that Siddhartha's mother was impregnated by a sacred white elephant who touched her side with a lotus; that when Siddhartha was born, he immediately began to talk, declaring himself a future Buddha; and that he also immediately began to walk, and everywhere he stepped lotus blossoms appeared. Miracles are said to have accompanied his birth: light flooded the world; the blind, deaf, dumb, and lame were healed; prisoners were freed; and the fires of Hell were quenched. Some Buddhists believe that the Buddha had lived many lifetimes before this birth, gradually acquiring wisdom and compassion, and culminating in the life we know as the Buddha.

[5] This tree became known as the Bhodi tree—that is, the Tree of Enlightenment. Located near the town of Gaya, the tree is now a pilgrimage site for Buddhists.

[6] Indian leaders are trying to eliminate the caste system, and the Indian Constitution prohibits "untouchability."

[7] The Buddha also rejected the Hindu scriptures, Hindu myths, and the belief in miracles.

[8] The leading Hindu gods and goddesses are: Brahma (not to be confused with Brahman), the Creator; Shiva, the Destroyer, but also the god of fertility; Vishnu, the Preserver or Sustainer; and Shakti (also known as Kali, Durga, Parvati, and Uma), the Divine Mother of the Universe. Some of the other Hindu gods and goddesses are: Lakshmi, goddess of prosperity and good fortune; Sarasvati, god of wisdom and music; Ganesh,

the symbol of good luck and prosperity; Indra, the god of the thunderbolt, clouds, and rain, and the ruler of heaven; Agni, the god of fire; and the sage, Manu.

[9] Mahayana Buddhism has many off-shoots, such as Japan's Zen Buddhism, Tibet's Vajrayana Buddhism, and China's Pure Land Buddhism.

[10] Theravada and Mahayana Buddhism differ regarding the writings which they accept as authoritative. The Buddha's teachings were first written down about 400-500 years after his death, during either the first century B.C. or the first century A.D., in Ceylon (now known as Sri Lanka). Those Buddhist scriptures were written in Pali, the language of ancient Ceylon, and consist of the *Sutra Pitaka* (Collection of Teachings), the *Vinaya Pitaka* (Collection of Disciplinary Rules), and the *Adhidharma Pitaka* (Collection of Higher Wisdom). Together they are known as the *Tripitaka*—that is, the Three Baskets. They are also known as the Pali Canon. These are the only writings accepted as scriptural by most Theravada Buddhists.

In contrast, Mahayana Buddhists are much more accepting of later—and more questionable—writings which they claim also represent the Buddha's teachings. Examples of writings accepted as scriptural by one or more branches of Mahayana Buddhism include: the *White Lotus of the True Dharma Sutra* (also known as the Lotus Sutra); the *Exposition of Vimalakirti*; the *Perfection of Wisdom Sutras*; the *Descent into Lanka Sutra*; the *World-Array Sutra*; the *Land of Bliss Sutras*; the *Flower Ornament sutra*; the *Bardo Thödol* (*The Tibetan Book of the Dead*); the jatakas, which are said to be stories from the Buddha's earlier lifetimes; and Zen Buddhism's *Hekigan roku* and *Mumonkan*. Many of these were written in Sanskrit, the language of the upper classes in ancient India.

[11] Buddhism is nearly extinct in today's India.

[12] "The Four Noble Truths," although a popular name, is probably an inadequate translation. A better translation might be, "The Four Exalted Fundamental Principles of Existence."

[13] Many Buddhists believe that the impact of negative karma can be minimized through remorse and atonement, such as altruistic deeds that help people, especially those who were hurt by your harmful actions.

Similarly, good deeds done with improper motives can diminish the good karma those deeds would ordinarily purchase.

[14] However, not all Buddhists would agree. For example, some Buddhists believe that, under the right circumstances, a person's consciousness can survive death and enter a kind of Heaven called the Pure Land—a belief which seems very close to the Christian concept of the eternal soul. Similarly, some Buddhists believe that the Buddha took many lifetimes to achieve enlightenment, which implies at least some degree of continuity of his soul.

[15] Undesirable rebirths include hell-beings and hungry ghosts, both of which involve much suffering. A pleasant rebirth would be as a human being, a god, or a demi-god.

[16] The Theravada tradition insists that "right livelihood" means becoming a monk and joining a *sangha*—a community of monks. The Mahayana tradition simply requires that a person's job not harm himself or others, directly or indirectly. The Buddha insisted that his followers, at a minimum, not pursue the following occupations: poison peddler, slave-trader, prostitute, butcher, brewer, armament maker, tax collector, and caravan trader.

[17] Hindus think of *Nirvana* as reunion with the pantheistic god Brahman, but of course the Buddha did not accept the existence of Brahman.

Chapter 10
DOES EVOLUTION DISPROVE CHRISTIANITY?

Does evolution disprove God's existence? Or does it perhaps render Him impotent—reducing Him to a mere spectator in the creation and development of life? In other words, has science eliminated God's role in creation? To answer these questions, we must be clear about what we mean by "creation" and "evolution." Let me illustrate with a story from my own experience.

I was brought up to believe that evolution is a historical and scientific fact. When I became a Christian, I didn't at first question this belief. Sometime later, I attended a debate about the truth of evolution between some university science professors and creationists. With much anticipation, I went to hear the facts and arguments each side could marshal, eager to learn the truth. But the professors cut the legs out from under the discussion within the first two minutes, by insisting on a definition of "evolution" similar to the following: "characteristics of organisms change in response to their environment." The debate disintegrated into two sides arguing over completely different issues. I felt cheated. So lest you feel cheated, too, let's define what I consider to be two different types of "evolution."

Microevolution and Darwinian Evolution. Characteristics of organisms *do* change in response to their environment. That is an observable fact which is about as controversial as saying that the Sun is bright. I will refer to the process by which these changes occur as "microevolution." Microevolution causes changes within species, [1] as various characteristics are favored or disfavored by the environment.

For example, the European Peppered moth *(Biston betularia)* in England changed colors over time. Dark moths became more plentiful during the Industrial Revolution, when factory soot created a blacker environment, making dark moths harder for predators to see. Microevolution has been documented many times, in various studies: mussels' shells have grown thicker in response to an invasive species of crab; the Blue Moon butterflies of Somoa developed resistance to a parasite that was killing most of the male butterfly population; people have been breeding dogs for thousands of years in order to make them good hunters or watchdogs, or just good companions.

The professors sought to define "evolution" as micro-evolution, knowing that this would ensure victory in the debate. But they were also avoiding the real issue.

Microevolution is not what non-scientists generally think of as "evolution." For most people, "evolution" refers to what Charles Darwin wrote about in 1859 in his famous book, *On the Origin of Species*. Darwin hypothesized that complex living organisms gradually developed from simpler organisms, through random genetic mutations and the mechanism of natural selection.

According to Darwin's theory, these random mutations would cause small changes in living organisms, and some of these changes would confer a reproductive advantage, resulting in the spreading of that beneficial change. Wings that enable a bird to fly would allow it to find food and avoid predators, giving it a better chance to survive and reproduce. The result would be more and more birds that can fly.

The accumulation of small changes over time would eventually alter the organism so much that it would become an entirely new species. Darwin believed that in this manner, single-celled organisms had gradually evolved into multicellular organisms, and those evolved into creatures of greater and greater complexity, including mankind. I will refer to this concept—that complex organisms evolved from simpler organisms, *through entirely natural means*—as "Darwinian evolution."

A related question is the "origin of life"—that is, where did life come from in the first place? Those who accept Darwinian evolution usually claim, or at least assume, that life also originated naturally through a series of chemical reactions. [2] I will therefore include the belief that life originated through entirely natural means as part of Darwinian evolution.

My purpose is not to disprove Darwinian evolution, because I believe that is impossible. Darwinian evolution is not subject to proof or disproof. It is ultimately a faith position. By "faith position," I mean a belief in something, or someone, that can never be objectively verified or proven to a reasonable certainty—in other words, something that must ultimately be accepted on faith.

A faith position cannot be disproved because the target keeps moving. If you believe in little green men from outer space, that is a faith position. We can discuss the facts underlying your belief, such as whether a particular UFO sighting was a real alien, a natural phenomenon, or a figment of someone's imagination. But even if I debunk 20 or 2,000 UFO sightings, I cannot disprove your belief that the aliens are "out there" somewhere and we just haven't found them yet. As we will see, the same is true of Darwinian evolution. But first we must take a brief look at the other side of the coin: Creation.

Creation. The first two chapters of Genesis say that God created the earth and everything in it in six days, and then rested on the 7th day. Using chronologies in the Old Testament, the 17th century Irish Bishop James Ussher calculated that the world was created in 4,004 B.C. Even today, some Christians argue that the universe is less than 10,000 years old. [3] If you insist on a literal interpretation of everything in the Bible, you will have trouble reconciling Genesis with what science tells us about ancient earth and the life it contained. However, we have good reasons to think the first two chapters of Genesis should not be taken quite so literally.

First, look at 2 Peter 3:8: "But do not let this one fact escape your notice, beloved, that with the Lord one day is as a thousand years, and a thousand years as one day." Psalm 90:4 is similar:

For a thousand years in Your sight
Are like yesterday when it passes by,
Or *as* a watch in the night.

This does not mean that God created the world in 6,000 years, rather than Genesis' six days, but that He is not obsessed about time like we are. He is, after all, eternal. He doesn't grow up, grow old, or die. So whether something takes one day or a thousand years or one-hundred-million years makes little difference to Him.

Now let's examine Genesis more closely. We measure a "day" by the rising and setting of the sun. For the Israelites, for whom Genesis was written, each new day began at sunset. But in Genesis 1:14-19, the sun was not created until the fourth day. The first three "days" had no sunrise or sunset, so they were not "days" as we think of that term. This is another clue that the first two chapters of Genesis should not be taken literally.

A non-literal interpretation of Genesis avoids the potential headaches created by a New Testament verse like Hebrews 1:2: "in these last days [God] has spoken to us in His Son, whom He appointed heir of all things, through whom also He made the world." [4] The author of Hebrews, probably writing in the latter half of the first century (i.e., between about 80 and 95 A.D.), tells his readers that they are in the "last days." To us, 2,000 years later, this looks like a mistake, particularly if we view Earth as only a few thousand years old. But if the Earth is actually billions of years old, then 2,000 years is little more than a moment in time by comparison—easily short enough for God to call it part of the "last days" of Earth.

Now think of God's purpose in giving us the Bible. It is not a history text or a scientific treatise. The Bible reveals God to His people. It tells us who God is and how we should respond to Him. God never intended Genesis to be a scientific explanation of the process of Creation.

Similarly, who is God's audience? If Moses was the author of Genesis, as tradition says, [5] then he wrote it at a time when the Israelites were just beginning their spiritual walk with God. They had only recently received the Law after being freed from slavery in Egypt, and had not yet entered the "promised land." [6]

Even if Genesis was written at a later time, it still preceded the prophets and Solomon's proverbs and David's psalms, to say nothing of the teachings of Jesus and the events of Pentecost. In terms of spiritual maturity, the Israelites were babies. God, in His mercy and humility, chose to speak to them in a way they could understand. Creation may be God's greatest miracle. The Israelites would have been hopelessly confused and overwhelmed by a sophisticated, scientific description of it. (In fact, we might be, too.) We don't try to teach physics, biology, and biochemistry to infants, and neither did God.

The first two chapters of Genesis teach the basic truth that everything we see was created by one God, who is good and powerful, and who intended this world to be better than it has turned out. With that in mind, let's return to Darwinian evolution.

Darwinian Evolution: Fact or Theory? Is Darwinian Evolution a fact or a theory? To answer that question, we must be clear about what is a "scientific fact." Those university science professors drove home to me the truth that a scientific fact is really a limited concept.

Science is based on the principles of experimentation and testing, observation, and verifiability. A scientific fact must have been **tested**, usually through **experimentation**. The experiment seeks to eliminate all variables which could affect the outcome, except the one variable which is being tested. The results of the experiment must then be accurately **observed**. [7] Finally, nothing can be accepted as scientific fact unless other scientists are able to **verify** it, by obtaining the same or substantially similar results using the same methods and procedures. An experiment or an observation which cannot be duplicated and verified by others has no scientific validity.

Regardless of how the evidence for and against Darwinian Evolution is sifted, one thing is clear: while microevolution is a well-established scientific fact, Darwinian evolution is not—and likely never will be. If Darwinian Evolution actually happened, it necessarily occurred in the past, when life originated and developed. And we cannot test, observe, or verify a past event unless someone invents a reliable time machine.

On the other hand, Darwinian evolution *is* a theory, in the scientific meaning of that word. To scientists, a "theory" is a reasoned—and usually an *accepted*—explanation for the observable scientific facts. The National Academy of Sciences defines a "theory" as "a well-substantiated explanation of some aspect of the natural world that can incorporate facts, laws, inferences, and tested hypotheses." [8] Unlike facts, "theories are not 'proven' but are corroborated, rejected, or modified in light of new data and how well they agree with accepted theories and principles." [9]

Darwinian evolution is a theory, and a widely accepted theory at that. But a theory is not a fact. If it were, it would be testable and verifiable. Ultimately, no matter how scientists try to dress it up, a theory is an opinion. And even widely held opinions can be wrong. At one time, a large number of people believed that the Sun revolved around the earth, because they saw the Sun moving across the sky. People made a logical deduction from the observed facts, and they were wrong. In the 19th and 20th centuries many scientists sought to justify white supremacy with scientific "evidence" demonstrating the superiority of the white race.

Scientists are not perfect. They are not immune to politics, biases, and unquestioned assumptions. Like the rest of us, they are merely human. That is why, in discussing Darwinian evolution, we must always be careful to distinguish between scientific fact and scientific theory.

The Three Assumptions Underlying Darwinian Evolution. Unfortunately, many scientists who accept Darwinian evolution are not so careful with their terminology. They speak of it as established "fact" which only religious zealots would doubt. Here are a few examples:

> Evolution is a fact. . . . Where there is legitimate debate it is over the mechanisms by which evolutionary change occurs. There are ways by which genetic change can take place by mechanisms other than natural selection and scientists argue about the relative importance of these, as they do about the rates of evolutionary change. Such arguments are the legitimate business of science, leading to hypothesis, experiment, observation and conclusion. They should not be confused with doubts about whether or not evolution has occurred. [10]

> Evolution is a fact in the same sense as it is a fact that Paris is in the Northern Hemisphere. [11]

> The creationist movement is part of a triumphal New Ignorance that rules in many places, the United States more than most. In fact, the majority of those determined to tell lies to children believe in Darwin's theory and understand how it works, without noticing. [12]

Even when Darwinian evolutionists try to be humble about their subject, their arrogance often bleeds through. Note how a Darwinian evolutionist defends the theory by comparing it to gravity, as if the former were as unassailable as the latter:

> Evolutionists are widely perceived as uncritical ideologues, devoted to suppressing all doubt about evolution. It's easy to see how this impression

> arose: evolutionists, after all, spend most of their public lives defending Darwin against endlessly recycled creationist arguments. So of course we appear hide-bound reactionaries. (So would physicists if the theory of gravity were dragged into court every other year.) [13]

Such arrogance seems to spring from three erroneous assumptions. The first is that the existence of microevolution proves Darwinian evolution. [14] Mr. Steve Jones (the author of the quote about "those determined to tell lies to children") cites the case of the human immunodeficiency virus (HIV) as proof of Darwinian evolution. Scientists tell us that the HIV has mutated in recent times from an animal virus into the deadly version that causes Acquired Immunodeficiency Syndrome (AIDS) in humans. But is this truly an example of an organism mutating into a different species, or merely a species changing its characteristics—like the black Peppered moth becoming dominant in England? Either way, this is a far cry from fish changing into land animals, or apes into men.

Another common assumption seems to be that the only alternative to evolution is a literal interpretation of Genesis. This assumption sets up a Creationist straw man that is easily discredited by almost universally accepted scientific beliefs, such as the age of the Earth. An intellectually honest person finds it difficult to believe that the earth is less than 10,000 years old when science provides abundant evidence that our planet's age must be much older. [15] However, I have already discussed several reasons why I believe a literal interpretation of Genesis is both unnecessary and unwise.

But the third assumption is the most critical: that there is no creative God who can or does intervene in nature—or that if there is, He is irrelevant to this discussion. This assumption, if accepted, leads to the almost inescapable conclusion that nature alone must be responsible for the origin and development of life on earth. [16] Darwinian evolution provides the most credible explanation—and perhaps the only credible explanation to date—for how this could have occurred in the absence of a creative God. But the Darwinian evolutionists have reached this conclusion by barring the only other credible explanation—that life originated and developed by the hand of God.

Of course, practicalities require that scientific investigation function in an atmosphere devoid of divine intervention, for such intervention is inherently unpredictable. Science can only determine what unaided nature will do, not what God will do. Yet ignoring God for some limited purposes is quite a different matter from denying or ignoring His existence altogether. [17] When scientists accuse Christians of embracing ignorance and telling lies to children, then the time has come to expose Darwinian evolution for what it is: a faith position, no different in its essentials from faith in God or faith in Jesus Christ.

With this in mind, let's consider the evidence for and against Darwinian evolution, beginning with the evidence in its favor.

Common Descent. The foundation of Darwinian evolution is the evidence for common descent. Common descent means that two species shared a common ancestor from which each descended. For instance, all reptiles are believed to have descended from a common amphibian ancestor, and birds are believed to have descended from a common reptilian ancestor. Similarly, mankind and chimpanzees are believed to have descended from a common ancestor which is now extinct. [18] The evidence for common descent is frankly overwhelming.

That evidence begins with the similarities and differences in the anatomies and characteristics of species. Biologists have observed these similarities and differences for many years, and have used them to classify species into families, orders, classes, phyla, etc.

Additional evidence comes from proteins, which are used by every form of life on Earth. Proteins are composed of amino acids. Beginning in the 1950's, scientists were able to compare the combinations of amino acids in the proteins used by each species. These comparisons demonstrate a lot of similarity between proteins of species which are thought to be closely related, and less similarity among species believed to be more distantly related.

Hemoglobin is one such protein. Hemoglobin transports oxygen within the bloodstream to all parts of the body. The amino acids of hemoglobin in humans and monkeys are identical in 141 out of 146 positions—that is, only five are different. Hemoglobin molecules in humans and horses have 17 differences; those of humans and chickens have 26 differences; and those of humans and frogs have 46 differences. [19]

DNA [20] also provides strong evidence for common descent. DNA is the genetic material that serves as the blueprint for the growth and development of an organism. In recent years, technology has enabled scientists to compare the DNA of different organisms, and the results are generally similar to that of the amino acid comparisons. As with proteins, many scientists believe that similarities in the DNA of different species demonstrate that they are descended from a common ancestor. [21]

In addition, identical *flaws* in specific DNA sequences have been found in different species, likely indicating that at some point they shared a common ancestor whose DNA contained that flaw.

Some viruses appear to leave a mark upon their host's DNA, which is then passed down to the host's descendents. If true, such marks in the genetic code of different species would seem to confirm that each species received the mark from a common ancestor who was infected by the virus.

Fossils provide some evidence to support common descent, through so-called "intermediates." These intermediates have characteristics common to different species, such as: (1) rhipidistians, which are fish with some skeletal features resembling amphibians; [22] (2) Therapsida—species with skeletal features that appear to be intermediate between reptiles and mammals; [23]

(3) Archaeopteryx, a fossil bird with teeth and claws, which are essentially reptilian features;[24] and (4) so-called "ape-men," such as Australopithecus, Homo habilis, Homo erectus, and primitive forms of Homo sapiens, like Neanderthal and Cro-Magnan man.[25]

Fossils not only provide evidence of common descent, but they also present a bigger problem for those who doubt Darwinian evolution: extinctions.

Fossils and Extinctions. Fossils reveal the existence of many creatures which are now extinct, such as dinosaurs, mammoths, and trilobites. And here, in my opinion, is where Darwinian evolutionists make their strongest case. Why have so many species gone extinct?[26] Couldn't God get it right the first time? Did He have to learn the creative process through trial and error? I do not dismiss this possibility out of hand. Life is unbelievably complex, as we will see. If God's omniscience and omnipotence are somehow diminished in our eyes because He worked out His plan for life on Earth with some experimentation, and sometimes changed His mind, then so be it. He still did it. However, perhaps God had reasons for these extinctions that He has not shared with us.

On the other hand, Christians certainly do not have a monopoly on unanswered questions in this field. In the midst of the Darwinian evolutionist's apparent triumph, he will still find himself struggling to answer many of the known facts about the fossil evidence, such as:

(1) Species in fossil records exhibit "stasis"—a lack of directional change from the time of their first appearance until their eventual extinction. In other words, fossils show that most species stay pretty much the same. Even DNA provides evidence of stasis. The common ancestor of frogs and fruit flies is said to have lived at least 535 million years ago. Yet a critical section of their DNA is so similar that it can be extracted from the fly's DNA and inserted into the frog's DNA, where it will function flawlessly. In fact, scientists have found that: "About a thousand genes are shared by every organism,

however simple or complicated." [27] Thus, these genes have not evolved, or even been modified, despite more than a billion years of change.

Many species alive today have remained essentially unchanged for millions of years. The coelacanth, a fish that lives in the waters of the western Indian Ocean, appears to be much like its ancestors 400 million years ago. The same can be said of sharks, the lungfish, and many others. [28] Seaweed is even more ancient, having been found in Chinese fossils that are more than 550 million years old.

(2) The "Cambrian Explosion," also known as "The Biological Big Bang," is a good example of the relative suddenness with which new species frequently turn up in the fossil records. Prior to the beginning of the Cambrian period, [29] fossils reveal only a few multicellular organisms. During the early Cambrian period, fossil evidence indicates that multicellular organisms are beginning to diversify—but the fossils also show that most of these are very tiny organisms. Then during the middle Cambrian, and within a period of only about five to ten million years, large numbers of complex fossilized animals appear, with widely differing body plans: mollusks, brachiopods, echinoderms, trilobites, and many other bizarre creatures. [30] Yet the fossil evidence reveals almost no trace of the evolutionary ancestors that Darwinian evolution requires.

Darwinian evolutionists counter that the fossil record is simply incomplete because the animals which fossilized did so because they had developed hard shells, whereas their evolutionary ancestors were soft-bodied creatures which did not fossilize easily. [31] However, the evolutionists' explanation simply prompts another equally perplexing question: why was there such an explosion of animals capable of fossil preservation within such a short time?

(3) Darwinian evolution postulates that organisms gradually change from one species to another, so we would expect the fossil record to be replete with many "intermediate" steps

between species. However, few have actually been found. Instead, species generally appear suddenly, fully formed, and quite distinct from anything that preceded them. [32] Bird fossils, for instance, do not show the gradual development of wings. Instead, wings suddenly appear intact on early bird species. [33] Even after decades of fossil hunting and countless recovered fossils, the potential intermediates are still the rare exception rather than the rule.

This gap in the fossil records is so striking that some scientists have devised hypotheses to explain them, including: (1) incomplete fossil records; [34] (2) "punctuated equilibrium," [35] which theorizes that most evolutionary changes occur outside the general species population—i.e., in small populations on the fringes, where fossil evidence is lacking; or (3) "saltation," a sudden, macro-evolutionary change in a single generation. (No evidence exists to support the possibility of saltation. In evolutionary terms, it amounts to a miracle.)

The Two Weaker Legs of Darwin's Three-Legged Stool. We now return to the subject of common descent—that is, that species which share certain characteristics are descended from a common ancestor.

Even if we accept the existence of common descent—and I believe the evidence in its favor is quite compelling—this does *not* prove Darwinian evolution or the absence of God's involvement in the process. God may have used the same pattern when creating similar species because following that pattern was easier or because it worked well. Or maybe He made some species similar in many of their characteristics simply because He wanted to.

Darwinian evolution postulates more than just common descent. The Darwinian evolutionary theory proposes that common descent *results from* random mutations generating beneficial changes, which natural selection then favors over time, leading to gradual improvements and advances. Thus, the Darwinian three-legged stool requires all three: common descent, random mutation, and natural selection. But scientific discoveries in more recent times have presented the Darwinian evolutionary theory with two immense difficulties: (1) life is far more complex than Darwin ever imagined, and (2) natural selection and random mutation have limitations that raise serious doubts about their ability to *construct* this remarkable complexity.

Problem #1 – The origin and incredible complexity of life

Charles Darwin published his book, *On the Origin of Species,* in 1859. In the following 100 years, many scientists in different fields came to accept the basic concept of Darwinian evolution, although they often held widely varying views of how it was supposed to have worked. In the mid-1950s Neo-Darwinism arose as an attempt to produce a consistent view of Darwinian evolution across the various branches of science. But they left one out—biochemistry, because the technology to study structures within the cell did not then exist. Now it does.

Biochemical evidence may be the biggest obstacle to the theory of Darwinian evolution to date. Darwinian evolution is based on the premise that complex organisms can gradually develop from simple organisms, through small mutational changes. Yet in recent years, biochemistry has revealed that so-called "simple" organisms such as bacteria are exceedingly complex, and that the differences between bacteria and even the simplest multicellular plants and animals are enormous.

Think of it this way. In Darwin's lifetime, and for many years thereafter, Darwinian evolution's concept of the gradual development of life on earth seemed to involve small mutational changes that were about as simple as jumping over a two-foot-wide ditch. But in more recent years, biochemistry has made that ditch much wider. The small jumps which Darwinian evolution postulates have turned out to be huge canyons. One such canyon is the mystery of how life began.

The Origin of Life. The building blocks of life are: (1) sugars, for energy; (2) fatty acids, which are essential components of cell membranes; (3) amino acids, from which proteins are constructed; and (4) nucleotides, which form DNA, the genetic code for the cell.

Proteins in living organisms are made up of combinations of twenty-three different amino acids. [36] For example, human myoglobin, a protein which stores oxygen, contains 153 amino acid molecules. At least 200,000 distinct proteins exist in the various life forms on Earth. The human body uses upwards of 50,000 different proteins.

In 1953 a young graduate student at the University of Chicago, Stanley Miller, working under the chemist Harold Urey, reported the results of an experiment that made headlines. Using a simulated pre-life earth atmosphere of methane, ammonia, hydrogen, and water vapor, a pool of water, and sparking electrodes to simulate lightning, Miller produced several kinds of amino acids—the building blocks for the proteins which are essential for life. Subsequent experiments were able to generate many of the amino acids utilized by living organisms, and Darwinian evolutionists were certain they were on the road to discovering the secret to the origin of life on earth. However, further experimentation has not only failed to solve the origin-of-life riddle, but has made the problem even more difficult to solve.

Proteins can easily be generated from amino acids, but not without special conditions, controls, and procedures of human design. When experiments seek to simulate early-earth conditions, proteins do not form. Some experiments have been able to generate "proteinoids"—molecules similar to proteins, but not true proteins—but these experiments are not generally accepted as valid in the scientific community because they utilize conditions not likely to have been present on pre-life earth. In addition, proteins do not self-replicate, so they lack the ability to reproduce like living organisms.

The complexity of the cell itself also presents tremendous difficulties for the Darwinian evolutionary theory about the origin of life. One of the simplest living organisms is the prokaryote, a single-celled organism which lacks a distinct cell nucleus. The only prokaryotes today are bacteria and blue-green algae. Cells which contain a distinct cell nucleus are called eukaryotes. The vast majority of the species which exist today—including all multi-cellular organisms, such as plants, fish, animals, and humans—are eukaryotes.

A prokaryotic cell performs all essential life functions, such as food ingestion, digestion, elimination of waste products, and reproduction. To perform these functions the prokaryotic cell contains many specialized structures, such as mitochondria, which produce a cell's energy; ribosomes for manufacturing proteins; and the Endoplasmic reticulum, to process proteins. Other cellular structures include: the Golgi apparatus, globular and helix proteins, endosomes, clathrin, secretory vesicles, and peroxisomes. [37]

When the cell was viewed as a simple, homogenous organism, it was not hard to visualize a bacterium randomly forming from organic molecules available in pre-Cambrian waters. But how does a cell with many specialized structures randomly form? Sir Fred Hoyle, a British astronomer, aptly described it "as ridiculous and improbable as the proposition that a tornado blowing through a junk yard may assemble a Boeing 747." [38]

The creation of life through nature alone seems even more improbable when we consider the complexity and fragility of DNA. The DNA for a single-celled bacterium contains "*1 million* bits of information—the equivalent of 125,000 words, or a 500-page book with 250 words of instructions on each page." [39] Human DNA is a thousand times more complex than bacteria DNA.

When an organism dies, the molecules that make up DNA soon begin to break down. For this reason, intact DNA is never found in fossils, even in those that are well-preserved in frigid or arid climates. Consider this statement from an admittedly pro-Darwin source: "Most creatures have a complex system of enzymes that repair DNA, which is such an unstable chemical that it would decay without constant help." [40] So how did the first DNA form on its own if its nature is to break apart?

Richard Dawkins, a noted Darwinian evolutionist, author, and atheist, concedes that "we know little more than Darwin did" about the origin of life, and admits that it may be a mystery mankind will never solve because it may be an event we can never replicate. [41]

The Development of Life. The questions for Darwinian evolution do not end with how life originated. Darwinian evolution relies heavily on the vast amounts of time available for life to evolve. As George Wald, a biologist, said: "Given so much time the 'impossible' becomes possible, the possible probable and the probable virtually certain." [42] But has there been *enough* time? Professor Arne A. Wyller, [43] author of *The Planetary Mind,* says no. Here's why.

A prokaryotic cell contains about one-hundred million atoms. A eukaryotic cell, by contrast, is ten to one-hundred times larger, and contains a cell nucleus which houses the cell's DNA. [44] After the appearance of the first prokaryote 3.8 billion years ago, more than two billion years passed before the first eukaryotic cell emerged about 1.4 billion years ago. The amoeba, a typical single-cell eukaryote, contains a variety of organelles which perform specialized functions within the cell. If nature needed more than two billion years to produce the "simple" complexity of an amoeba-like organism, [45] how did nature manufacture between 200 million and two billion multicellular species in only about one-third of that time? [46]

The development of multicellular life forms required more sophistication than simply using proteins [47] to join individual single-celled organisms. In multicellular creatures cells perform different functions: "Even the simplest of multicellular forms are made up of several different kinds of cells, whereas the most complex ones may harbor as many as 200 different types of cells." [48] Not surprisingly, this means that the individual cells are interdependent—that is, they cannot live apart from the whole. And when creatures began reproducing sexually, about 1.1 billion years ago, cell specialization took another giant leap forward.

Yet even bigger problems remain for the Darwinian evolutionist. The development of life on earth at times seems to move at breathtaking speed compared to the two billion years required to construct the first eukaryote. About one-hundred million years ago a wide variety of flowering plants appeared—not gradually, as Darwinian evolution would postulate, but with such rapidity that paleobiologists refer to it as "explosive radiation." [49]

The first amphibian, the lungfish, developed lungs and limbs for crawling on land about 350 million years ago, only fifty million years after the first jawed fish. Reptiles arrived about seventy million years later, fully able to live and reproduce on land because of their watertight skin and hard-shelled egg. The first mammal appeared about eighty million years after the first reptile, with at least two fantastic innovations: a warm-blooded metabolism that allowed it to live in colder climates and hunt for food at night, and the amazing placenta that nourishes the developing young in the warmth and relative safety of their mother's body.

And then there is Hawaii. The oldest of the major Hawaiian islands, Kauai, is only five million years old, while the youngest—Hawaii, also known as "The Big Island"—is about one-tenth that old. Yet the islands have a wide variety of plant life that is found nowhere else on the planet—eighty such species on the

Big Island alone. The Hawaiian Islands are also home to more than 500 species of flies, and more than 1,000 species of snails, that exist only on those islands. How has this diversity evolved in such a relatively short amount of time? [50]

Professor Wyller does not believe that Darwinian evolution can adequately explain this seeming acceleration in the development of life:

> Every new turn of evolutionary breakthroughs is more and more complex and occurs in a shorter and shorter time span. When we take this fact into account, the outlandishness of the chance hypothesis becomes more and more flagrant and improbable. [51]

The Development of Human Intelligence. The most remarkable development of all, except perhaps life itself, is the incredible human brain. The modern human brain contains more than one-hundred billion nerve cells, compared with 7,000 in bees and a few hundred million in most mammals. The nerve cells of the human brain communicate with each other and with the rest of the body through both electrical and chemical means, the latter through the use of more than fifty varieties of neurotransmitter molecules.

This extraordinary organ has developed with unbelievable speed compared to most evolutionary changes. Modern man's brain is three times the size of that of *Australopithecus,* who first appeared only four million years ago. *Homo habilis,* which dates from about two million years ago, had a brain slightly less than half the size of modern man. [52] Beginning about 500,000 years ago, human brains grew "at an extraordinary rate, until 100,000 years ago when they reached their present size." [53]

Such rapid development seems astonishing enough by itself. But the problem is compounded by the effects of population growth. Until about 10,000 years ago, "[mankind's] total numbers do not appear to have exceeded a few thousand at any one time." [54] Are we then to believe that Darwinian evolution, operating on only a few thousand individuals at a time, over the course of only a few million years, [55] manufactured the most sophisticated organ possessed by any living creature? Professor Wyller is understandably skeptical:

> Now that we have examined the brain, with its culmination in the development of the human brain over only 2 million to 3 million years, we see the Darwinian paradigm face its most formidable challenge: accounting for the appearance of human intelligence by a pitiful few throws of the dice. [56]

Consider also that a few million years is far less time for human evolution than for most other species because we reproduce so infrequently. A human generation is measured in years, not days or months, since human children require many years to reach puberty. [57]

Problem #2 – The evidence raises serious doubts about whether random mutations and natural selection are capable of creating such complexity.

Mutations. Mutations may be severely limited in their ability to construct the complexity that life exhibits. To fully understand why, we need to discuss what a mutation is and how it happens. It begins with proteins.

Proteins are used by all forms of life, for a wide variety of purposes. The human body builds and uses proteins such as collagen for skin and connective tissue, rhodopsin to act as the photo-receptor in the eye, hemoglobin to transport oxygen, enzymes to build or break down chemicals the body needs, etc. Some proteins even act as switches to activate or deactivate processes like blood-clotting.

All of these amazing proteins are built using various combinations of amino acid molecules. Those molecules have different properties that are critical to constructing proteins. For example, some amino acids are oily and therefore try to avoid water, while others are attracted to water; some are negatively charged and some are positively charged. When amino acids are combined into a single protein, their different properties cause the protein to fold into a distinctive shape that enables it to carry out a particular function in the cell. Human hemoglobin, for instance, consists of four protein chains that fold into a pyramid shape, which enables it to bind to four oxygen molecules at a time.

DNA contains the blueprint for building proteins. For our purposes, the critical components of DNA are its four nucleotides: adenine (A), cytosine (C), guanine (G), and thymine (T). A combination of three of these nucleotides will code for a specific amino acid, just as a combination of 1s and 0s tells your computer which letter to print. The sequence of the nucleotides in the DNA determines which amino acids are produced and in what order—and this in turn controls what protein is built.

DNA is organized into genes, each of which codes for a different protein, and the genes are organized into chromosomes. The human genome—the complete set of all human genes—contains about three billion nucleotides. A mutation usually refers to a change in only *one* of those nucleotides, although mutations can also result in a duplication or rearrangement of a gene or even a chromosome.

Not all of these nucleotides are created equal. Some enable cells to manufacture the amino acids needed to produce proteins. [58] Others comprise genes that control other genes, by turning them on or off as needed. And the vast majority of nucleotides in the human genome are part of DNA that performs neither of these functions. Such DNA is called "noncoding DNA." [59]

In humans, only about one-hundred million nucleotides are in areas of the genome that are critical to the functioning of the cells. So when random mutations occur, only a relatively small percentage are likely to be in this critical area of the genome—and those mutations will probably be detrimental.

A Mathematical Problem for Mutations. Darwinian evolution postulates that random mutations are the architects of new proteins, new organs, and new structures in an organism. In the real world, however, most mutations are harmful—a fact that even the most ardent Darwinian evolutionists concede. In other words, most mutations do not enhance the functioning of a protein, but diminish its effectiveness.

So while natural selection can favor a helpful mutation, its primary function appears to be to eliminate harmful mutations.

In addition, because natural selection is driven by functionality rather than intelligence, it will frequently favor a mutation which is not truly advantageous, but is merely the lesser of two evils. A case in point is the ongoing battle between humans and *Plasmodium falciparum*—commonly known as malaria.

Malaria bacteria invade healthy red blood cells and feed on their hemoglobin. If the body's hemoglobin is sufficiently depleted, the person dies. The human body combats malaria through mutations that alter some or all of the body's red blood cells. These mutations act in one of two ways: they either inhibit malaria's ability to enter the red blood cells, or they help the body recognize the invaded cells more quickly so that they can be eliminated before the infection spreads. Such mutations include the well-known sickle cell trait, thalassemia, and others. [60]

Since the immune system is primarily responsible for defending the body against disease, the most constructive mutation would seem to be one that enhances the immune system to combat malaria. But none of these mutations do that. Instead, they combat malaria by altering the body's red blood cells. And each mutation is harmful in the sense that the altered cells do not operate as efficiently as they otherwise would. Aside from the protection these mutations provide against malaria, all are essentially harmful. [61] Natural selection favors them only because the alternative is worse.

Malaria also mutates, and because it reproduces so quickly and in enormous numbers, it has been able to defeat every drug mankind has sent against it. Yet these mutations appear to be destructive as well. The mutation that enabled malaria to acquire resistance to the drugs quinine and chloroquine disappears when the drugs are no longer used. This demonstrates that it is not really an improvement, because natural selection eliminates it when the drugs are not present.

Malaria exists only in the tropics because it has never been able to generate a mutation that would enable it to survive in cold weather. Nor has it been able to generate a mutation that could overcome the defenses the human body has erected against it. Such constructive mutations appear to be beyond the ability of nature to create.

The human immunodeficiency virus (HIV) and the bacteria *Escherichia coli* (*E. coli*) do the same. Just like malaria, HIV and *E. coli* combat threats to their survival, such as new drugs, through mutations that damage the normal functioning of the organism, but which nevertheless enable it to survive.

Michael J. Behe is a biochemist and a Professor of Biological Sciences at Lehigh University. In his book, *The Edge of Evolution: The Search for the Limits of Darwinism*, Professor Behe suggests that the reason for this apparent inability of random mutations to create truly constructive changes rests in the principles of mathematical probability. To understand his argument, we must delve even deeper into the world of proteins.

Most proteins consist of a large number of amino acid molecules. Human hemoglobin has 574 of them. A mutational change to a single nucleotide can easily damage or destroy the functioning of a protein by altering a critical amino acid within it. This is how parasitic organisms like malaria and HIV are able to defeat drugs, and how the human body has been able to combat malaria effectively. In each case, the specific protein exploited by the parasite or the drug is modified and thereby rendered invulnerable. The resulting protein doesn't function as well, but its benefits for survival outweigh its reduced efficiency.

On the other hand, a mutational change that will generate a new beneficial protein will almost certainly require *simultaneous* alterations of multiple nucleotides in the same gene. Professor Behe believes that this creates a mathematical roadblock, because such simultaneous mutations are so unlikely as to be virtually impossible.

But perhaps the mutations don't have to occur simultaneously. Suppose they could occur innocuously at their own pace and eventually come together to create new, functional proteins. Many Darwinian evolutionists have now embraced that theory—that is, that constructive mutations occur in the noncoding DNA, the section of DNA which appears to serve no functional purpose. Mutations of the nucleotides in this area do not generally harm the functioning of the organism, and therefore can exist and accumulate without being automatically eliminated by natural selection.

Yet what are the odds that these random mutations will actually be able to generate a functional protein of meaningful complexity? Douglas Axe, Ph.D., an engineer with the Medical Research Council Centre at Cambridge, computed the odds of random mutations generating a functional protein composed of only 150 amino acids, and came up with the figure of one in 10^{77}. That is a one followed by seventy-seven zeroes. [62] You would have a better chance of winning the Powerball lottery *five times in a row*. [63]

Perhaps because of these mathematical odds, some Darwinian evolutionists no longer believe that significant changes in organisms result from entirely random mutations. Instead, they are focusing on other possibilities, such as mutations in so-called master genes—that is, genes that control and affect other genes—and genes that may be susceptible to numerous and frequent mutations. But whether such mutations can actually generate the changes Darwinian evolution requires is still open to serious doubt.

If random mutations are somewhat hamstrung in their ability to achieve Darwin's evolutionary aspirations, the third leg of the three-legged stool, natural selection, may be even more limited.

The limits of natural selection. Each creature's characteristics are determined by its genetic material—i.e., its DNA. When a creature is able to survive and reproduce, part of its genetic material is passed down to its offspring and is thus preserved. [64] If an organism possesses a characteristic, or a combination of characteristics, which gives it a better chance of surviving and reproducing, then that organism is well positioned to transmit those characteristics to succeeding generations. Similarly, characteristics which *decrease* an organism's chances of surviving and reproducing tend to be eliminated. Thus, advantageous characteristics are preserved and spread throughout later generations. This is natural selection.

Natural selection results in changes *within species,* when variations in characteristics such as coloration or size are favored or disfavored by the surrounding environment. From this, Darwin deduced that natural selection, in combination with random mutational changes accumulated over time, would also cause new species to arise. He then concluded that this process would ultimately result in the wide variety and incredible complexity of the forms of life that exist today.

However, Darwin's theory may expect too much of natural selection, for it has some significant limitations. For one thing, natural selection is blind. It is not intelligent and cannot plan for the future. So natural selection will only favor characteristics which promote survival *now.* As we will see, this is an important limitation, because a mutational change that could be useful in the future, but is not immediately helpful, is unlikely to be preserved.

And if such a change is actually detrimental, natural selection will simply eliminate it.

Also, natural selection can only favor or disfavor characteristics which already exist. It cannot *create* new characteristics. In Darwinian theory, creating new characteristics is primarily the job of random mutations, and that task turns out to be quite formidable, as we have seen.

Another limitation of natural selection is that the changes it favors are often not permanent. Thus, while the characteristics of species do change in response to the environment, when circumstances reverse themselves so do the favored characteristics. In England the dark-colored European Peppered moths became much more plentiful during the Industrial Revolution when factory soot helped camouflage them. But when government regulations cleaned up the environment, the lighter moths again became dominant.

How Does Perfection Evolve? I also believe many proponents of Darwinian evolution exaggerate and oversimplify the impact of natural selection. One aspect of this oversimplification is their focus on single characteristics. But that's not how the real world works.

In the real world, organisms have many characteristics, and natural selection does not so much favor a single characteristic as it favors an *organism*. Natural selection is like a voter who must choose between political candidates. Just as each candidate will have some positions the voter likes, others he dislikes, and some he doesn't care about, an organism will possess some characteristics that are beneficial for survival, others which are potentially detrimental, and some which are essentially neutral.

If the organism survives and prospers, all of its characteristics will be passed on to its descendants—the bad with the good. Natural selection cannot choose certain traits to preserve, while eliminating others, any more than a voter can vote for specific policy positions rather than the candidate as a whole.

Unlike a human animal breeder, natural selection lacks the intelligence to promote and preserve beneficial traits while weeding out flaws. While we can easily see how breeding can result in continuous improvements in a species, natural selection doesn't breed. It simply weeds. So we would not expect natural selection to achieve perfection, or anything approaching it. Yet that is exactly what we so often see in nature.

In Chapter 5 of their book, *What Darwin Got Wrong,* Professors Jerry Fodor and Massimo Piattelli-Palmarini [65]—who are confirmed Darwinian evolutionists, by the way—cite numerous cases of "nature" achieving perfection, or near perfection, in the characteristics of organisms.

One example is the diameter of capillaries in vertebrates, which achieves the most efficient balance between "the maximization of the inner and outer exchange surfaces, while minimizing distances of internal transport." [66] Similarly, the fractal-like structure of the circulatory system is seen in many other contexts—lungs, gills, leaves, kidneys, etc.—because it is simply so efficient. Brains, nervous systems, and methods of locomotion are not merely functional, but seem to have achieved maximum functionality when balanced against the cost to the organism.

Creatures display such perfection not only in their characteristics, but in their behavior. When honey bees search for food, some go out as scouts to look for suitable locations, while others remain in the hive to exploit information the scouts bring back. When scientists analyzed the optimal ratio of scouts to exploiters under various circumstances, they found that honey bees are consistently at or near those optimal levels.

Or consider the behavior of *Ampulex compressa,* which is a type of wasp. It deposits its eggs in a cockroach, which the wasp guides to its prepared nest. To accomplish this, the wasp must inflict two stings on the much larger cockroach, at different times and in different locations on the roach's body. The first sting temporarily paralyzes it, and the second seemingly enthralls it, enabling the wasp to guide the roach to the nest, where it will become the first meal for the baby wasps.

How these ideal characteristics and complex behaviors naturally "evolve" is a mystery. After all, natural selection is not intelligent. It cannot choose the "best" trait, for it cannot *choose* anything. But we can't even say that natural selection *favors* a particular trait. What it actually does is favor the most advantageous *combination of traits* for the environment in which an organism operates. Many scientists seem to gloss over these difficulties by oversimplifying how natural selection works in the real world.

And the oversimplification of natural selection does not stop there.

Would Natural Selection Truly Favor Wings? We can easily see how flight confers a tremendous advantage on birds, insects, and bats. Wings enable them to escape enemies and find food, and therefore reproduce in greater abundance than their flightless competitors. But virtually all Darwinian evolutionists will concede that wings had to develop gradually, and that flight was not possible until late in their development.

Yet early "wings" that were useless for flight would not seem to confer any reproductive advantage. In addition, wings do not enable birds to fly unless accompanied by changes such as greatly reduced body weight—which birds achieve through hollow bone structure and loss of teeth—and bipedalism that frees the "arms" to act as wings. Stubby "wings" without these other modifications could easily be an evolutionary *disadvantage*, and thus would be eliminated by natural selection long before actual wings could develop.

Even if primitive "wings" provided some trivial evolutionary advantage, that would not ensure survival. Any mutation might easily be extinguished in its infancy if its bearer succumbs to an early death as a result of disease, accident, predators, the presence of a harmful mutation, or a variety of other calamities. But a mutation that confers only a slight advantage would be especially vulnerable since it contributes so little to the organism's chances of survival.

Thus, many mutations which might be potential enhancements will not survive, either because they are not beneficial—or not beneficial enough—or because their recipient is simply unlucky.

Consider a soldier in an army who acquires a better weapon. If all around him are fighting with swords and he obtains a gun, his chances of survival are greatly enhanced. But what if his "better" weapon is merely a slightly sharper sword? Will this improve his chances of survival significantly? Some Darwinian evolutionists seem to treat every beneficial mutation as if it were a gun in a sword fight.

The problem of irreducible complexity. Natural selection runs into an even bigger problem when we consider what Professor Behe calls "irreducible complexity."

In his book, *Darwin's Black Box: The Biochemical Challenge to Evolution*, Professor Behe points out that any mutational change in an organism must have "minimal function" in order for natural selection to favor it. In other words, the modified biological system must be able to satisfactorily perform the task required of it, or the system will fail to promote survival of the organism.

For example, if a mutational change comes up with a sophisticated new blood-clotting protein *that doesn't work*, the animal will bleed to death, will not reproduce, and the mutational change will die out. It does no good to argue that in another 1,000 generations, after further mutational changes and the generation of other new proteins, this protein will actually result in an improvement to the organism. The mutational change will die out long before it can become beneficial. Natural selection will not favor any change which does not *immediately* contribute to survival.

The need for *minimal function* becomes a problem for Darwinian evolution because of "irreducible complexity," a term coined by Professor Behe, by which he means: "a single system composed of several well-matched, interacting parts that contribute to the basic function, wherein the removal of any one of the parts causes the system to effectively cease functioning." [67] All necessary parts of an irreducibly complex system must come into existence at once, because if any of those essential components is missing, the whole will not perform its required function. And if the system lacks minimal function, natural selection will not favor it.

The gradual development of an irreducibly complex system through incremental steps is problematic for Darwinian evolution. If I need four proteins to produce an effective blood clotting system, the mutational development of any one of those proteins without the other three will not work. The animal still bleeds to death. Darwinian evolution needs all four, and it needs all four to "evolve" at the same time.

But as we have seen, even a single beneficial new protein is difficult for Darwinian evolution to achieve. Development of four at once would not be Darwinian evolution—it would be a miracle. For this reason, any irreducibly complex biological system poses serious problems for the Darwinian evolutionist. So are there any irreducibly complex biological systems? In fact, there are many. One example is the cilium.

The Cilium. The cilium is a hair-like projection from a cell which is used for locomotion or for moving liquids over the cell. In simple terms, the cilium is composed of three parts: (1) eleven cylindrical, parallel microtubules made from a protein called "tubulin"; (2) several other proteins which bind the microtubules together; and (3) a "motor protein," called "dynein." Without any one of these three components, the cilium will not function. The microtubules form the structure of the cilium. The binding proteins keep the microtubules together as a whole, creating the cilium's back-and-forth movement when the microtubules are excited. The motor protein makes the whole structure move. If only one of these components were produced through Darwinian evolution, natural selection would not favor it because it lacks minimal function—one of these components is useless without the other two.

The actual construction of the cilium also demonstrates irreducible complexity. The cilium is built by many different proteins working together, including: (1) proteins which form the structure of the cilium; (2) the intraflagellar transport (IFT) particle, which seizes the structural proteins and releases them at the proper location; (3) kinesin-II, which carries the IFT particles toward the tip of the cilium, (4) dynein, which carries the IFT particles back from the tip of the cilium; and (5) transition fibers, which screen out unnecessary materials from the construction area. The lack of any of these proteins will sabotage the construction of the cilium.

But the problems get even worse for the Darwinian evolutionists. The cilium actually contains more than 200 different kinds of proteins. And the simplest independent life form we know of—the bacteria—has a kind of rotary propeller that it uses for locomotion (called a "flagellum") that is even more complex than the cilium.

Blood clotting. The seemingly simple process of blood clotting actually involves many different proteins, which are triggered one after another, in a cascade of protein activation. This complex system ensures that blood clots are triggered only when needed, and only to the extent they are needed. [68]

The last four proteins in the cascade—fibrinogen, thrombin, Stuart factor, and accelerin—form an irreducibly complex system. Without fibrinogen, thrombin, or Stuart factor, no clot is formed, and without accelerin the clot forms much too slowly and the animal bleeds to death. None of these proteins perform any function outside of blood clotting, so a mutation that generated one, two, or even three of the proteins would not provide minimal function, and would thus be eliminated by natural selection. But a combination of mutations that created all four proteins in a single generation would be unexplainable in terms of Darwinian evolution alone. As we have seen, the creation of four new proteins by random mutation would be so mathematically improbable as to be virtually impossible.

By the way, the entire system gets even more complicated when you consider the many proteins which are involved in stopping the blood clotting process, hardening the clot, and gradually re-moving the clot.

If you want to read a more detailed explanation of these irreducible complexities, as well as examples of others, I recommend Mr. Behe's books, *Darwin's Black Box: The Biochemical Challenge to Evolution* and *The Edge of Evolution: The Search for the Limits of Darwinism.*

The Darwinian Evolutionists' Response. I will not pretend that most Darwinian evolutionists accept these criticisms as valid. They do not. Mr. H. Allen Orr, a strong critic of Mr. Behe's books, concedes the existence of irreducible complexity, but argues that these biochemical systems gradually evolved from simpler systems, just as a heart or a lung supposedly evolved from more primitive organs, and that what we have now is merely the irreducibly complex *end result* of that evolution.

Darwinian evolutionists contend that the proteins involved in blood clotting evolved from proteins which served other functions prior to their adaptation. The evolutionists point to organisms whose more primitive blood-clotting mechanism functions in the absence of one or more of these proteins.

Indeed, Darwinian evolutionists have suggested possibilities for the development of many irreducible complexities. The evolutionists can certainly tell us how such complexities *might* have evolved, but that is quite different from proving what *actually* happened. The scientists are simply making an educated guess. This is no doubt a valid exercise, especially if God is left out of the picture, but educated guesses are not facts.

Mr. Orr concedes that "we have no guarantee that we can reconstruct the history of a biochemical pathway." [69] That is not surprising, since reconstruction of past events can be exceedingly difficult or impossible, especially in the absence of eyewitnesses. But that is my point. If Darwinian evolutionists cannot prove that irreducible complexity occurred through unaided nature, then their explanation must be taken on faith.

And therein lies the problem with the Darwinian evolutionists' reply to Mr. Behe—indeed, the problem with many of their arguments. They ask us to put our faith in science, while they denounce the most credible alternative explanation for the facts—God—because it is based on faith.

Did You Know We Are Playing a Game? Mr. Douglas J. Futuyma, another scientist who is critical of Mr. Behe, points out that irreducible complexity is everywhere, and then uses this as a reason to denounce Mr. Behe's position:

> . . . these are but a tiny fraction of the "irreducibly complex" molecular adaptations to be found among vertebrates, insects, plants, and other forms of life. Behe, then, must be forced to see the designer's handiwork everywhere. Life must present him with countless instances of supernatural intervention—of miracles.
>
> *When scientists invoke miracles, they cease to practice science.* Were a geologist to cite plate tectonics, a chemist hydrogen bonds, or a physicist gravity as an instance of the miraculous, he or she would be laughed out of the profession. Moreover, they would not be doing their job, which is to seek answers by posing and testing explanatory hypotheses. [70]

Mr. Futuyma's argument is flawed because plate tectonics, hydrogen bonds, and gravity are present realities, which can be studied, tested, and verified in real time. The origin and development of life are in the past. We cannot test and verify the Darwinian evolutionists' explanations for these events without a time machine. On what grounds then do we accept one untestable and unverifiable explanation (Darwinian evolution) and reject the other (God)? This is the heart of the matter, and one scientist frankly explains it as a game:

> Science, fundamentally, is a game. It is a game with one overriding and defining rule:
>
> > Rule No. 1: Let us see how far and to what extent we can explain the behavior of the physical and material universe in terms of purely physical and material causes, without invoking the supernatural.
>
> Operational science takes no position about the existence or non-existence of the supernatural; it only requires that this factor is not to be invoked in scientific explanations. Calling down special-purpose miracles as explanations constitutes a form of intellectual "cheating." [71]

If this is a game, then Darwinian evolutionists have stacked the deck. Before the game begins, they rule God out-of-bounds. The only acceptable explanation for the origin and development of life becomes the "scientific" one.

Now this is fine if the rules of the game are known by everyone and carefully explained up front—indeed, if everyone is told we are playing this "game." But we must never disguise or mistake this game as a search for Truth. Nor should anyone denounce as ignorant or dishonest those who don't wish to play.

Conclusion. Professors Fodor and Piattelli-Palmarini astutely point out that Darwinian evolutionary theory has much more in common with history than science. When we look back at human history, archeology and scholarship can often tell us *what* happened, but determining the *how* and *why* are frequently problematic, especially in the absence of reliable eyewitness accounts.

And so it is with Darwinian evolution. Science has been able to tell us a lot about what happened in the past: organisms that came into being, organisms that went extinct, and even what those organisms probably looked like. But determining how life originated and developed is a much tougher question. And unlike human history, we don't have any eyewitnesses or recorded history to help us.

Just to be clear, I see no conflict between Christianity and many commonly accepted scientific beliefs, like the idea that the Earth is billions of years old. I can even accept the possibility of species evolution—i.e., that God allows some new species to be formed through entirely natural means. [72] And I have no problem with scientists who say that life could have originated and developed through nature alone. But when they assert that life *must* have originated and developed through nature alone, they go well beyond what the facts will support.

Of course, we must never confuse Darwinian evolution with Truth. Indeed, many scientists, like Professor Wyller and Professor Behe, have concluded that Darwinian evolution alone is an inadequate explanation for life's complexities, and that the answers must lie elsewhere. Some scientists have conjectured that matter is somehow able to self-organize itself and thereby catalyze the development of life. Others, like Professor Wyller and Professor Behe, believe that this development is being assisted by some type of intelligence. Professor Wyller attributes this intelligence to an impersonal "Mind Field," [73] whereas Professor Behe believes that this intelligence is God.

So why do some adherents of Darwinian evolution speak as if they possess a monopoly on truth on this subject? Perhaps many reasons could be given, but I believe it all boils down to this: Darwinian evolution has become their philosophy, their paradigm, or even their religion. Scientists holding this position ignore, ridicule, or summarily reject those who believe otherwise. Professor Wyller correctly identifies this as faith, no different in its fundamentals than religious faith: "the past and present states of evolutionary theory bear much more resemblance to religious faith than to hard-nosed natural science." [74]

I believe God is responsible for the origin of life, and that we must attribute most, and perhaps all, species creation to Him. Certainly the uniqueness of mankind—our emotions, our intellect, our reason, our spirit—is God's handiwork. As Genesis says, He created us in His image. [75]

Fundamentally, the choice between Christianity and Darwinian evolution is *not* a choice between faith and science. This is really a choice between two different faiths: faith that science will one day provide all the answers versus faith that there are some answers only God can provide. I choose the latter, because I find the Biblical claim that God created life to be far more credible than Darwinian evolution.

Endnotes for Chapter Ten, "Does Evolution Disprove Christianity?"

[1] The simplest definition of "species" is based on reproductive ability—i.e., members of the same species are capable of mating with each other and producing young that can also reproduce. If a male and female cannot successfully mate in this way, they are members of different species. Of course, this definition is only useful for species that reproduce sexually. However, most of the Earth's living organisms do reproduce in this way.

[2] For example: "Almost all biologists agree that life originated spontaneously by natural processes on our planet from the same chemicals of which living organisms consist today, such as carbon, nitrogen, oxygen, and hydrogen." Ayala, *Am I a Monkey?*, 61.

[3] For example, see the articles, "Young Earth Creationism" and "Don't Call Us Young-earth Creationists . . . ," cited in the bibliography.

[4] See also Acts 2:17; 1 Peter 1:20, 4:7; and 1 John 2:18.

[5] The Bible does not actually say that Moses wrote Genesis, or any of first five books of the Bible. It does say that he wrote down the laws which he received from God (Exodus 24:3-4 and Deuteronomy 31:9, 31:24-26), and that he *spoke* the words which became the book of Deuteronomy (Deuteronomy 1:1).

[6] Moses died before the Israelites entered Canaan. See Deuteronomy 34:1-6. See also, Numbers 27:12-23, and Deuteronomy 3:21-29 and 4:21-22.

[7] Sometimes careful observation is all we have, such as when biologists are studying animals in their native habitat, or when geologists are studying rock formations.

[8] National Academy of Sciences, 1998, *Teaching About Evolution and the Nature of Science,* Washington, D.C.: National Academy Press, p. 7, as quoted in Scott, *Evolution vs. Creationism,* p. 14.

[9] Scott, *Evolution vs. Creationism,* p. 238.

[10] Berry and Hallam, *Encyclopedia of Animal Evolution,* Preface.

[11] Dawkins, *Greatest Show on Earth,* p. 10.

[12] Jones, *Darwin's Ghost*,p. 2.

[13] Orr, "Darwin v. Intelligent Design (Again)."

[14] A related assumption is that the existence of common descent proves Darwinian evolution. Francisco J. Ayala refers to "the fact of evolution, that is, that organisms are related by common descent. . . ." Ayala, *Am I a Monkey?*, p. 20. Professor Ayala does not address the possibility that common descent could result from the actions of a Creator rather than from natural causes.

[15] Scientists estimate that Earth is about four-and-a-half to five billion years old.

[16] Another alternative is that life was introduced by an alien species from another world. But this creates a chicken-and-egg problem of where and how those aliens originated.

[17] I do not mean to imply by this that all Darwinian evolutionists are atheists, or that none believe in God. I'm sure that neither is true.

[18] The common ancestor of humans and chimpanzees lived at least five million years ago, and perhaps six to seven million years ago. Zimmer, *Evolution*, 329; Ayala, *Am I a Monkey?*, p. 3.

[19] Some scientists believe that a correlation may exist between the number of differences in some proteins and the amount of time since the two species are believed to have shared a common ancestor. This presumed correlation led to the "molecular clock theory"—i.e., that such a correlation is caused by proteins accumulating mutations at a steady rate over time.

[20] DNA stands for deoxyribonucleic acid. In the vast majority of organisms, DNA contains the genetic material for the organism.

[21] For example, the DNA of humans and chimpanzees differs by only one to four percent (1% - 4%), depending on how such differences are measured. In other words, human DNA and chimp DNA are identical in 96% to 99% of their genes.

[22] For example, Tiktaalik is a fish whose fossilized remains were recently found in northern Canada. Tiktaalik had primitive lungs and a skeleton sturdy enough to allow this fish to move around on land and in very shallow water. Other rhipidistians include *Eusthenopteron*, *Panderichthys*, *Acanthostega*, and *Ichthyostega*.

[23] However, mammals may not have actually descended from reptiles. Both may have developed from a common ancestor.

[24] Archaeopteryx lived about 165 million years ago. A possible intermediate between Archaeopteryx and modern birds is Unenlagia, which lived about ninety million years ago. Unenlagia was featherless and probably flightless, but had a shoulder joint like that of a modern bird's wing. A small dinosaur with a feathered tail, but no wings, has also been found. However, birds as we know them—with feathers and wings capable of flight—appear suddenly about sixty-five million years ago, around the time dinosaurs became extinct.

[25] Genesis talks of the creation of man in both Chapters One and Two. In Genesis 1:26-27, God makes man in His own image. Some have misinterpreted these verses to mean that God created man in His *physical* image. This cannot be correct, since God is Sprit and we are flesh. Instead, we are created in God's *spiritual* image, with the capacity to think, to make moral choices, and to love. Most importantly, we can choose whether or not to surrender ourselves to God, as He asks us to.

In Genesis 2:7, God breathes into man the breath of life and man "became a living being." The Hebrew word for "being" is *nephesh,* which literally means, "soul." Adam was different from Australopithecus, Neanderthal, and all other ape-men in that he was no longer just an animal. Adam was a spiritual being like God, with an eternal soul. And so are all of his descendants.

[26] According to scientists, at least five major mass extinctions—in which more than fifty percent of the then-living species became extinct—have occurred in Earth's history: (1) at the end of the Ordovician Period, about 440 million years ago; (2) at the end of the Devonian Period, about 370 million years ago; (3) at the end of the Permian Period, about 240 million years ago; (4) at the end of the Triassic Period, about 210 million years ago; and (5) at the end of the Cretaceous Period, about sixty-five million years ago. The species currently on Earth may represent only one percent of the species that have existed since life began—the other ninety-nine percent are extinct.

[27] Jones, *Darwin's Ghost*, p. 284

[28] Other examples of these "living fossils" include: platypus, horseshoe crab, fairy shrimp, giant tortoise, Ryukyu rabbit, lampshell, chambered nautilus, latimeria, neoceratodus, diverse damselfly, okapi, onychophoran, ginkgo, araucaria, equisetum, cycas, metasequoia, pika, and *Parnassius* butterfly.

[29] The beginning of the Cambrian period is roughly between 545 million years ago and 600 million years ago, depending on the source consulted. The Cambrian period ended about 500 million years ago.

[30] Stephen C. Meyer, author of *Darwin's Doubt,* points out that these creatures probably required more than fifty (50) different types of cells—a staggering jump in complexity over single-celled organisms which had only one type of cell, or even the primitive multicellular creatures such as sponges which utilized only about ten different types of cells. Such complexity required more than 100 times as much genetic information in these organisms' DNA, compared to that of single-celled organisms. Meyer, *Darwin's Doubt,* p. 163.

[31] On the other hand, fossilized bacteria and plants from a much earlier time have been found, so soft-bodied creatures were certainly capable of becoming fossilized.

[32] Steve Jones, the author of *Darwin's Ghost,* a decidedly pro-Darwin work, admits:

> The fossil record—in defiance of Darwin's whole idea of gradual change—often makes great leaps from one form to the next. Far from the display of intermediates to be expected from slow advance through natural selection, many species appear without warning, persist in fixed form, and disappear, leaving no descendants. Geology assuredly does not reveal any finely graduated organic chain, and this is the most obvious and gravest objection which can be urged against the theory of evolution.

Jones, *Darwin's Ghost,* p. 191

[33] The same can be said of bats, as well as the change of whales from land to sea creatures.

[34] Dedicated Darwinian evolutionists rightly point out that most individuals do not become fossils because conditions were not suitable at the time of their demise, that many fossils are lost or destroyed by erosion or

other geological changes after the fossils are deposited, and that many more fossils have not been found because they are in locations which are not easily accessible. Yet despite these problems, a great many fossils have been preserved and discovered.

[35] In simplest terms, punctuated equilibrium refers to long periods of stasis (equilibrium) with little or no evolutionary changes, which are interrupted (punctuated) by shorter periods of rapid evolutionary change. According to the theory, equilibrium occurs in a species' mainstream population group, where favorable mutations are diluted or extinguished by sheer numbers. Rapid evolutionary changes occur in smaller population groups—cut off by geographic separation from the mainstream group—where favorable mutations can spread quickly.

[36] There are twenty "standard" amino acids, which are produced by genes in DNA. They are: alanine, arginine, asparagine, aspartic acid, cysteine, glutamic acid, glutamine, glycine, histidine, isoleucine, leucine, lysine, methionine, phenylalanine, proline, serine, threonine, tryptophan, tyrosine, and valine. The three "non-standard" amino acids are: selenocysteine, pyrrolysine, and *N*-formylmethionine.

[37] The **Golgi apparatus** stores proteins until they are ready to be used elsewhere in the cell. **Globular and helix proteins** play a central role in passing nutrients and waste products through the cell membrane. **Endosomes** store nutrients. **Clathrin**, a protein composed of more than a thousand amino acids, transports nutrients within the cell. **Secretory vesicles** store materials which are to be expelled from the cell. **Peroxisomes** metabolize fats. This is far from a complete list of cellular structures.

[38] Berry and Hallam, *Encyclopedia of Animal Evolution,* p. 142

[39] Wyller, *The Planetary Mind,* p. 47.

[40] See Jones, *Darwin's Ghost,* p. 113.

[41] Dawkins, *The Greatest Show on Earth,* pp. 416-422. Dawkins rejects the idea that proteins are the key to solving this quandary, since they are not self-replicating. Instead, Dawkins places his hope in the "RNA World theory"—that life originated through the spontaneous formation of RNA—an idea which he finds "plausible." *Ibid.,* pp. 420-421. RNA is ribonucleic acid, which carries the genetic information in some viruses and also plays a key role in manufacturing proteins in all living cells.

[42] Wyller, *The Planetary Mind*, pp. 63 and 159-160, quoting *The Centre of Life*, by L. L. Cudmore (Quadrangle New York Times Book Co., New York, 1977), p. 138.

[43] Professor Wyller received a Ph.D. in Astronomy from Harvard University and a doctorate of Philosophy from the University of Oslo. He served as a Professor in Astrophysics at the Royal Swedish Academy for twenty years, and also taught at colleges and universities in Norway, South Korea, France, and the United States.

[44] Prokaryotes reproduce asexually, by simple cellular division—that is, one cell splits into two. Aside from mutations, the "offspring" is a clone of its "parent." Most eukaryotes reproduce sexually, from the mating of a male and female.

[45] Scientists believe part of the delay in the development of eukaryotic organisms was due to a lack of atmospheric oxygen.

[46] To anyone who would object that technology has advanced in exactly that way, with increasing rapidity over time, I submit that this argues in favor of God's involvement in the development of life. We know that technology is the product of intelligence, and its ever-increasing pace is the result of people learning from and building upon advancements that came before. But nature and random mutations do not "learn." Perhaps God does.

[47] Proteins such as pectin in plants, and collagen, elastin, and reticulin in animals

[48] Wyller, *The Planetary Mind,* p. 79.

[49] Wyller, *The Planetary Mind,* p. 91

[50] The Darwinian response is that the Hawaiian Islands were free of predators and thus were an inviting environment in which plants and insects could flourish and evolve. But this response does not really address the primary question—how did it all happen *so fast*?

[51] Wyller, *The Planetary Mind,* p. 102.

[52] *Australopithecus* and *Homo habilis* are "hominids"—that is, human ancestors who lived *after* our lineage split from that of chimpanzees. Other hominids include *Homo erectus,* which first appeared approximately 1.5 million years ago and disappeared from most of the Earth about 250,000

years ago; Neanderthal (*Homo neanderthalensis*), which lived from about 200,000 to 30,000 years ago; and *Cro-Magnon,* which came on the scene about 90,000 years ago.

[53] Zimmer, *Evolution,* p. 347. The rapid development of language—which began no more than 500,000 years ago, and perhaps as recently as 50,000 years ago—is equally astonishing. It was accompanied by a repositioning of the larynx lower in the throat, freeing up the tongue to make a wide variety of sounds useful for speaking.

[54] Berry and Hallam, *Encyclopedia of Animal Evolution,* p. 130. Another author agrees: "Its [the human race's] average size over most of its history may have been a mere ten to twenty thousand people." Jones, *Darwin's Ghost,* p. 324.

[55] For those who would consider a few million years to be ample time for sophisticated evolutionary change to occur, consider this. The Mediterranean Sea has been filling and drying out throughout its history. The modern Mediterranean Sea is about five million years old. It was last created when the Atlantic Ocean filled it through the Strait of Gibraltar. When the Suez Canal opened in 1869, species from the Red Sea began to rapidly replace the native species of the eastern Mediterranean because after five million years they had not evolved and adapted to their warm water habitat. They still resembled their cold water ancestors in the Atlantic Ocean. As one evolutionist puts it: "The locals *have had no time*—nor, in the absence of competition, much need—to respond to the challenges presented by their home's warm and salty waters since the sea last filled." (Jones, *Darwin's Ghost,* p. 239, emphasis added)

[56] Wyller, *The Planetary Mind,* pp. 140-141

[57] Darwinian evolution must not only account for the amazing brain development within this very short time, but also the many other differences between humans and other primates, such as: (1) our spinal cord connects to the brain through a hole (the foramen magnum) in the bottom of the skull, rather than in the back of the skull as in other primates, enabling humans to stand upright and still look forward; (2) unlike other primates, our skull has a soft spot at birth and doesn't fully harden until we are adults, allowing our brains to continue to grow well after birth; (3) we have much smaller jaws and teeth, and much less prominent brow

ridges, giving our face a straighter appearance; (4) our big toe is not opposable as in other primates, so it is well suited for walking upright, but not for grasping; and (5) the vaginal canal in other female primates points backward, so that males mount from the rear, whereas in humans the canal points down and forward, facilitating face-to-face coitus.

[58] This type of DNA is called coding DNA.

[59] Some noncoding DNA performs other functions, and some performs no known function.

[60] Those others are: hereditary persistence of fetal hemoglobin (HPFH), hemoglobin-C, and defects in otherwise beneficial proteins such as glucose-6-phosphate dehydrogenase, band-3-protein, and Duffy antigen

[61] Several of these mutations can in fact be deadly. Without medical treatment—and sometimes even with treatment—a child who inherits the sickle cell trait, thalassemia, or the band-3-protein defect from *both* parents will not generally survive into adulthood.

[62] For a more detailed discussion of Dr. Axe's statistical methods and results, see Meyer, *Darwin's Doubt*, Chapter 10, "The Origin of Genes and Proteins."

[63] According to Nick Stockton, "The Fascinating Math Behind Why You Won't Win Powerball," the odds of winning Powerball are one in 292 million—which is 2.92 times 10^8. The odds of winning twice in a row would be one in 292 million times 292 million, or one in 8.5264 times 10^{16}. The odds of winning five times in a row would be approximately one in 2.12 times 10^{42}. And we are still not close to one in 10^{77}.

[64] In the case of asexual organisms, *all* of its genetic material is passed down to its offspring.

[65] Jerry Fodor is a professor of philosophy and cognitive science at Rutgers University. Professor Piattelli-Palmarini is a professor of cognitive science at the University of Arizona.

[66] Fodor and Piattelli-Palmarini, *What Darwin Got Wrong*, p. 79.

[67] Behe, *Darwin's Black Box,* p. 39. Professor Behe later offered an alternate definition which focuses on the *formation* of a system, rather than on its *function*: "An irreducibly complex evolutionary pathway is one that contains one or more unselected steps (that is, one or more necessary but

unselected mutations). The degree of irreducible complexity is the number of unselected steps in the pathway." By "unselected," Professor Behe means a mutation not favored by natural selection, such as a mutation that neither harms nor benefits the organism. See Behe, "*In Defense of the Irreducible Complexity of the Blood Clotting Cascade.*"

[68] This is not meant to imply that the blood-clotting system always works perfectly. Sometimes blood clots do form when or where they are not supposed to, such as when they cause a stroke.

[69] Orr, "Darwin v. Intelligent Design (Again)."

[70] Scott, *Evolution vs. Creationism,* p. 182, quoting: Futuyma, Douglas J., 1997, "Miracles and Molecules," *Boston Review* 22 (1):29-30. (Emphasis added)

[71] Scott, *Evolution vs. Creationism,* p. 252, quoting Dickerson, Richard E., 1992, "The Game of Science," *Journal of Molecular Evolution* 34:277-279.

[72] For example, laboratory experiments have reportedly produced a new species of Venezuelan fruit fly by breeding them under controlled conditions for several years. See Scott, *Evolution vs. Creationism,* p. 42, citing Dobzhansky, Theodosius, and O. Pavlovsky, 1971, "Experimentally Caused Incipient Species of *Drosophila,*" *Nature* 230:289-292. Similarly, mosquitos living in the London subway system are reportedly now a different species than their surface cousins. See Scott, *Evolution vs. Creationism,* p. 43, citing Byrne, Katharine, and Richard A. Nichols, 1999, "*Culex pipiens* in London Underground Tunnels: Differentiation Between Surface and Subterranean Populations," *Heredity* 82:7-15.

[73] Of this "Mind Field," Professor Wyller says: "To me, the Mind Field resides in a mental energy field suffused throughout the entire Earth—the visual manifestation of which may be the life forms created. But those life forms live and die independently of the Mind Field. . . ." Wyller, *The Planetary Mind,* p. 234.

[74] Wyller, *The Planetary Mind,* p. 150.

[75] Genesis 1:26-27, 5:1

Chapter 11
APOCALYPSE SOON

> "But of that day or hour no one knows, not even the angels in heaven, nor the Son, but the Father *alone.* Take heed, keep on the alert; for you do not know when the *appointed* time will come."
>
> —Mark 13:32-33

Before you read the title and dismiss me as a nut who retreats to a mountaintop at midnight to await the Second Coming of Christ, read the quote just below the title again. "No one knows" exactly when Christ will come again, and I certainly do not claim such knowledge. I am just trying to read the signs of the times. [1]

People have been predicting the end of the world for thousands of years, [2] and it hasn't happened yet. But things may be different today. The prophets of doom this time are not religious fanatics, but scientists. They warn us that our world-wide addiction to fossil fuels—oil, coal, and natural gas—is heating up our air and oceans, generating problems that will one day prove difficult, or even catastrophic, for the human race if we don't change our ways.

And so far, we aren't changing our ways. Indeed, our use of fossil fuels is increasing. According to statistics from the 2016 BP Statistical Review of World Energy, world oil consumption increased by 12% from 2005 to 2015; natural gas consumption increased by 25% during that same ten-year period; and coal consumption increased by 23%. [3]

The U.S. Energy Information Administration projects that consumption of petroleum and other liquid fuels will increase by 36.4% by 2040 compared to 2011 levels. Similarly, natural gas consumption will increase by 73.8% over 2011 levels, and coal consumption will increase by 18.6%. [4]

If we continue down this path, the future predicted by the climate scientists bears some striking similarities to what Jesus said would precede the end times. But we will get to that. First, we need a basic understanding of what the scientists are telling us.

Basic Climate Change Facts. Carbon is one of the building blocks of life; all living organisms contain carbon. When plants and animals die, that carbon is trapped and buried with them. Oil, coal, and natural gas were at one time dead plants and animals, until time, heat, and pressure transformed them. Thus, each of these fossil fuels contains carbon. When they are burned as fuel, the carbon combines with the oxygen in the air to form carbon dioxide—CO_2. (Carbon dioxide consists of one carbon atom, "C," joined to two oxygen atoms, "O_2"—thus, CO_2.) Combustion of fossil fuels releases billions of tons of CO_2 into the atmosphere every year.

So what's so bad about CO_2? In small quantities it is actually a remarkable molecule—vital, in fact, for all plant life on earth. Plants use CO_2, water, a few nutrients, and the Sun's energy to grow through a process called photosynthesis, releasing oxygen in the process—which is convenient for us, since that is what we breathe.

Also, without CO_2 and other "greenhouse gases," such as methane, the earth would be a much colder place. Greenhouse gases absorb some of the heat energy from the Sun before it escapes into space, just as a greenhouse traps heat inside. Because of greenhouse gases like CO_2 the average temperature on earth is about 58° Fahrenheit. [5] Without them, the average temperature would be a numbing two to four degrees below zero. That's about 35 degrees *below* the freezing point of water. During the last ice age (which ended 10,000 years ago), when ice covered much of the northern United States and northern Europe, the average temperature on earth was only about 10 degrees cooler than it is today. Without CO_2 and other greenhouse gases, Earth would be an ice planet.

But too much of a good thing nearly always causes problems, and CO_2 is no exception. Just ask the planet Venus, whose atmosphere of at least 95% carbon dioxide generates an average temperature well over 800°. Venus is closer to the Sun than we are, but that alone does not explain why Venus is hot enough to melt lead. The planet Mercury is only about half as far from the Sun as Venus, yet has a much lower average temperature. [6] The difference is CO_2. Mercury has almost no atmosphere, so a lot of the heat it receives from the Sun escapes into space. Venus' atmosphere traps almost all of that heat.

Before the Industrial Revolution began in the eighteenth century, Earth's atmosphere had about 280 parts per million (ppm) of CO_2. In other words, if you had sampled a million molecules from the atmosphere then, about 280 of them would have been carbon dioxide molecules. But that number has been steadily climbing since humans began pumping CO_2 into the air. In 2013, CO_2 exceeded 400 ppm, and continues to increase by about two to three ppm annually. [7] That extra CO_2 has driven up the average temperature on earth almost two degrees since 1880, when such records began to be kept.

Scientists believe this situation will continue to get worse—probably a lot worse. The Intergovernmental Panel on Climate Change is a group of more than 2,000 scientists worldwide. Their 2014 report projects that average global temperatures [8] will increase between 0.5° and 1.25° over the next two decades, compared with the period of 1986-2005, and could be as much as 7-8° warmer than that 20-year period by the end of this century. [9]

It's Only Getting Worse. We are adding CO_2 and other greenhouse gases to the atmosphere faster all the time. One reason is that developing countries such as China, Brazil, and India are devouring fossil fuels to power their growing economies, even as developed areas like the United States, Europe, and Australia continue to guzzle these fuels as they have for decades.

Another reason is population growth. In the early 1960s three billion people shared this planet. Now the world population exceeds seven billion, and is expected to reach nine billion by 2050. As we add more people, total energy use increases, even if per capita energy usage doesn't change (although per capita energy use has also increased).

The pressure of population growth and the demands of modern society have led to the destruction of large swaths of vegetation in favor of agriculture and development. We have destroyed more than half of Earth's tropical rain forests. Such destruction is a double blow: it hurls CO_2 into the atmosphere by releasing the carbon stored in the vegetation, while also killing plants that absorb huge quantities of CO_2 from the atmosphere.

Fire also releases CO_2, because the carbon in plants and trees binds with oxygen in the air when they burn, generating CO_2. Whether man or nature starts the fire, hotter temperatures will create conditions in which fire thrives and spreads, by drying out vegetation and decreasing precipitation in some locations.

And it gets worse, because as the earth warms a lot of carbon that is currently confined in "carbon sinks" will get released into the atmosphere. Billions of tons of CO_2 and methane are locked away in the permanently frozen ground (permafrost) of Siberia, Alaska, the Arctic, and many high-elevation areas. This permafrost holds the remains of dead plants which never fully decomposed due to the frigid temperatures. But as temperatures rise, some of this permafrost is thawing. And as it does, those dead plants will finish decomposing, releasing previously suspended CO_2 and methane into the atmosphere. With warmer global temperatures, this will become more common, especially since temperatures in the polar regions are rising faster than global temperatures generally.

Speaking of carbon sinks, a tremendous volume of CO_2 is dissolved in the vastness of the oceans. But warm water cannot hold as much CO_2 as cold water. So as the oceans warm—which is already happening, by the way—they will either release some of that CO_2 into the atmosphere or simply absorb less of the CO_2 we are emitting. Either way, the amount of CO_2 in the air will increase more rapidly.

Then there is the albedo effect. The albedo of a surface measures how much sunlight it reflects. Snow and ice reflect eighty to ninety percent of the sun's energy back into space. Darker surfaces reflect less—often a lot less. Ocean water reflects less than ten percent.

As temperatures rise, the ice in the Arctic Ocean is melting. The summer Arctic ice has been retreating at a rate of about eight percent per decade since 1979, and may entirely disappear by 2060. As water replaces the Arctic ice, much more of the sun's energy will be absorbed, which adds to global warming. Similarly, since ice and snow reflect more sunlight than almost anything else on dry land, retreating ice and snow will also change the albedo of land surfaces.

Warming temperatures could also mean less phytoplankton. Phytoplankton is a microscopic sea plant that helps keep CO_2 under control, and is vital for life on earth. Through photosynthesis, phytoplankton removes CO_2 from the air and fixes the carbon into organic form—as much as a hundred million tons of carbon a day—releasing oxygen in the process. About one-half of the oxygen on earth comes from phytoplankton. But studies have shown that the growth of phytoplankton is inhibited by global warming in several ways: (1) warm water doesn't circulate vital nutrients as well as colder water, so the phytoplankton has less to feed on; (2) some of the carbon in the ocean turns into carbonic acid, making the water more acidic, and this damages some types of phytoplankton; and (3) in the Arctic, phytoplankton grows at the edge of sea ice, so less ice probably means less phytoplankton.

And It Could Get Much Worse. Scientists also warn of catastrophic scenarios that are unlikely to occur in your lifetime or mine, but which will be disastrous if or when they do. The release of "clathrates" is one such nightmare possibility.

Clathrates are methane molecules. Huge quantities of clathrates are trapped in ice crystals on and under the deep ocean floor. Estimates range as high as 55 quadrillion cubic yards of the stuff. (That's 55 with 15 zeros after it!) This methane is kept under control by pressure and low temperatures at the bottom of the ocean. But if the deep ocean were to warm sufficiently, some scientists believe this methane could one day be freed from its underwater prison. Since methane is twenty times as efficient as CO_2 in trapping the sun's heat, global warming could escalate exponentially if these clathrates escape.

Another frightening possibility is the collapse of South America's Amazon rain forest, which could one day be doomed by the combination of increasing CO_2 and higher temperatures. The Amazon basin receives an average of 60 to 120 inches of rainfall each year. This large quantity of rain results in part from a process called transpiration, which occurs when water evaporates from a plant as it opens its stomata to take in CO_2. The quantity of plant life in the Amazon basin is so great that a lot of the moisture in the air results from transpiration. Without this process, the air would be drier, and less rain would fall. But in a cascade of unfortunate events, increasing CO_2 levels shorten the length of time plants must open their stomata, which reduces evaporation due to transpiration, and this in turn decreases rainfall.

In addition, climate computer models predict that higher global temperatures will promote more frequent El Niño-like conditions, decreasing rainfall across the Amazon basin. By 2100, this combination of higher temperatures, higher CO_2 levels, and decreasing rainfall could devastate the rain forest, leaving behind only grasses, shrubs, and even desert vegetation in some places. And then comes the most painful news of all: the plush rain forest vegetation that used to be a carbon repository begins to give up its carbon after it dies, adding huge quantities of CO_2 to the atmosphere and exacerbating the problem of global warming.

What the Future Could Look Like. So what does all this added CO_2 mean to you, your children, and your children's children? For starters it means some locations will be warmer and wetter, while others will be hotter and dryer. Heat waves and droughts will occur more often—and be harsher—in areas which are prone to them. And since warmer air can hold more moisture, storms and hurricanes will be more severe. These storms will send rain, snow, and ice in heavier quantities in some locations, and greatly increase the risk of flooding in coastal and low-lying areas.

More flooding will likely increase the spread of various diseases—like cholera, which is caused by bacteria that thrive in fecal-contaminated water, a common problem when flooding occurs. Flooding can also promote the spread of the plague, by driving flea-infested rats into close proximity with humans. Mosquitoes breed in stagnant water, so flooded areas will be more prone to the diseases mosquitoes carry, such as malaria, yellow fever, dengue fever, West Nile virus, encephalitis, and the Zika virus. Warmer temperatures will also increase the mosquitoes' range, which is often limited by colder temperatures. As temperatures rise, mosquitoes will carry these diseases to higher elevations and locations closer to the polar regions—places that were once too cold. Since low temperatures also act as a barrier to the ticks that carry Lyme Disease, global warming will promote the spread of that illness, too. People who live in hotter, dryer climates could suffer as well, because meningitis thrives in warm, dry conditions.

Climate change will impact people's health in other ways. A 2016 report by the U.S. government predicts that higher average temperatures will degrade air quality by increasing fine particles (from increased frequency and intensity of wildfires), ozone, and airborne allergens, causing problems for people with respiratory conditions, asthma, and allergies. [10]

The same report predicts an increased risk for waterborne illnesses, from such causes as the growth and spread of harmful algae and bacteria due to warmer water temperatures, and contamination of freshwater and some seafood from excessive rain runoff and storm surges. [11] Mental health could also be adversely impacted, because the dangers and destruction that accompany weather-related disasters often cause anxiety, depression, and post-traumatic stress, especially among children, the elderly, and other highly vulnerable groups. [12]

Many species, plant and animal, will face extinction because of their inability to adapt to the changing climatic conditions. Coral reefs are suffering—and many have been destroyed—because they are sensitive to the warmer, more acidic oceans that global warming produces. Trees are being lost, and many more will be lost, because their natural enemies—diseases, insects, and fire—flourish in warmer weather.

Ice at the poles and in glaciers is melting due to warmer temperatures, and this will certainly get worse. Melting ice will cause ocean levels to slowly rise. However, ocean levels are rising even without the ice melt, simply due to the fact that water expands as it warms. In the short term, these rising sea levels will make storm surges more dangerous. In the long term, higher water levels could be disastrous for many islands and coastal areas.

Warmer temperatures and more CO_2 may be beneficial for farmers in some colder climates, such as Canada and Russia. This is primarily due to the longer growing season, but also because plants grow marginally better, up to a point, as CO_2 levels increase. Unfortunately, these gains will be more than offset by crop damage elsewhere caused by flooding, heat waves, drought, fire, and plant diseases.

Climate change can affect food distribution—warmer temperatures promote spoilage, and weather disasters can disrupt transportation infrastructure and delivery systems. So food shortages may be inevitable. And as if that isn't bad enough, higher levels of CO_2 decrease the nutritional value of such food staples as rice and wheat by lowering the amount of protein and essential minerals in these foods. [13]

Water shortages will be more frequent and more acute, especially in traditionally dry climates, because of a combination of more frequent drought conditions, saltwater contamination from rising sea levels, increased pollution from flooding, and the loss of glaciers which often provide summer freshwater.

Finally, many experts warn that problems caused by global warming—such as food shortages, water shortages, and refugees displaced by storms and flooding—will greatly increase the dangers of conflict around the globe. And one of the nations at risk for more severe droughts is China, home to more than a billion people and powerful armed forces.

Signs of the Times. We are already seeing some of these signs now. The world is getting hotter. The Goddard Institute for Space Studies (GISS), part of the United States' National Aeronautics and Space Administration (NASA), publishes statistics on world temperatures. Those statistics tell us that the hottest year worldwide since 1880 [14] occurred in 2016, when the mean average global temperature was 1.9° warmer than the mean average in 1880. GISS statistics also show that the 17 hottest years on record have all occurred during the past 19 years (1998-2016). [15]

The European summer of 2003 was so hot that tens of thousands of people died from the heat. A heat wave in southeast Australia in 2009 killed 300 people, and heat-related bushfires killed another 173. Scientists tell us that in another 60 years such heat waves may be common.

As you would expect, a hotter world melts ice. Antarctica's Larsen-B ice shelf provides a stark illustration. The Larsen-B ice shelf was a huge mass of ice along Anarctica's coast, about the size of the country of Luxembourg. [16] Yet the ice was so weakened by melting that in February, 2002 it collapsed into the ocean in only a few weeks.

Melting ice is also causing glaciers worldwide to shrink. Some have already disappeared, such as Bolivia's Chacaltaya glacier. In the not-too-distant future, Montana's Glacier National Park will appear to be misnamed because the glaciers will all be gone.

Wildfires and droughts are on the rise in many areas. The 2014 IPCC Report notes that wildfires have increased in frequency in the western United States, Canada, Portugal, Greece, the Amazon region of South America, and Africa's Mt. Kilimanjaro. [17] In 2005, the worst drought in 40 years struck the Amazon. In 2012, hot and dry conditions in Colorado caused the worst wildfire season in a decade, while the central and eastern portions of the United States suffered through record summer heat. In January 2014, the governor of the State of California declared a state of emergency due to that state's unprecedented drought conditions.

The first decade of the new century (2001-2010) saw more Category 5 hurricanes (the most severe type of hurricane) in the Atlantic Ocean than in any decade since records have been kept. History had never recorded a hurricane in the South Atlantic until March 2004, when a hurricane struck Brazil. In 2005, the North Atlantic saw three Category 5 hurricanes—Katrina, Rita, and Wilma—for the first time in a single season, along with two Category 4 storms. Indeed, Category 4 and 5 storms have nearly doubled in recent years. [18]

Mosquitoes now trouble cities like Nairobi, Kenya, and Harare, Zimbabwe, which used to be inhospitable for them due to cold temperatures at the higher altitudes. Mountain pine beetles in British Columbia and spruce bark beetles in Norway are killing millions of trees because cold weather no longer controls the beetle population.

And if all of this results from an increase of less than two degrees, what will happen by 2100, when CO_2 levels could be well above 500 ppm and global average temperatures could be several degrees higher than today? No one knows with certainty what havoc these hotter temperatures will inflict on us and our fellow travelers on Planet Earth. [19] But without doubt the problems we are currently experiencing will grow worse—probably a great deal worse.

New Testament Prophecy. So what does all of this have to do with Jesus and the New Testament? Did He foresee any of this? I believe so. In the synoptic Gospels (Matthew, Mark, and Luke), the authors recount a conversation Jesus had with some of His disciples about what would happen before His ultimate return "on the clouds of the sky with power and great glory." (Matthew 24:30) [20] Jesus talks about a time of suffering worse than any the world has ever known [21]—tribulation so great that "unless those days had been cut short, no life would have been saved." (Matthew 24:22) [22] But Jesus also talks about what comes before that great tribulation—what He calls "birth pangs." (Matthew 24:8) [23] In Matthew and Mark, these birth pangs include three elements: wars, famines, and earthquakes. [24] Luke adds a fourth: diseases. [25]

With the exception of earthquakes, these "birth pangs" are exactly what climate scientists predict will be in our future if we do not control greenhouse gases. Warmer global temperatures are already increasing the number and severity of droughts, heat waves, deluges, and major storms, as well as flooding and insect activity. Global warming will cause these problems to grow worse, one day leading to food and water shortages, as well as increasingly widespread epidemics. In such a world, conflict and wars would be almost inevitable. Thus, three of the four birth pangs—famine, disease, and wars—are predictable outgrowths of what climate scientists are telling us today.

But what about earthquakes? There are two possible explanations. The literal New Testament Greek, *seismos*, means a "commotion." [26] This word usually refers to an earthquake. However, in the context of Biblical prophecy the term can also refer to a political commotion or insurrection. Thus, we have the image of not only wars *between* nations, but of violent upheavals *within* nations, as people struggle to survive amidst growing hardship.

However, if the term "earthquake" is taken in its literal sense, consider this: the number of man-made earthquakes is on the rise. From 1970 to 2000, the U.S. Geological Survey recorded an average of 20 earthquakes of magnitude 3.0 or greater in the United States each year. But in the four years from 2010 through 2013, 450 such earthquakes occurred—an average of more than 100 per year. *Time* magazine recently reported that Oklahoma experienced 907 magnitude 3.0 earthquakes in 2015 compared to just one in 2007, and that the state now has more such earthquakes than California. [27]

One likely cause of this dramatic increase is the injection of waste water deep underground. The water lubricates places where stress has built up in underground rock formations, causing movement—that is, earthquakes. Injection of waste water underground is frequently incidental to the process of hydraulic fracturing, or "fracking," which is an increasingly common method of extracting fossil fuels from deep underground. To be fair, these man-made earthquakes are a tiny fraction of the tens of thousands of magnitude 3.0 or greater earthquakes that occur annually worldwide. So, for now at least, man's influence on earthquakes appears to be trivial. But 200 years ago man's impact on the climate was trivial.

The Great Tribulation? Let's also revisit another part of Jesus's prophecy, the part that comes after the "birth pangs." He predicted a time of suffering worse than any mankind has ever known. [28] Climate scientists are echoing this prophecy with warnings that out-of-control global warming could eventually trigger catastrophes on a scale we've never seen before. And we are not merely talking about killer heat waves, mega-droughts, or Category 5 hurricanes.

What would happen if nine percent of the world's ice melted? That's the amount of ice in Greenland. If all of that ice became water, ocean levels would rise as much as twenty-three feet, swamping low-lying islands and many coastal cities such as Miami and New Orleans.

Now imagine flooding that was ten times worse. Antarctica holds about ninety percent of the world's ice, so the resulting ice-melt would raise sea levels 170 to 200 feet! If this were to happen, New York City and almost all of Florida would be under water. Such melting would take a long time to complete, measured in centuries rather than decades. But if we continue warming the planet, that outcome will eventually become inevitable.

As Greenland's ice melts, it could trigger another kind of catastrophe in Europe. If you look at a globe, you will notice that Great Britain is about as far north as Canada. Yet the British enjoy a much warmer climate thanks to the Gulf Stream, the fastest ocean current in the world. The Gulf Stream transports warm water from near the equator up to the North Atlantic, where it thaws England and some other parts of Europe.

This heat conveyer belt keeps moving due to the relative salinity of ocean water, because water that is saltier is also heavier. As the warm Gulf Stream travels north, a lot of heat and water ascend into the atmosphere through evaporation. The remaining water becomes much saltier, and therefore heavier, so it sinks to the ocean floor in the North Atlantic in vast quantities before beginning its journey back to the south. This sub-surface waterfall in turn pulls more water northward.

But this tremendous flow of water can be interrupted if a sufficiently large body of freshwater intervenes. The freshwater dilutes the salinity of the Gulf Stream's current, preventing it from sinking. The waterfall stops, and so does the northern flow of water. This makes Europe much colder, because the heat stays down south.

Does this seem far-fetched? It isn't. It has actually happened. About 13,000 – 14,000 years ago, after several thousand years of retreating and melting ice, a huge ice dam in North

America burst. Freshwater behind the dam rushed down the St. Lawrence River into the North Atlantic and disrupted the Gulf Stream. Europe was plunged back into an ice age (called the "younger Dryas") for 1,000 years. Average summer temperatures in parts of northern and western Europe dropped as much as 16°.

Climate scientists tell us that a similar disruption of the Gulf Stream is unlikely during this century. But the salinity of the water in the North Atlantic has been slowly decreasing, the result of melting ice and increased precipitation in that area, so the possibility does exist.

Conclusion. When I was a young and ignorant baby Christian—and still under the influence of Hal Lindsey's best-seller, *The Late Great Planet Earth*—I believed Christ's Second Coming would probably occur during my lifetime. I now doubt that. In fact, I don't even think the "birth pangs" will come in my lifetime unless global warming speeds up considerably.

But as the effects of climate change grow worse, the birth pangs will become more evident, if we do not blind ourselves to them. We will see more severe heat waves and more serious droughts, leading to **famines** more tragic than any we've witnessed before. Hurricanes and storms will cause more suffering, more flooding, and more **disease**. The growing misery will trigger **unrest** within countries, and **wars** between nations, as people fight over scarce resources needed for survival.

Reading the signs of the times, I fear we will blindly go on burning fossil fuels and making the problem worse, until disaster becomes inevitable. We will eventually approach the point of our own extinction, "but for the sake of the elect those days will be cut short." (Matthew 24:22) And then Christ will come again, from the sky, [29] like a flash of lightning. [30] Just don't ask me exactly when that will occur. I don't make predictions like that, and I don't like mountaintops at midnight.

Endnotes for Chapter Eleven, "Apocalypse Soon"

[1] See Matthew 16:3.

[2] See, for example, the entertaining web site, "A Brief History of the Apocalypse."

[3] Oil consumption increased from 84.726 million barrels per day in 2005 to 95.008 million barrels per day in 2015; natural gas consumption increased from 2.7743 trillion cubic meters in 2005 to 3.4686 trillion cubic meters in 2015; and coal consumption increased from 3.1306 billion "tonnes oil equivalent" in 2005 to 3.8399 billion "tonnes oil equivalent" in 2015. *2016 BP Statistical Review of World Energy*, pp. 9, 23, and 33.

[4] These statistics are derived from U.S. Energy Administration's International Energy Outlook 2016, Appendix A, Table A2, "World total energy consumption by region and fuel, Reference case, 2011-2040."

[5] For convenience, all temperatures are in degrees Fahrenheit. To convert Fahrenheit to Celsius, subtract 32° and then multiply by 5/9, or go to the National Weather Service's Fahrenheit to Celsius Converter, found at http://www.wbuf.noaa.gov/tempfc.htm.

[6] Mercury is about 36 million miles from the Sun and has an average temperature of about 380°. Venus is about 67 million miles from the Sun.

[7] The average monthly carbon dioxide level at Hawaii's Mauna Loa Observatory in March 2017 was 407 ppm, according to the National Oceanic and Atmospheric Administration. See https://www.esrl.noaa.gov/gmd/ccgg/trends/.

[8] "Average global temperature" refers to global mean surface air temperatures.

[9] See, for example, the following portions of 2014 IPCC report:

(1) **IPCC**, 2014: *Climate Change 2014, Part A*, pp. 13, 57-58, 62, 138, 178-179, 189.

(2) Kirtman, B., *et al.*, *Near-term Climate Change*, pp. 955, 1012.

(3) Collins, M., *et al.*, *Long-term Climate Change*, pp. 1031, 1055-1056.

[10] USGCRP, 2016, *Impacts of Climate Change on Human Health*, Chapter 3 (pp. 70-86)

[11] *Ibid.*, Ch. 6 (pp. 158-175)

[12] *Ibid.*, Ch. 8 (pp. 218-231)

[13] *Ibid.*, Ch. 7 (pp. 190-205)

[14] This is based on average mean global temperatures, with a "year" measured from January through December.

[15] NASA's "Global Land-Ocean Temperature Index"

[16] Luxembourg has 2,586 square kilometers, or 998 square miles.

[17] See **IPCC**, 2014: *Climate Change 2014, Part A*, pp. 30-32, 44-46, 1005-1006.

[18] In fairness, some scientists argue that this apparent increase in severe hurricanes may be the result, in whole or in part, of better methods of detection and tracking, such as satellite technology. See NASA's "Hurricanes: The Greatest Storms on Earth."

[19] The uncertainty arises from the many variables that must be taken into account in trying to predict future occurrences. Two of the most important variables are:

1. Clouds. Higher temperatures and warmer ocean water will increase evaporation, which should result in more clouds. But clouds have two opposite effects. Because they consist of water vapor—a potent greenhouse gas—high, thin clouds trap the sun's energy, warming the planet. On the other hand, low thick clouds cool the planet because of their albedo effect—that is, they reflect more of the sun's energy than they trap. At this time, no one knows which will be the more impactful of the two.
2. Greenhouse gas levels. Uncertainty remains concerning how fast greenhouse gas levels will rise, due to such factors as the increasing use of fossil fuels by developing countries, energy conservation efforts, and the rate of growth of alternative energy sources, such as solar and wind power.

[20] See also Mark 13:26 and Luke 21:27.

[21] Matthew 24:9-21; see also Mark 13:95-6, 13:9-19, and 13:21-22

[22] See also Mark 13:20.

[23] See also Mark 13:8.

[24] Matthew 24:6-7 and Mark 13:7-8

[25] Luke 21:10-11

[26] Strong's Talking Greek & Hebrew Dictionary, in Bible Explorer 4.0.

[27] Sanburn, J., "The Faults of Oklahoma," *Time*, p. 36.

[28] Matthew 24:9-22; Mark 13:95-6, 13:9-22

[29] Matthew 24:30

[30] Matthew 24:27

Chapter 12
WHY REASONABLE PEOPLE SHOULD CONSIDER CHRISTIANITY

"He who loves his life loses it, and he who hates his life in this world will keep it to life eternal."

—John 12:25

Personally, I don't want to die. And I think the same is true for most of us. We enjoy life—and we fear death. In short, we want to be immortal. Yet this truth confronts us: immortality is beyond our grasp.

Most of the time we live with this truth by ignoring it or denying it. We speak hyperbolically of an athlete's achievements lasting "forever," or of an actress becoming "immortalized," when the truth is that their accomplishments will be treasured for a generation or two, and then gradually forgotten. We use creams, ointments, and cosmetic surgery to slow the visible effects of aging, and try to extend our lives through healthy living. We pretend that Death will never come for us—until someone's passing, or perhaps our own debilitation, forces us to face our inescapable fate. Everyone who has ever lived has eventually died. [1] So will you. And so will I.

Christianity offers us a way of escape from this inevitable doom, through the promise of eternal life. Maybe that sounds too good to be true. But if there is even a possibility that you could gain immortality, shouldn't you at least take a closer look at Christianity?

In this book I have tried to give you an intellectual foundation for Christian faith. Yet I suspect most people find their way to Christ as a kind of last resort, because on their own they cannot find the peace and joy and lasting happiness that they crave. That was true for a friend of mine who grew up as a Christian, but later lost her faith and left the church. After awhile she realized that she was no longer happy or content. Life apart from Christ was frustrating and unfulfilling. So she came back. She decided to trust God again because she realized that she was happier when she did so.

This has been the common experience of many who have stepped out on faith. To their surprise, they find that life in Christ is more fulfilling, more hopeful, more joyful, and yes, even more fun than the life they left behind. Saint Augustine had a similar experience, and he summed up the importance of faith when he said: "Seek not to understand that you may believe, but believe that you may understand." [2]

Personally, I had a lot of misconceptions about Christianity in my youth. Until I was twenty years old, I was convinced that Christianity was a religion for fools and nitwits—for people who turned off their brains when they entered a church.

Yet I knew that something vital was missing in my life. The idea of eternity distressed me intensely, because it made my own existence seem hopelessly short, trivial, and meaningless. Death both frightened and attracted me. Suicide seemed like a way to stop the emotional pain—but God rescued me before I found the courage to attempt it.

I found Christ through prayer. My prayer was not unlike Gideon's, [3] except without the certainty that anyone was listening. I asked God, if He was real, to show me the truth. And He did. I am convinced that God answered my prayer because He knew that I was earnestly seeking the Truth—and that I would accept the Truth if I found it.

Since then, my experiences and my own study of the subject have convinced me of the truth of Christianity almost beyond any possible doubt. But my knowledge and experiences are unlikely to convince you. I have tried to give you some idea of where to look, and perhaps what to look for, but you must ultimately search for yourself.

Why Reasonable People Should Consider Christianity

God does not lead everyone to Truth in the same way. However, I am certain of this: anyone who sincerely seeks the Truth will find it, one way or another. As God told the exiles in Babylon through Jeremiah the prophet:

> "You will seek Me and find *Me* when you search for Me with all your heart."
>
> —Jeremiah 29:13

Or as Jesus said:

> "Ask, and it will be given to you; seek, and you will find; knock, and it will be opened to you. For everyone who asks receives, and he who seeks finds, and to him who knocks it will be opened. Or what man is there among you who, when his son asks for a loaf, will give him a stone? Or if he asks for a fish, he will not give him a snake, will he? If you then, being evil, know how to give good gifts to your children, how much more will your Father who is in heaven give what is good to those who ask Him!"
>
> —Matthew 7:7-11 [4]

God eagerly waits to rescue all who do not wish to die. He has promised to give salvation and eternal life to any who will love Him and commit themselves to Him. That is why reasonable people should consider Christianity.

Endnotes for Chapter Twelve, "Why Reasonable People Should Consider Christianity"

[1] Two possible exceptions are Enoch and Elijah. See Genesis 5:24 and II Kings 2:11.

[2] Durant, *The Story of Civilization, Vol. 4,* p. 70 (citing "Comment. in Joan. Evang., xxix, 6; Sermon 43")

[3] See Judges 6:36-40.

[4] See also, Luke 11:9-13 and Acts 17:27.

BIBLIOGRAPHY

"8 Examples of Evolution in Action." Listverse.com web site, found at: http://listverse.com/2011/11/19/8-examples-of-evolution-in-action/ (last viewed 1/30/2017).

"About the Amazon." Panda.org web site, found at: http://wwf.panda.org/what_we_do/where_we_work/amazon/about_the_amazon/ (last viewed 1/23/2017).

Adam Clarke's Commentary, in *Bible Explorer 4.0* software (WORDsearch 2006).

Ali, Maulana Muhammad, trans. "The Holy Qur'an," at: http://en.wikisource.org/wiki/Quran_%28Progressive_Muslims_Organization%29 (last viewed 1/2/2017).

"Amino Acid," at: http://en.wikipedia.org/wiki/Amino_acid (last viewed 1/2/2017).

Arnold, Eberhard, ed. *The Early Christians*. Grand Rapids, Michigan: Baker Book House, 1970, 1972, paperback ed. 1979.

Arthur, K., and staff of Precept Ministries International, Chattanooga, Tennessee, compilers. *The New Inductive Study Bible: Updated New American Standard Bible*. Eugene, Oregon: Harvest House, 2000. Copyright for Scripture text, marginal notes, and references held by The Lockman Foundation, La Habra, California, 1995.

Asimov, Isaac. *Asimov's Guide to the Bible, the Old and New Testaments*. New York: Avenel Books, 1967, 1969, 1981.

"Ask a Biologist: Protein Parts," on the web site of Arizona State University, at: http://askabiologist.asu.edu/venom/building-blocks-protein (last viewed 1/2/2017).

Ayala, Francisco J. *Am I a Monkey?: Six Big Questions About Evolution*. Baltimore: John Hopkins University Press, 2010.

Bainton, Roland H. *Christendom: A Short History of Christianity and its Impact on Western Civilization*, New York: Harpers & Row, 1964.

Barnes' Notes on the New Testament, in *Bible Explorer 4.0* software (WORDsearch 2006).

Behe, Michael J. *Darwin's Black Box: The Biochemical Challenge to Evolution*. New York: The Free Press, 1996.

———. *In Defense of the Irreducible Complexity of the Blood Clotting Cascade: Response to Russell Doolittle, Ken Miller and Keith Robison*. Discovery Institute, 7/31/2000, at:

http://www.arn.org/docs/behe/mb_indefenseofbloodclottingcascade.htm (last viewed 3/23/2017).
———. *The Edge of Evolution: The Search for the Limits of Darwinism.* New York: Free Press, 2007.
Berry, Professor R. J. Berry and Professor A. Hallam, eds. *The Encyclopedia of Animal Evolution*. New York: Facts on File, 1987.
Bettenson, Henry, Ed. *Documents of the Christian Church*, 2nd Ed. London: Oxford Univ. Press, 1977.
Bijlefeld, Willem A. "Wahhabism," at *http://mb-soft.com/believe/txo/wahhabis.htm*.
Black, Henry Campbell, M.A. *Black's Law Dictionary*, 5th Ed. St. Paul, Minnesota: West Publishing Co., 1979.
Borenstein, Seth, Associated Press. "Little link between drilling, quakes." *Fort Worth Star-Telegram*, June 16, 2012, p. 4A.
BP Statistical Review of World Energy, June 2016. 65th edition, found at: https://www.bp.com/content/dam/bp/pdf/energy-economics/statistical-review-2016/bp-statistical-review-of-world-energy-2016-full-report.pdf (last viewed 4/17/2017).
Braasch, Gary. *Earth Under Fire: How Global Warming is Changing the World*. Berkeley, California: University of California Press, 2007.
Brain, Marshall. "If the polar ice caps melted, how much would the oceans rise?," at:http://science.howstuffworks.com/environmental/earth/geophysics/question473.htm (last viewed 1/5/2017).
Bruce, F.F., M.A., D.D., F.B.A. *The New Testament Documents: Are They Reliable?*, 5th ed. Grand Rapids, Michigan: Eerdmans Publishing Co., 2003.
Bulfinch, Thomas. *Bulfinch's Mythology Illustrated: The Age of Fable, The Age of Chivalry, Legends of Charlemagne*. New York: Avenel Books, 1979.
"The Cambrian Explosion," from *The Evolution Library*, http://www.pbs.org/wgbh/evolution/library/03/4/l_034_02.html (last viewed 1/2/2017).
Chalice Hymnal. St. Louis: Chalice Press, 2003.
Chambers, Richard L., ed. "The Ottoman Empire: 1600-1923," *http://www.turizm.net/turkey/history/ottoman3.html* (last viewed 1/2/2017).
Cheney v. State, 755 S.W.2d 123 (Tex.Crim.App. 1988)

Collins, M., R. Knutti, J. Arblaster, J.-L. Dufresne, T. Fichefet, P. Friedlingstein, X. Gao, W.J. Gutowski, T. Johns, G. Krinner, M. Shongwe, C. Tebaldi, A.J. Weaver and M. Wehner, *2013: Long-term Climate Change: Projections, Commitments and Irreversibility*. In: *Climate Change 2013: The Physical Science Basis. Contribution of Working Group I to the Fifth Assessment Report of the Intergovernmental Panel on Climate Change* [Stocker, T.F., D. Qin, G.-K. Plattner, M. Tignor, S.K. Allen, J. Boschung, A. Nauels, Y. Xia, V. Bex and P.M. Midgley (eds.)]. Cambridge University Press, Cambridge, United Kingdom and New York, NY, USA.

"Colorado Wildfires 2012: Stunning NASA Map Shows Severe Heat Wave Fueling Wildfires." *HuffPost Denver*, posted 6/30/2012, found at http://www.huffingtonpost.com/2012/06/30/waldo-canyon-fire-2012-st_n_1639836.html (last viewed 1/21/2017).

A Commentary on the Holy Bible, in *4.0*software (WORDsearch 2006).

"Commonly Asked Questions and Facts." Rainforest Foundation U.S. web site, found at: http://www.rainforestfoundation.org/commonly-asked-questions-and-facts(last viewed 1/23/2017).

Corduan, Winfried. *Neighboring Faiths: A Christian Introduction to World Religions*. Downers Grove, Illinois: InterVarsity Press, 1998.

Cremin, Dr. Aedeen, chief consultant. *The World Encyclopedia of Archaeology*. Buffalo, New York: Firefly Books, 2007.

Cubasch, U., D. Wuebbles, D. Chen, M.C. Facchini, D. Frame, N. Mahowald, and J.-G. Winther, 2013: Introduction. In: Climate Change 2013: The Physical Science Basis. Contribution of Working Group I to the Fifth Assessment Report of the Intergovernmental Panel on Climate Change[Stocker, T.F., D. Qin, G.-K. Plattner, M. Tignor, S.K. Allen, J. Boschung, A. Nauels, Y. Xia, V. Bex and P.M. Midgley (eds.)]. Cambridge University Press, Cambridge, United Kingdom and New York, NY, USA.

Dawood, N.J., trans. *The Koran*. London: Penguin Books, 1999.

Dawkins, Richard. *The Greatest Show on Earth: The Evidence for Evolution*. New York: Free Press, 2009.

DeSalle, Dr. Rob, ed. *Epidemic! The World of Infectious Disease*. New York: The New Press, published in conjunction with The American Museum of Natural History, 1999.

DeWeerdt, Sarah E."What's a Genome?," *at:* http://www.genomenewsnetwork.org/resources/whats_a_genome/Chp1_1_1.shtml#genome1 (last viewed 1/2/2017).
"Don't Call Us Young-earth Creationists. . . ." Answers in Genesis web site, found at: https://answersingenesis.org/creationism/young-earth/young-earth-creationists/ (last viewed 1/30/2017).
Durant, Will. *The Story of Civilization, Volume III: Caesar and Christ*. New York: Simon and Schuster, 1944).
———.*The Story of Civilization: Volume IV, The Age of Faith*. New York: Simon and Schuster, 1950.
———. *The Story of Civilization: Volume VI, The Reformation*. New York: Simon and Schuster, 1957.
Durant, Will, and Ariel Durant. *The Story of Civilization: Volume VII, The Age of Reason Begins*. New York: Simon and Schuster, 1961.
———. *The Story of Civilization: Volume VIII, The Age of Louis XIV*. New York: Simon and Schuster, 1963.
———. *The Story of Civilization: Volume X, Rousseau and Revolution*. New York: Simon and Schuster, 1967.
———. *The Story of Civilization: Volume XI, The Age of Napoleon*. New York: Simon and Schuster, 1975.
"Early & Medieval History of Sicily," *http://www.bestofsicily.com/history2.htm* (last viewed 1/2/2017).
Ellsworth, William, Jessica Robertson, and Christopher Hook. "Man-Made Earthquakes Update." U.S. Geological Survey web site (posted January 17, 2014), found at: http://www.usgs.gov/blogs/features/usgs_top_story/man-made-earthquakes/(last viewed 1/23/2017).
Emerick, Yahiya. *The Complete Idiot's Guide to Understanding Islam*. Indianapolis: Alpha, A Pearson Education Company, 2002.
Erickson, Jon. *Ice Ages, Past and Future*. Blue Ridge Summit, Pennsylvania: TAB Books, 1990).
———. *Dying Planet: The Extinction of Species*. Blue Ridge Summit, Pennsylvania: Tab Books, 1991.
Eusebius. *The Ecclesiastical History of Eusebius Pamphilus, Bishop of Caesarea, in Palestine*. Translated from the original by Isaac Boyle. Grand Rapids, Michigan: Baker Book House, first printing 1955, 12th printing 1984).
Farrer-Halls, Gill. *The Illustrated Encyclopedia of Buddhist Wisdom*. Weaton, Illinois: Quest Books, Theosophical Publishing House, 2000.

Flannery, Tim. *The Weather Makers: How Man is Changing the Climate and What it Means for Life on Earth*. New York: Atlantic Monthly Press, 2005.

Fodor, Jerry, and Massimo Piattelli-Palmarini. *What Darwin God Wrong*. New York: Picador, 2011.

Friedman, Thomas L. *Hot, Flat, and Crowded: Why We Need a Green Revolution—and How it Can Renew America (Release 2.0)*.New York: Picador / Farrar, Straus and Giroux, 2009.

Gard, Richard A., ed.. *Buddhism*. New York: George Braziller, 1962.

Geisler, Norman L., and Paul K. Hoffman, eds. *Why I Am a Christian: Leading Thinkers Explain Why They Believe*. Grand Rapids, Michigan: Baker Books, a Division of Baker Book House, 2001.

"Global Analysis – Annual 2013." National Oceanic & Atmospheric Administration's National Climatic Data Center, found at: http://www.ncdc.noaa.gov/sotc/global/2013/13(1/23/2017).

"Global Analysis – Annual 2016." National Oceanic & Atmospheric Administration's National Climatic Data Center, found at: https://www.ncdc.noaa.gov/sotc/global/201613(1/23/2017).

"Global Land-Ocean Temperature Index," through March 2017, published by the National Aeronautics and Space Administration's Goddard Institute for Space Studies, at:http://data.giss.nasa.gov/gistemp/tabledata_v3/GLB.Ts+dSST.txt (last viewed 4/18/2017).

Gould, Stephen Jay. *Ever Since Darwin: Reflections in Natural History*. New York: W. W. Norton & Company, 1979.

Hallick, Richard B. "Introduction to DNA Structure," at: https://kem3.com/esrp/IntroDNAStr/IntroductiontoDNAStructure.html (last viewed 1/2/2017).

Henry, Matthew. *Matthew Henry's Commentary on the Whole Bible*. Edited by Rev. Leslie F. Church, Ph.D., F.R.Hist.S. Grand Rapids, Michigan: Regency Reference Library, Zondervan Publishing House, 1961.

"History of Bulgaria," *http://www.bulgaria.com/history/bulgaria/liber.html* (since incorporated into "Bulgaria," at https://en.wikipedia.org/wiki/Bulgaria)(last viewed 12/2/2016).

Hopfe, Lewis M. *World Religions (Growing Christians Series)*. Nashville: Graded Press, 1987.

Hopkins, Jeffrey, Ph.D., ed. & trans. *Becoming Enlightened, by His Holiness the Dalai Lama*. New York: Atria Books, a Division of Simon & Schuster, 2009.

"How many Proteins exist in human body?" *Innovateus.net* web site, found at: http://www.innovateus.net/health/how-many-proteins-exist-human-body (last viewed 8/7/2017).

"Hurricanes: The Greatest Storms on Earth." NASA Earth Observatory web site, found at: http://earthobservatory.nasa.gov/Features/Hurricanes/hurricanes_3.php (last viewed 1/21/2017).

"International Energy Statistics."Compiled by the U.S. Energy Information Administration, and found at:http://www.eia.gov/cfapps/ipdbproject/iedindex3.cfm?tid=1&pid=1&aid=2&cid=regions,&syid=2008&eyid=2012&unit=TST (last viewed 1/23/2017).

IPCC, 2014: *Climate Change 2014: Impacts, Adaptation, and Vulnerability. Part A: Global and Sectoral Aspects. Contribution of Working Group II to the Fifth Assessment Report of the Intergovernmental Panel on Climate Change*[Field, C.B., V.R. Barros, D.J. Dokken, K.J. Mach, M.D. Mastrandrea, T.E. Bilir, M. Chatterjee, K.L. Ebi, Y.O. Estrada, R.C. Genova, B. Girma, E.S. Kissel, A.N. Levy, S. MacCracken, P.R. Mastrandrea, and L.L. White (eds.)]. Cambridge University Press, Cambridge, United Kingdom and New York, NY, USA, 1132 pp.

IPCC, 2014: *Climate Change 2014: Impacts, Adaptation, and Vulnerability. Part B: Regional Aspects. Contribution of Working Group II to the Fifth Assessment Report of the Intergovernmental Panel on Climate Change* [Barros, V.R.,C.B. Field, D.J. Dokken, M.D. Mastrandrea, K.J. Mach, T.E. Bilir, M. Chatterjee,K.L. Ebi, Y.O. Estrada, R.C. Genova, B. Girma, E.S. Kissel, A.N. Levy, S. MacCracken, P.R. Mastrandrea, and L.L. White (eds.)]. Cambridge University Press, Cambridge, United Kingdom and New York, NY, USA, pp. 688.

Jamieson-Fausset-Brown Bible Commentary, in *4.0* software (WORDsearch 2006).

Johnson, Phillip E. *Darwin on Trial*. Downers Grove, Illinois: InterVarsity Press, 1993.

Jones, Steve. *Darwin's Ghost: The Origin of Species Updated*. New York: Random House, 2000.

Keller, Werner. *The Bible as History: A Confirmation of the Book of Books*. Translated by William Neil. New York: William Morrow & Co., 1956.

Kirtman, B., S.B. Power, J.A. Adedoyin, G.J. Boer, R. Bojariu, I. Camilloni, F.J. Doblas-Reyes, A.M. Fiore, M. Kimoto, G.A. Meehl, M. Prather, A. Sarr, C. Schär, R. Sutton, G.J. van Oldenborgh, G. Vecchi and H.J. Wang, 2013: Near-term Climate Change: Projections and Predictability. In: Climate Change 2013: The Physical Science Basis. Contribution of Working Group I to the Fifth Assessment Report of the Intergovernmental Panel on Climate Change [Stocker, T.F., D. Qin, G.-K. Plattner, M. Tignor, S.K. Allen, J. Boschung, A. Nauels, Y. Xia, V. Bex and P.M. Midgley (eds.)]. Cambridge University Press, Cambridge, United Kingdom and New York, NY, USA.

Kitzmiller v. Dover Area School District, 400 F.Supp.2d 707 (U.S. District Court, M.D. Pa. 2005).

Kolbert, Elizabeth. *Field Notes from a Catastrophe*. New York: Bloombury Publishing, 2006.

Kreeft, Peter, and Ronald K. Tacelli. *Handbook of Christian Apologetics*.Downers Grove, Illinois: Intervarsity Press, 1994.

Krukonis, Greg, Ph.D., and Tracy Barr. *Evolution for Dummies*. Hoboken, New Jersey: Wiley Publishing, 2008.

Lambert, David, and the Diagram Group. *The Field Guide to Prehistoric Life*. New York: Checkmark Books, 1994

Landaw, Jonathan and Stephen Bodian. *Buddhism for Dummies*. Hoboken, New Jersey: Wiley Publishing, 2003.

Latourette, Kenneth Scott. *A History of Christianity, Volume I: Beginnings to 1500*. New York: Harpers and Row, 1953, 1975).

Leeming, David Adams. *The World of Myth*. New York: Oxford University Press, 1990.

Lewis, C.S. *The Best of C.S. Lewis*. Grand Rapids, Michigan: Baker Book House, copyright 1952, by Macmillan Co.

Licona, Michael. *The Resurrection of Jesus: A New Historiographical Approach*. Downers Grove, Illinois: InterVarsity Press, 2010.

The Life Application Concise New Testament Commentary, in *Bible Explorer 3.0* software (WORDsearch).

Linder, Doug. "Bishop James Ussher Sets the Date for Creation," 2004, http://law2.umkc.edu/faculty/PROJECTS/FTRIALS/scopes/ussher.html (last viewed 1/23/2017).

Lindsey, Hal, with C.C. Carlson. *The Late Great Planet Earth*. New York: Bantam Books, 1973, published by arrangement with Zondervan Publishing House.

Little, Paul E. *Know Why You Believe*. Wheaton, Illinois: Victor Books, a division of SP Publications, 1967, 1980.

"Luxembourg." Wikipedia web site, found at: http://en.wikipedia.org/wiki/Luxembourg (last viewed 1/23/2017).

"Massimo Piattelli-Palmarini, Homepage of." University of Arizona, found at: http://dingo.sbs.arizona.edu/~massimo/ (last viewed 2/23/2017).

May, Elizabeth, and Zoë Caron. *Global Warming for Dummies*. Mississauga, Ontario: John Wiley & Sons, 2009.

Mayr, Ernst. *What Evolution Is*. New York: Basic Books, a Member of the Perseus Books Group, 2001.

Mays, James L., general ed. *Harper's Bible Commentary*. San Francisco: Harper & Row, 1988.

McBirnie, William Steuart, Ph.D. *The Search for the Twelve Apostles*. Wheaton, Illinois: Living Books, Tyndale House Publishers, 1973.

McDowell, Josh, ed. *Evidence That Demands a Verdict*, San Bernardino, California: Campus Crusade for Christ, 1972.

———. *More Evidence That Demands a Verdict*, San Bernardino, California: Here's Life Publishers, Inc., 1975, 1981; copyright by Campus Crusade for Christ.

———. *The New Evidence That Demands a Verdict*. Nashville: Thomas Nelson Publishers, 1999.

Meyer, Stephen C. *Darwin's Doubt: The Explosive Origin of Animal Life and The Case for Intelligent Design*. New York: HarperOne, an Imprint of HarperCollins, 2013.

Microsoft ENCARTA 98 Encyclopedia (1998 ed.).

Microsoft ENCARTA "Virtual Globe" software (1998 ed.).

Moore, Randy, and Janice Moore. *Evolution 101*. Westport, Connecticut: Greenwood Press, 2006.

Morison, Frank. *Who Moved the Stone?* Grand Rapids, Michigan: Lamplighter Books, Zondervan Publishing House, 1958; first published in 1930 by Faber and Faber.

National Academies of Science, Engineering, and Medicine. 2015. *Review of the Draft Interagency Report on the Impacts of Climate Change on Human Health in the United States*. Washington, DC: National Academies Press, available at http://dx.doi.org/10.7930/J0R49NQX (last viewed 1/23/2017).

National Academy of Sciences and Institute of Medicine. *Science, Evolution, and Creationism.* Washington, D.C.: The National Academies Press, 2008.

National Aeronautic and Space Administration (NASA). "NASA scientists react to 400 ppm carbon milestone," NASA.gov, May 21, 2013, found at: https://climate.nasa.gov/400ppmquotes/ (last viewed 4/28/2017).

———. "Graphic: The relentless rise of carbon dioxide," found at: https://climate.nasa.gov/climate_resources/24/ (last viewed 4/28/2017).

National Oceanic and Atmospheric Administration (NOAA). "Trends in Atmospheric Carbon Dioxide," found at: https://www.esrl.noaa.gov/gmd/ccgg/trends/ (last viewed 4/28/2017).

Nelson, Chris. "A Brief History of the Apocalypse," at http://www.abhota.info/index.htm.

New Unger's Bible Dictionary, in *Bible Explorer 3.0* software (WORDSearch).

"Noncoding DNA," at: http://en.wikipedia.org/wiki/Noncoding_DNA (last viewed 1/2/2017).

Orr, H. Allen. "Darwin v. Intelligent Design (Again)," *Boston Review*, at http://bostonreview.net/archives/BR21.6/orr.html (last viewed 2/1/2017).

Osborn, Kevin, and Dana Burgess, Ph.D. *The Complete Idiot's Guide to Classical Mythology*. New York: Alpha Books, a Division of Macmillan General Reference, a Simon & Schuster Macmillan Company, 1998.

Palmer, R. R., and Joel Colton. *A History of the Modern World,* 4th ed. New York: Alfred A. Knopf, 1971.

Pfeiffer, Charles F., and Everett F. Harrison, eds. *The Wycliffe Bible Commentary*. Chicago: Moody Press, 1962.

"The Physical Carbon Pump." University of California at San Diego *Climate Change: Earth's Climate System*, found at: http://earthguide.ucsd.edu/virtualmuseum/climatechange1/06_1.shtml (last viewed 1/21/2017).

"Punctuated Equilibrium." PBS.org, found at: http://www.pbs.org/wgbh/evolution/library/03/5/l_035_01.html (last viewed 2/3/2017).

"Punctuated Equilibrium." Wikipedia.org, at: https://en.wikipedia.org/wiki/Punctuated_equilibrium (last viewed 2/3/2017).

"Quran." Progressive Muslims Organization, trans. Found on the web site Wikisource, at: http://en.wikisource.org/wiki/Quran_%28Progressive_Muslims_Organization%29 (last viewed 4/15/2017).

RapidTables Fahrenheit to Celsius Converter, athttp://www.rapidtables.com/convert/temperature/fahrenheit-to-celsius.htm (last viewed 1/5/2017).

Ross, Nancy Wilson. *Three Ways of Asian Wisdom: Hinduism, Buddhism, Zen and Their Significance for the West*. New York: Simon and Schuster, 1966.

Ryrie, Charles Caldwell, Th.D., Ph.D. *The Ryrie Study Bible: New American Standard Translation*, with annotations. Chicago: Moody Press, 1978.

Sanburn, Josh. "The Faults of Oklahoma." *Time*, Volume 187, No. 10, March 21, 2016.

Schneider, Stephen H. *Science as a Contact Sport: Inside the Battle to Save Earth's Climate*. Washington, D.C.: National Geographic, 2009.

Scott, Eugenie C. *Evolution vs. Creationism: An Introduction*. Westport, Connecticut: Greenwood Press, 2004.

Scott, Dr. Gene, "My Search for the Truth About the Resurrection of Jesus Christ," *The Twin Peaks Sentinel*, Dolores Press, March 1986, reprinted from Vol. 1 of *Jesus Christ . . . Super Nut or Super-Natural?*

Shakir, M.H., trans. *The Qur'an,* 12th U.S. ed. Elmhurst, New York: Tahrike Tarsile Qur'an, 2001.

"Sickle Cell Anemia." The New York Times Health Guide, found at: http://www.nytimes.com/health/guides/disease/sickle-cell-anemia/prognosis.html (last viewed 2/23/2017).

Silver, Jerry. *Global Warming & Climate Change Demystified*. New York: McGraw Hill, 2008.

Simanek, Donald. "Bishop Ussher Dates the World: 4004 BC." Lock Haven University web site, found at: https://www.lhup.edu/~dsimanek/ussher.htm (last viewed 1/23/2017).

Smith, Huston, Professor of Philosophy, Massachusetts Institute of Technology. *The Religions of Man*. New York: Harper & Row, 1958.

Stockton, Nick. "The Fascinating Math Behind Why You Won't Win Powerball." Wired.com, posted 1/12/2016, and found at: https://www.wired.com/2016/01/the-fascinating-math-behind-why-you-wont-win-powerball/

Strobel, Lee. *The Case for Christ: A Journalist's Personal Investigation of the Evidence for Jesus*. Grand Rapids, Michigan: Zondervan Publishing House, 1998.

———. *The Case for the Real Jesus: A Journalist Investigates Current Attacks on the Identity of Christ*. Grand Rapids, Michigan: Zondervan, 2007.

Strong's Greek-Hebrew Dictionary, in *Bible Explorer 4.0* software (WORDsearch 2006).

Strong's Greek Lexicon search result for *pistis*, found at http://www.eliyah.com/cgi-bin/strongs.cgi?file=greeklexicon&isindex=pistis (last viewed 4/13/2017).

Tennesen, Michael. *The Complete Idiot's Guide to Global Warming, 2d. Ed*. New York: Alpha, a member of Penguin Group (USA), 2008.

"Thalassemias." The Cleveland Clinic Foundation, found at: http://my.clevelandclinic.org/health/articles/thalassemias (last viewed 2/23/2017).

"Trends in Atmospheric Carbon Dioxide." National Oceanic & Atmospheric Administration's Earth System Research Laboratory, Global Monitoring Division, found at: http://www.esrl.noaa.gov/gmd/ccgg/trends/global.html (last viewed 1/23/2017).

Tyson, Peter. "If Polar Ice Vanished." NOVA, PBS.org, posted 4/21/1998, found at http://www.pbs.org/wgbh/nova/earth/mapping-sea-level-rise.html (last viewed 1/21/2017).

Understanding Science & Nature: Evolution of Life. Alexandria, Virginia: Time-Life, 1992.

United States Census Bureau. "U.S. and World Population Clock." Census Bureau web site, found at: https://www.census.gov/popclock/ (last viewed 4/29/2017).

United States Energy Information Administration (USEIA). "International Energy Outlook 2016." USEIA web site, found at: https://www.eia.gov/outlooks/ieo/, including Appendix A, Table

A2, found at: https://www.eia.gov/outlooks/ieo/pdf/ieotab_2.pdf (last viewed 4/17/2017).

USGCRP, 2016: *The Impacts of Climate Change on Human Health in the United States: A Scientific Assessment*. Crimmins, A., J. Balbus, J.L. Gamble, C.B. Beard, J.E. Bell, D. Dodgen, R.J. Eisen, N. Fann, M.D. Hawkins, S.C. Herring, L. Jantarasami, D.M. Mills, S. Saha, M.C. Sarofim, J. Trtanj, and L. Ziska, Eds. U.S. Global Change Research Program, Washington, DC, 312 pp. http://dx.doi.org/10.7930/J0R49NQX.

"Vicious wildfires spread to Colo. tourist centers." Associated Press (posted 6/23/2012), found at http://www.denverpost.com/2012/06/23/vicious-wildfires-spread-to-colo-tourist-centers/ (last viewed 1/21/2017).

Walsh, Bryan."The Golden Age: Could Europe and China's fracking forays remake global energy?." *Time*, May 21, 2012, pages 47-48.

———. "King Coal's Comeback," by Bryan Walsh, *Time*, June 11, 2012, pages "Business 1-4."

———. "Warning: The Next Global Security Threat Isn't What You Think." *Time*, Volume 189, No. 18, May 15, 2017.

"What Is Faith?" TruthorTradition.com, found at http://www.truthortradition.com/articles/what-is-faith (last viewed 4/13/17).

"What is the average rainfall in the Amazon rainforest?" Reference.com web site, found at: https://www.reference.com/science/average-rainfall-amazon-rainforest-3b9dd9d8a49357# (last viewed 1/23/2017)

Williams, John Alden, ed..*Islam*. New York: George Braziller, Inc., 1961.

Wyller, Arne A. *The Planetary Mind*. Aspen, Colorado: MacMurray & Beck, 1996.

"Young Earth Creationism" Conservapedia.com web site, at: http://www.conservapedia.com/Young_Earth_Creationism#Age_of_the_Universe_and_Earth_-_General_Overview (last viewed 1/30/2017).

Zakaria, Rafiq. *The Struggle Within Islam: The Conflict Between Religion and Politics*. London: Penguin Books, 1988.

Zimmer, Carl. *Evolution: The Triumph of an Idea*. New York: Harper Perennial, 2006.

ABOUT THE AUTHOR

Who I am. I am a happily married husband of thirty-four years, father of two, and lawyer by trade. I spent twelve years on active duty with the U.S. Navy, and another fourteen in the U.S. Naval Reserve, all of it in the Judge Advocate General's Corps. After leaving active duty, I made my living as an attorney in private practice.

I have been a Christian for more than forty-one years. During that time, studying the Bible and Judeo-Christian history has been my hobby, and at times my obsession. I am not a Bible scholar, a historian, or a scientist, but I have read many books and articles in those fields in an effort to better understand God's word and God's world.

My Faith Journey. I grew up as an agnostic. At about age 15, I briefly and naively embraced Christianity, but my newborn faith quickly fizzled when my father assailed it with tough questions for which I had no answers (many of which are addressed in this book).

Unfortunately, when I talked to Christian friends and acquaintances, I found that they had no satisfactory answers, either—only the lame response, "you just have to believe." But I could not "just believe" in a religion that seemed so foolish and nonsensical. On the other hand, I had no satisfactory alternative. The other world religions seemed to suffer from the same flaws as Christianity—or worse. Deism offered only a non-communicative God who was apparently indifferent to His creation. Christianity, as foolish as it appeared, made more sense than that.

I can remember being intensely disturbed by the thought of eternity. The incredible vastness of time and the endless expanse of space diminished my own existence to a desperate triviality. I craved immortality, but saw no way to attain it. Thoughts of suicide invaded my mind—if I must die anyway, what difference would it make when or how that occurred? In a hundred years, no one would care anyway. Suicide would at least end the struggle, the pain, and the feelings of hopelessness. But I lacked the courage to attempt it.

Convinced that Christianity was a lie, I evangelized on behalf of my hope-crushing dogma. During my early college years, I aggressively confronted matriculating Christians with the absurdity of their religion. I asked them those tough questions, and repeatedly found that even these intelligent and educated believers could not defend their faith. I didn't know it at the time, but I was attacking a caricature of Christianity. Yet the Christians I encountered never challenged this flawed image of their religion—until I met B.P.

B.P. was a Christian who had thought about and studied these same questions, and he had answers. He made me see that I was shooting at a mirage. The religion for which I had such contempt could be found only in church traditions, dusty books, and bad sermons—not in the New Testament. B.P. convinced me that Christianity made sense, and therefore that it *might* be true. He opened my mind. God would do the rest.

Still, I was not yet a Christian. I could not—or would not—acknowledge that Christianity was true, and without that conviction I could not honestly commit my life to Christ. Perhaps in exasperation at my stubborn refusal to see the Light, B.P. challenged me to pray, and to ask God to show me the Truth. And I did.

Like Gideon (Judges 6:36-40), I set out a fleece in the form of a prayer that I asked God to answer. The nature of that prayer I will keep to myself for now. For our purposes, I need only say that God not only answered the prayer, but He answered it in a way that humbled me and left me little room to doubt the answer or to plead coincidence. In an instant God broke my resistance and my will. I gave my life to Christ that same day: January 3, 1976, in St. Louis, Missouri.

My studies and experiences since then have only reinforced what I discovered to be true that day. I have now read the

New Testament many times, yet am still awed by the incredible wisdom and honesty it contains. I have studied the historical evidence for Christ's resurrection, and can only conclude that if the story is a fabrication, Jesus's disciples were the most brilliant, audacious, and foolish liars in history. I have seen God perform a miracle to restore the health of my newborn baby boy overnight in response to many prayers. How can I doubt such a magnificent God?

May God bless you, and may you be a blessing to others. (Genesis 12:2-3.)
Don

www.ingramcontent.com/pod-product-compliance
Lightning Source LLC
Chambersburg PA
CBHW051821040426
42447CB00006B/310
* 9 7 8 0 9 9 9 2 3 3 5 0 4 *